SICILIAN
SPLENDORS

Discovering the Secret Places
That Speak to the Heart

John Keahey

THOMAS DUNNE BOOKS
St. Martin's Press
New York

THOMAS DUNNE BOOKS.
An imprint of St. Martin's Press.

SICILIAN SPLENDORS. Copyright © 2018 by John Keahey. All rights reserved.
Printed in the United States of America. For information, address St. Martin's
Press, 175 Fifth Avenue, New York, N.Y. 10010.

www.thomasdunnebooks.com
www.stmartins.com

Library of Congress Cataloging-in-Publication Data

Names: Keahey, John, author.
Title: Sicilian splendors : discovering the secret places that speak to the heart
   / John Keahey.
Description: First edition. | New York : St. Martin's Press, 2018. | "Thomas
   Dunne Books." | Includes bibliographical references and index.
Identifiers: LCCN 2018022343| ISBN 9781250104694 (hardcover) | ISBN
   9781250104700 (ebook)
Subjects: LCSH: Keahey, John—Travel—Italy—Sicily. | Sicily (Italy)—
   Description and travel. | Sicily (Italy)—History, Local. | Sicily (Italy)—
   Social life and customs.
Classification: LCC DG864.3 K44 2018 | DDC 914.5804/93092—dc23
LC record available at https://lccn.loc.gov/2018022343

Our books may be purchased in bulk for promotional, educational, or business use. Please contact your local bookseller or the Macmillan Corporate
and Premium Sales Department at 1-800-221-7945, extension 5442, or by
email at MacmillanSpecialMarkets@macmillan.com.

First Edition: November 2018

10   9   8   7   6   5   4   3   2   1

Per i miei compari Siciliani,
Leonard Chiarelli and Alissandru (Alex) Caldiero.

For years their help, support, stories, and love of their culture
have sustained me throughout my work.

And, again, for Connie-Lou Disney,
whose loving support keeps me on track.

CONTENTS

PREFACE

Cities [and villages, one must assume] *don't have their own energy. It derives from the density of their history, from the power of their literature and arts, of the emotional richness of human events that take place against that background.*

—Elena Ferrante,
Neapolitan author

To Live in Sicily—or to wander among its small villages and towns—is to repeatedly step into and out of the past. There are remnants everywhere, commingled with the modern, of the seventeen or so civilizations that have swept over this island for more than three thousand years: The yellowish foundation stones in that medieval-era structure perched along the edge of the village square might be Greek; the smaller stones sitting tight together atop that foundation could be from a Roman, or perhaps Byzantine or Arab, structure, its materials reused often more than once by Norman, or French, or Spanish builders, each into their own style and within their own era.

As a child, traveling with parents through the Intermountain West, I would spot a pine tree in a place where a sign would claim it was a hangout for robbers and other villains of the late 1800s. In my childish mind, I thought that tree, exactly as I was seeing it, would have been there a hundred years earlier, perhaps used to tie a horse or, worse, to hang a ne'er-do-well. I had no concept of how time changes landscapes, towns, and villages—over a century or over millennia. Eventually I understood what the classical scholar M. I. Finley taught me: "The human mind plays strange tricks with time perspectives when the distant past is under consideration: Centuries become as years and millennia as decades."

He points out that, like all of us, I suppose, the Greeks had no idea that as they moved westward, ten generations after the war with Troy, and colonized places in southern Italy and Sicily that they were doing anything that was historically significant. They simply wanted to establish places in which to live, work, and enjoy life. They would change the untrammeled, wide-open, rich landscape they encountered by building hamlets, villages, and cities and absorbing indigenous peoples into their culture. Many of those places, over time, would be destroyed by opposing armies, rebuilt over and over throughout the ages to what we see today, our brief stop in time's continuum. And their names would change, often dramatically, to reflect the different cultures that the island absorbed.

As I travel around Sicily, year after year, I often remember what I read, long ago, by Don Whitehead, a World War II cor-

respondent for the Associated Press. He described what he saw
in Sicily during the Allied invasion in the summer of 1943: "Sicily
had a gray look to it. Even the people had a gray, worn appearance. Their towns perched on hilltops like ragged caps stuck
on the hoary heads of gray old men."

Today, a traveler does not see this Sicily. The towns no longer
look that way, and the people certainly do not. Visitors—and
even today's younger residents—must imagine what it looked
like during that emotionally and physically destructive war, just
as it takes imagination to piece together the ruins of Greek
temples at Selinunte or Agrigento. It is difficult for the casual
observer to try to imagine what the Greek towns might have
looked like before becoming the ruins that now are buried under
scrub-covered hillsides or locked beneath the once-medieval but
now-modern historic centers of places like Catania or under Agrigento, with its ugly postwar sprawl. Occasionally, I can find a
gnarly olive tree that locals say is two thousand years old and
imagine a Greek farmer leaning against it as he eats his noonday
meal in the warm Sicilian sun.

The closest I came to being lost in imagination as a world-
wise adult was when I stood, in 1986, between two columns on
the platform of the Temple of the Dioscuri (Castor and Pollux) at
Agrigento's Valley of the Temples. I stretched my arms out like
the biblical Samson while a friend shot a photo. Standing on that
platform, I had tried to visualize what must have been around
me three thousand years earlier. I returned nearly three decades
later, climbed up, and again stretched my arms out between the
same two columns for another photograph. In comparing them
side by side, I saw how dramatically I had changed, physically,

from my early forties to my late sixties. The temple, its ruins still
scattered as before, had not changed a bit.

There is a lot of the ancient Greek world tossed about in Sicily. The Greeks were the first historical colonizers of southern
Italy and Sicily that the conquering Romans later called Magna
Graecia, or Great Greece. These early Greeks displaced and absorbed many of the indigenous peoples that had wandered there
from throughout the Mediterranean during Europe's darkest
prehistory. In more recent times—the eighteenth and nineteenth
centuries after a series of other conquerors had come and gone,
and come again—Italy and Sicily were the focus of well-to-do
Europeans who wanted to absorb some of that ancient ambi-
ence.

A friend, Franco De Angelis, a professor of archaeology and
Greek history, writes that these Greek ruins drew Grand Tour
travelers to Italy and Sicily primarily because Greece, then part
of the Ottoman Empire, was not as accessible. The activities of
these travelers "often centered around writing travelogues,
studying and illustrating art and architecture . . . and absorbing
as much of Greek antiquity and its survival as possible." I have
not spent a lot of time in Greece, but I suspect that there are more
Greek ruins in Sicily—and many of them better maintained—
than in Greece.

Some of the many conquerors of this island in the center of
the Mediterranean world—Greeks, Byzantines, Muslims, Normans, Germans, Spanish—left distinct marks on the land and
the people. Others, such as the Romans, Vandals, and French,
did not thoroughly integrate with the native islanders and left
fewer marks. The DNA mostly associated with Sicilians whose

family lines flow well back into antiquity comes from the Greeks, who blended in over the centuries with the island's original population, and the Muslims and Christian Berbers from North Africa.

Sicilians today make up a rich minestrone of many of these cultures, and many fiercely maintain their identity as Sicilians and not Italians. After all, it was the northern Italians who were the island's last conquerors, leading to the unification of Italy between 1860 and 1870.

Early in my experiences as a traveler, I often was frustrated because places I expected to be one way—the way I had imagined them to be as a child—were really quite different, much more modern, say, than I expected. The more I traveled, and the more I learned to toss off those early expectations and "see" each place and particularly its people in the context of what it now is, the more enjoyable those trips became. I learned to go beneath guidebook descriptions and the perfunctory writing of some magazine and newspaper travel sections and see what lies beneath the surface in foreign places. Concentrating on the people and their cultures, rather than just castles, ruins, and restaurant recommendations, became the goal.

This never-ending exploration and particularly my relationship with the people are what keep me coming back. I am comfortable here. I know how to communicate and how to get around. No matter where I go, I know how not to act like a stranger or a tourist. Other places outside of this charmed land are worthy as well; I occasionally take a Sicily/Italy break and spend time elsewhere in Europe and even in my own country.

Despite my having no known ancestry here, Italy and Sicily

keep summoning me. Sicily in particular draws many Americans with Sicilian blood in their veins to their ancestral villages and cousins, aunts, and uncles they didn't know they had. Others, possessed with a strong sense of history, can find a lot of "ancientness" in the stones of Sicily. America, with its settlement by Europeans only five hundred or so years ago, really is in its nonnative infancy compared to the thousands of years of Italian, Sicilian, and European historical and proto-historical occupation. Recently, I came across these words of my writer-who-travels friend, Thomas Swick, who, as always, says it perfectly:

In the past, the most important quality in a traveler was a sense of adventure; today, it is a sense of wonder. We have all become inundated, the world a little overexposed. But for those who travel wide-eyed in an age of information overload, the revelations are more potent (if not more numerous) for being unexpected. And they still await, for no amount of images and data can shatter the preeminence of the personal encounter.

Here it is, then, finally, we were in this Sicily, the goal of our journey, the subject of our discussions for many months, here in its entirety under our feet. . . . This is the home of the gods of Greek mythology. Near these places, Pluto abducted Persephone from her mother in this wood we just crossed, Ceres suspended her rapid chase and, tired of her fruitless search, she sat down on a rock and, although a goddess, she wept, the Greeks say, because she was a mother. Apollo has guarded the herds in the valleys, and these groves and extending to the seashore have echoed the pan flute, the nymphs are lost in their shadows and breathed their fragrance. Here Galatea escaped Polyphemus, and Akis, on the verge of falling under the blows of his rival, enchanted yet these shores and there left his name. . . . In the distance you can see the lake of Hercules and the rocks of the Cyclops. Sicily, the land of gods and heroes!

—Alexis de Tocqueville

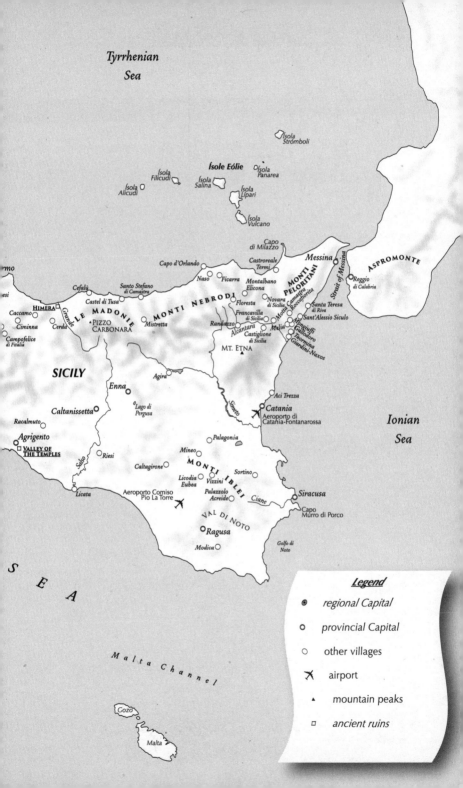

Tyrrhenian
Sea

*Isola
Strómboli*

Ísole Eólie   D*Isola
Panarea*

*Isola
Filicudi*   *Isola
Salina*

*Ísola
Alicudi*   *Ísola
Lípari*

*Isola
Vulcano*

Capo
di Milazzo

*Castroreale
Termi*   **Messina**

Capo d'Orlando   *Naso* *Ficarra*   *Montalbano
Elicona*   **MONTI
PELORITANI**   *Reggio
di Calabria*   **ASPROMONTE**

HIMERA   *Cefalà*   *Santo Stefano
di Camastra*   *Novara
di Sicilia*   *Santa Teresa
di Riva*

Caccamo   *Castel di Tusa*   **LE MADONIE**   **MONTI NEBRODI**   *Floresta*   *Sant'Alessio Siculo*

Ciminna   *Cerda*   ▲ **PIZZO
CARBONARA**   *Mistretta*   *Francavilla
di Sicilia*   *Savoca* *Gaggi*

*Campofelice
di Fitalia*   *Randazzo*   *Alcantara*   *Melia*   *Giardini-Naxos*

*Castiglione
di Sicilia*

SICILY   *Agira*   ▲ **MT. ETNA**

Enna

Caltanissetta   *Lago di
Pergusa*   *Aci Trezza*

Racalmuto   ✈ **Catania**
*Aeroporto di
Catania-Fontanarossa*

Agrigento   *Palagonia*   **Ionian
Sea**

Mineo   **VALLEY OF
THE TEMPLES**   *Riesi*   *Sortino*

Caltagirone   *Licodia
Eubea* *Vizzini*   **MONTI IBLEI**   **Siracusa**

Licata   *Aeroporto Comiso
Pio La Torre*   *Palazzolo
Acreide*   *Ciane*   *Capo
Murro di Porco*

✈   **VAL DI NOTO**

Ragusa   *Golfo di
Noto*

Modica

S E A

M a l t a   C h a n n e l

Gozo

Malta

SICILIAN
SPLENDORS

ONE

Street of the Pagan

Throughout the history of the human race no land and no people have suffered so terribly from slavery, from foreign conquests and oppressions, and none have struggled so irrepressibly for emancipation as Sicily and the Sicilians. Almost from the time when Polyphemus promenaded around Etna, or when [Demeter] taught the Siculi the culture of grain, to our day, Sicily has been the theater of uninterrupted invasions and wars, and of unflinching resistance. The Sicilians are a mixture of almost all southern and northern races; first, of the aboriginal Sicanians, with Phoenicians, Carthaginians, Greeks, and slaves from all regions under heaven, imported into the island by traffic or war; and then of Arabs, Normans, and Italians. The Sicilians, in all these transformations and modifications, have battled, and still battle, for their freedom.

—Karl Marx and Friedrich Engels
Collected Works, Vol. 17

M<small>Y FIRST</small>, and what I thought would be one of my most important vows—stay on blue highways; avoid the autostrada—was about to be broken. The clock was quickly moving forward; by noon, after leaving Palermo around 9:00 A.M. on SS113, I was only as far east along the Tyrrhenian coast as Cefalù.

Traffic through the small coastal towns was heavy. Cars and produce trucks were parked haphazardly along the narrow streets, as is typical in such places in Italy's far south. Vehicles from opposite directions would squeeze past each other, often with side mirrors pulled in to allow an extra inch or two of clearance. Or, a car in front would simply stop while the driver conversed with a friend on a sidewalk. I learned long ago to act like a Sicilian while driving in such an environment: There is no sense in honking; the conversation will eventually end, and the driver will move on. Sicilian friends over the years, when I expressed frustration over a bureaucratic snafu or getting hung up in impossible traffic, often would advise me, *"Tranquillo, John. Tranquillo!"* You will get there eventually. No reason to get agitated.

At this pace, my plan to reach Castiglione di Sicilia on the south slope of the Peloritani Mountains by midafternoon would fail. It would take until long after dark to navigate the final stretch into a town I had never before visited and that looked on my iPhone map to be made up of a maze of narrow, meandering, one-way streets.

So, with a shake of my head, I broke away from the coastal highway, which winds delightfully through villages and olive groves, and entered the sterile north–south Palermo–Messina autostrada with its miles of dark tunnels and high speeds. It was a wise decision. Those miles flashed by. Within thirty minutes, I was at Capo d'Orlando and the autostrada's connection to SS116, where I could leisurely begin the climb over the western edge of the Peloritani Mountains in Sicily's far northeast. I could wind my way over the top and down to the base of the north slope of Europe's largest active volcano, Etna, and into Castiglione. This tiny village would be my home for nearly two weeks as I visited it and a handful of mountain villages in the first phase of my search for the essence of Sicily's small towns.

I have traversed Sicily and portions of the Italian peninsula many times over the years, nearly always by automobile and, unless absolutely pressed for time, which is almost never, I studiously avoid the autostrada. Paying occasional tolls is not the issue; as on American interstates, it is the fast highway's avoidance of small places that bothers me. You see a hilltop village in the distance and long to explore it, but you are past the exit before you know it, or there is no specific exit.

By following state, provincial, and local roads, you are forced to slow down. And discover. Such small, narrower roads go everywhere, giving the traveler a chance to stop, enjoy a *caffè* in a local bar, or eat lunch or dinner in a family-run trattoria with perhaps only a half-dozen tables. The autostrada offers only garishly lighted truck stops and commercial cafeterias.

On this day, in early March with windy gusts and occasional rain splatters, SS116 carried me up, up, up on a road that sometimes felt like I was driving around the rings of a corkscrew. Despite being a state road, the equivalent of a federal highway in the United States, it is, like most roads in Sicily, often just wide enough for cars to pass in opposite directions, and ill maintained. Occasionally, warning markers show that a part of the roadway is slipping off a steep embankment, or there may be short stretches of gravel-only road surface. Many curves are nearly blind, requiring use of the car's horn to alert opposing drivers. This always takes me some getting used to, but within a day or so I tend to begin driving like a Sicilian, downshifting, then upshifting at will through the curves, laying on the horn as a warning to anyone approaching. On the portions where only one vehicle can go at a time, it becomes second nature to guess when the car coming at you will pause so you can go by, or when you should do the pausing.

High near a summit of the first line of Peloritani Mountains, I stopped just past the village of Naso. The observation point overlooked, far below, the tiny enclave of Ficarra, and far beyond to the north, the Tyrrhenian Sea and a cluster of three of the seven Aeolian Islands: Salina, Lipari, and Vulcano. It was a pleasing view, the cover of high clouds diffusing the light so each island stood out in soft, dark relief against what the Greek storyteller Homer, in the *Iliad* and the *Odyssey,* called a "wine dark sea."

This highway passes through the Parco Regionale dei Nebrodi, now protected, ostensibly, from overdevelopment. Once this land, like the neighboring Madonie Mountains farther to the west, was carpeted with vast swaths of pine and hardwood forest. Over the centuries, unthinking deforestation to feed the gigantic maw of shipbuilding required by Mediterranean empires that long raped, pillaged, and looted Sicily for their own gain cleared off these mountains with no thought given to replanting. And Sicily, centuries ago, offered a much cooler climate than it experiences today, so these forests stand little chance of reestablishing.

The first three months of 2016 were cold and wet, then gradually warming, and the mountains occasionally were covered with snow at their high points, but Sicily's reality is that such winters are the exception. And summers are blazingly hot, giving special meaning to the expressions "burned-over land" and the "Africanization" of Sicily. The Sicilian fir, native to these mountains, is virtually gone. One source says, incredibly, that only twenty-one mature trees of that particular species remain. Replanting fails because of continued heavy livestock grazing and gradual climate shifts to hotter and drier.

Over the top of the last southward ridge, SS116 dropped down into a great plain along the bottom edge of Mount Etna's north slope. As I curled my way down through the Peloritani foothills, I passed flocks of sheep and herds of cattle grazing on slopes that were likely terraced to sustain crops hundreds, if not a thousand or more years ago. Many of those *terrazze* today are overgrown and unplanted, occasionally punctuated by crumbling stone houses and huts. It was obvious that many of the farms have long been abandoned, with families leaving for the Americas or Australia in the late nineteenth and early twentieth centuries. Still others left after competing World War II armies swept through with the destruction such events bring. Many never came back to reclaim the property or the second homes in town. Their descendants, being fully raised Americans or Australians, may have had no interest in or even no knowledge of their ancestors' abandoned property. And so the land and decaying structures sit while the population of these places declines. If they are taken over with an eye toward reoccupying them, either by later generations or strangers, restoration seems preferable, maintaining the character of medieval neighborhoods. Few have the American penchant for tearing down something so old and building a modern structure. There are some restored homes that look ancient on the outside, but whose interiors are completely modern.

The only evidence of crops was in small, private gardens that produce enough vegetables for an extended family or, perhaps, for occasional sale in a village's weekly market. Cows, sheep, and goats prowl these overgrown swaths of green generated by winter snows and rain—land that will turn brown and dry by July and August and is prone to frequent wildfires.

I parked on a high turnout overlooking the town of Randazzo, a junction point in my drive to Castiglione, and watched a sheepherder and his dogs push his flock up a steep hill, along a slight *terrazza* leading to a pasture, already green in early spring. The flock disappeared over the crest of a bump in the land caused millennia ago by a now-dormant vent to the gases rumbling deep within Etna.

Randazzo is a medieval town, heavily modernized after World War II, but still with its requisite medieval churches and a handful of ancient buildings that survived the war or that have been restored. It has been a major crossing point for vast armies over the centuries. It was through here that the Spanish king, Peter of Aragon, after landing far to the west at Trapani, marched with his army in late summer 1282 en route to Messina on the northeast coast. He had offered to help rebellious Sicilians depose the French during an event that became known as the Sicilian Vespers in exchange for him becoming king of Sicily. And nearby, in 1719, at the village of Francavilla, the ruling Spanish fought and lost to the Austrians in one of the biggest battles on the island since Roman-Carthaginian times. It was during what historians call the War of the Quadruple Alliance. Messina then fell, and the Austrians besieged Palermo. The Austrians' victory was short-lived. Just fourteen years later, the Spanish returned, taking

Naples in 1734, and Sicily the following year. Francavilla, which grew up around a late-eleventh-century abbey, had "di Sicilia" added onto its name in 1863 to distinguish it from seven other Francavillas found throughout Italy.

Randazzo is one of the major population centers in the area closest to Etna's main crater, but lava flows over the centuries have graciously spared it. Several years ago, I drove along the town's edge en route elsewhere and, while the town didn't appeal to me, the area around it did. It was early July during that long-ago trip, and vast stretches of well-irrigated vineyards shimmered in all directions with intense skies free of clouds. Etna wine is produced here and elsewhere along Etna's vast flank, and the countryside hangs heavy with well-ordered vines.

Various roads cut through younger swaths of lava rock in stages of turning into that productive volcanic soil. Hundreds of years from now, new fields will grow out of the soil produced from the black rock disgorged as lava from deep within Sicily's northeastern edge a few thousand years ago. Small plants and bushes already are taking hold in these old lava fields, including the hearty ginestra, known in English as "broom," and its powerful roots that nature uses to inexorably break the lava apart. Meanwhile, lava stone is used for rock walls dividing land and bordering roadways, and, since ancient times, in buildings, temples, and churches.

Thanks to the respite I got by jumping onto the autostrada, I still had plenty of daylight left to help me find my way into Castiglione di Sicilia, known by the Sicilian name Castigghiuni before Sicily was unified with mainland Italy in 1860. Rome, the new conqueror, like it did with Francavilla, added the "di Sicilia" so the Sicilian version would not be confused with the handful of other Castigliones on the peninsula.

Just moments after I left Randazzo and sooner than I expected it, the turnoff popped up around a blind curve ahead. I made a sharp left and just ahead, high on a hill and scrunched into a saddle with what appeared to be the remains of a castle at one lofty end, clusters of mostly pale yellow buildings emerged in this village called Castiglione. Packed helter-skelter across the face of the mountain saddle, these structures showed themselves off in the increasing peachlike glow of midafternoon light.

For a few miles, the road passed vineyards closed off behind strong fences and large iron gates, through patches of freshly pruned olive trees, and, occasionally, those untouched fields of ancient lava flows. Within a few moments, the asphalt gradually, then suddenly, steepened as I moved off the valley floor, carved eons ago through ancient lava by the Alcantara River. The state highway made its way up into the town, tapering down to one very steep lane within a few hundred feet. I pressed along, hoping a car would not meet me wanting to come down. I got lucky, and the street crested a hill and lowered down into a tiny town square with a series of other streets shooting off in confusing directions. Some were one-way, others two-way, but all were narrow and lined with parked cars that shriveled down the driving space even more.

I could see I would have an adventure finding my bed-and-breakfast, Borgo Santa Caterina, which had the strange additional name of *albergo diffuso*. I pulled alongside a cluster of elderly men standing, as they usually do in small Italian and Sicilian towns, in front of a bar. Glancing inside, I could see tables of men, middle-aged and elderly, playing cards.

"*Buonasera. Dovè la Borgo Santa Caterina?*" Then I added on the phrase that I picked up from the B and B site: "*C'e 'albergo diffuso.'*" I had no idea what that term meant, but the men immediately knew. "Ahh, Valentino!" one said, giving the hotel owner's name on my confirming email. "*Sì,*" I said, thrilled to know they knew him and the hotel. One man then rattled off a series of directions in what sounded more like Sicilian than Italian, but I got the drift. Go down this street, turn left, turn left again, and go up the street. . . . There I lost the drift, but I figured I would take it a step at a time. Years of traveling by car in Italy and Sicily gave me a willingness to be bold.

Waving and shouting my gratitude, I took off. Within a few moments I was back, driving past the same group of men. I had simply made a circle rather than going down another road. I waved, they smiled and nodded, but I didn't stop. I tried it again, this time opting for a lower road at a small junction. There, near the edge of the village center, was a hotel sign with an arrow pointing right. I turned and drove about 150 feet. The road quickly squeezed down to almost less than a single lane, but ahead was the brightly painted front door. I pushed a button in the car that automatically brought the side mirrors in—the street was that narrow—and stopped at the door, where the driveway opened up enough to allow me to climb out.

Inside, the clerk Rosario greeted me in English. He filed my passport information and went out with me to retrieve my luggage. Hauling it up to my room was when I learned what *albergo diffuso* meant. Three short stair flights (I hate to use the word "narrow" again, but they were) later, with landings leading off in different directions to different buildings, finally got me to where I would sleep for the next eleven days.

This was not a traditional hotel with all the rooms under one roof. And there certainly was no elevator. The buildings, while separate, were in a cluster. "Twisting and narrow," for steps leading up hills to local streets, is commonplace in these Sicilian hill towns first built in the early Middle Ages or laid out even centuries before, sometimes by Greeks, other times by Romans, Arabs, or Normans. After all, how wide did a road back then need to be for a carriage, or a donkey-driven cart when buildings could be built right up to the road's edge? Tearing down medieval buildings to make roads wider is virtually unheard of there, except perhaps on occasion in large cities.

Then I had to move my car. "Parking is back there," Rosario said, pointing to the wider part of the street. He saw my consternation. I came in okay, but backing up would be much harder. I am not good at it. "I will do it for you," he said with a hopeful smile. "I do this all the time." No, I said confidently. Then, in strong Italian, *"Proverò* (I will try)."

That bravado lasted a few minutes. Although the earth had not moved since I first drove in, a building on one side and a low rock wall on the other seemed much tighter as I backed out. Rosario stood behind, motioning with his hand, then quickly shaking his head and yelling, "Stop! Stop!" I pulled forward, got out, and motioned him in. It took him ten seconds, and my car was free of that cursed driveway, never to darken it again. I parked a few dozen feet down the road up against a high stone wall covered

with heavy vines, walked back to my room, showered, and
changed my shirt before navigating those three stairways down
to the reception area, where Rosario was fixing a nice late lunch
of pasta *pomodoro*.

A nap was in order. Castiglione, now in the midst of a *riposo
pomeridiano,* or afternoon rest, would be empty of people; shops
and the one or two bars would be shuttered. Rosario told me
nothing much would be happening until around five thirty or six
o'clock "at the earliest." It was late February, the skies were darkened with gray clouds and a light rain—Sicilians refer to such
moisture as a *chioviri assuppaviddrani,* or a "peasant-drenching
drizzle"—and I figured it was worth it to wait.

My large room was warm, the bed looked comfortable. It was
in a restored medieval building two levels higher than the building with Rosario's reception desk and breakfast area. The street
above the complex leads to the upper part of the village, which
has its own central piazza, a bar, various markets, and the village's
only bank. I unpacked, dove in beneath the covers, and slept for
a good three hours—plenty of time to work out the kinks of a
long day's drive on twisting mountain roads.

Nap over and dressed for Sicily's late winter wetness, I made my
way to the street level and began the fifteen-minute walk to the
lower center. The light rain persisted. I imagined that the expression "peasant-drenching drizzle" referred to a time long ago
when field-workers had to stay on the job despite the wetness,
while the landowner remained indoors in front of a fireplace or
rode around in a covered carriage.

The walk was slightly downhill, and there was just enough late-afternoon light to make out, just beyond, a seven-hundred-year-old sandstone tower, called U Cannizzu in Sicilian. New friends a few days later told me that a lightning strike at some point long ago had split the tower; a large cement patch holds it together. This tower and the ruins of the twelfth-century Norman castle high above the village dominate the scene and underscore a sense of history that the traveler can never get away from in Sicily.

The panorama of vineyards and almond groves far beyond, laid out against the north slope of Etna and cut through by a silver sliver of road leading to the out-of-sight coast of the Ionian Sea far below, are changed little, I suspect, from how the land looked hundreds of years ago.

The gas station at the bottom of Santa Caterina's street, Via XXIV Maggio, was open, so I knew *riposo* was over and there would be activity in the lower heart of the hillside village. I turned left onto the village's main street, which took me past a small garage lit up with a welder's sparks. A helmeted man with the torch glanced up as I walked by, raised his protective hood, smiled, and gave a short wave to this complete stranger. I would see him nearly every day that I spent in Castiglione, and each time he would nod in growing recognition as I wandered into town for an evening meal at the one *ristorante,* or to pick up a few items from the druggist or small grocery store, or simply to sit on a small park bench among teenagers and elderly men enjoying the dwindling twilight.

During that first walk, I noticed a ceramic tile bolted to a wall.

It featured a person's name, in light blue paint on an off-white background, and a date: August 18, 1943. I saw similar tiles scattered throughout the village. I asked around, and found out that they marked where sixteen Castiglionesi were executed at the hands of retreating German soldiers following the Allied invasion of Sicily five weeks earlier, on July 10. What made the deaths particularly barbarous was the reality that Germany and Italy were still World War II allies when this tragedy occurred.

British and Canadian troops were fighting the Germans all along Sicily's eastern coast toward Messina. American troops were sweeping diagonally across Sicily much farther to the northwest, toward Palermo. Units of the retreating army had stopped, briefly, in Castiglione. Townspeople, caught in the midst of this Allied invasion, were hungry. A German truck carried food for the troops, and some locals pilfered supplies from it. The outraged Germans executed people in various locations around Castiglione, wounded twenty, and briefly held two hundred hostages. Each marker, installed just a few years before my 2016 visit, identifies a spot where a villager was shot. One marker carried the identity of an elderly woman who had been thrown, for some inexplicable reason, from her tiny balcony high above the street onto the pavement below.

This atrocity, committed against Italians while Italy was still a German ally—Italy did not surrender to U.S. and British forces until two weeks later—was the first of 180 German massacres of innocent civilians on Italian soil over the next twenty-one months of the war. Historian Massimo Storchi points out that, ironically, the last massacre carried out by Germans on the peninsula took place in Bolzano, in Italy's far north, on May 3, 1945, the day *after* German forces in Italy surrendered to the Allies. There, fifteen people were murdered.

Many Italian and Sicilian villages have war memorials in their town centers, marking one war or another and listing the names of the dead from those towns. This is to be expected for those in uniform. But when plaques mark the spots where innocent men, women, and children were gunned down in twentieth-century memory, it gives the sensitive traveler pause. While wandering Castiglione di Sicilia's streets and alleyways over nearly two weeks, I suspect I encountered all sixteen of those ceramic plaques. All the people I talked to during my visit, young and old, know the story of what happened in their village.

Nearly all know older history as well. Townspeople told me about Castiglione's once-thriving Jewish Quarter, dating back to at least the thirteenth through fifteenth centuries. Its remaining, crumbling, and mostly unoccupied buildings are just off the curiously named street Via Pagana, or street of the pagan. Cettina Cacciola, an executive with Castiglione's tourist office, pointed it out to me and said simply, "This is not a Christian street." She didn't mean it as a negative comment; it simply marked the place where non-Christians lived and where medieval Catholics rarely trod.

This discovery led to another story that offers insight into why the abandoned Jewish district was left alone over the centuries. In 1491, the town's Catholic priest led a procession of the faithful, complete with a statue of the dead Christ. The procession made its way to a house in the ghetto, next door to the home of Rabbi Biton, who viewed the Christian procession as a slight to Jews.

No one today knows the motive of the priest to lead his procession there. Perhaps it was to provoke a confrontation or simply to assert the church's authority.

Someone, from a window of the rabbi's house, threw a stone at the priest. It missed him and hit the statue, breaking off one of Christ's arms. The faithful were outraged, and two brothers—Andrea and Bartolomeo Crisis—attacked and killed the rabbi. The news of this isolated event traveled far. Ferdinand and Isabella, the royalty of Spain, heard about this attack and lavished praise on the brothers. In 1492, these same rulers who supported Christopher Columbus in his expedition to the New World created the Spanish Inquisition. Initially it tested whether Jews who had converted to Christianity, known as *conversos* on the Iberian Peninsula and *neofiti* in Sicily, really were true believers who hadn't simply converted for convenience.

Ferdinand and Isabella later decreed that the unconverted Jews of Castiglione, as well as Jews all over Sicily, be banished from the island. Jewish assets were confiscated and divided between the church and the island's noblemen. These expelled peoples had been an economic force in Castiglione and Sicily. Their departure led to economic repercussions that plagued the island for years.

Cettina, following our walk along Via Pagana, piled me into her car and drove to the village outskirts, turning onto a single-lane country road with a sign and arrow pointing to Cuba Bizantina. This was an Orthodox church, one of the earliest and most important in Sicily, locally known as Cuba of Santa Domenica.

It is very old, perhaps dating back to perhaps the twelfth century, when the Normans ruled and allowed Orthodox houses in this part of Sicily.

I had driven, on my own, in search of this historic structure a few days earlier, getting badly lost the first time and finding it when I decided to turn right onto a cobbled pathway instead of left. The heavy, steel-webbed front door was padlocked; I could only walk around the structure, small by most church standards, and imagine what the inside was like. The exterior is dark, rough stone, some native but others mostly chiseled-out lava rock. There is evidence that mortar was used and some bricks.

Cettina had a key. She opened the heavy, rust-encrusted doors, and we stepped inside and gazed around at the slightly crumbling walls. The structure itself was rigidly geometric, and the interior was in the form of a stubby Latin cross with three apses. Two side apses would have had small chapels. The pillars were square and delineated the center sanctuary from the two shallow sides. The window in the rear apse, behind where the altar would sit, faced east. This placement, I learned later, captured the light of a full moon around the time of Easter.

Here and there, on the walls and inside the dome, were faint traces of color, all that remained of what I was sure were glorious frescoes by unknown artists. I enjoyed the solemnity of that interior, standing where the altar once stood, feeling the coolness of the air in contrast to the Sicilian heat outside. After a while, we closed up those large, swinging doors and walked around where I had been a few days earlier. A low, broken wall framed what would have been an addition onto the main structure—the space now overrun with weeds. Around the back, there was scant evidence of more scattered stones. Cettina told me there once was a convent in that small space. Obviously, many of the convent's stones, over the centuries, had been commandeered and reused by farmers for fences and huts.

The term *"cuba"* was new to me. I later discovered that it was a style used in Eastern Orthodox churches, after the fall of the Roman Empire. The Byzantines of Constantinople took over control of the island in A.D. 536, building several of these Greek Orthodox churches. When the Muslims took over three centuries later, they, like the accommodating Normans, allowed many of them to function for the region's Christians, particularly in the island's east.

Cettina motioned for me to follow her along a side road and then onto a footpath. We covered perhaps a few hundred yards across a boulder-strewn field; the sound of rushing water rose up, and within a few minutes we were alongside a small river, full of late winter rain, weaving its way among boulders and small rocks and kicking off light spray from a myriad of small, shallow waterfalls. "This is the Alcantara," Cettina told me in Italian. "It is one of my favorite places to be."

I was familiar, from a previous journey to Sicily, with the Alcantara River. But the part I saw then was farther downstream to the east, where it had slashed its way deep into a wide gorge, the Gole dell'Alcantara, next to the town of Francavilla di Sicilia. At that time, I watched as Sicilians and tourists splashed about in waist-deep water flowing through towering walls of stunning, multicolored lava that had poured across the original streambed, millennia after millennia, eruption after eruption. Free of that long-ago obstacle, the Alcantara races around the southern end of the Peloritani Mountains and toward the Ionian Sea near Giardini-Naxos.

Cettina's favorite section, brimming with runoff fresh from the slopes of the Nebrodi Mountains and next to the Cuba Bizantina, was as small and wild as a mountain stream in the American Rockies. Here, there was no hint of what it would become perhaps fifteen miles farther east. Weeks later, someone told me that this river was beginning to grow, once again, a species of native trout—a freshwater fish that had all but disappeared as Sicily's rivers, some even navigable in the distant past, dried up over the centuries. The Alcantara, at thirty-two miles long, is one of the last constantly flowing rivers in all of Sicily. Others—there are at least twenty-eight listed for Sicily—are dry much of the year. Two large ones, flowing with spring rains and snowmelt but dry later, are the River Salso, which rises in the Madonie Mountains and flows south to Licata, and the Grande, which follows a leg of the autostrada and dumps into the sea near Imera on the north coast. Strangely, in ancient times these two rivers flowing in opposite directions shared the ancient name: the Himera.

On days when I stayed in Castiglione, I often walked around the "street of the pagan," meditating on the Inquisition and its torturous effect on thousands of people. Over time, it would be brutally expanded far beyond simply uncovering false converts among the Jews as Inquisitors went after those lifelong Christians they thought were heretical. Along the tiny street, I would choose a low wall and sit studying the abandoned buildings, clumps of yellow wildflowers and other plants spilling out of cracks in their honey-colored stone walls and underfoot in twisted, potholed walkways. The roofs, in various stages of collapse, reminded me of a passage I read in a book by Sicilian-Tuscan writer Dacia Maraini: "this desolation of roofs on which anything and everything grows, from chives to fennel, from capers to nettles." She was describing the battered roofs of abandoned structures in the eighteenth century; not much was different on this spot in the twenty-first century. None of the windows had glass, allowing interiors to become filled with birds' nests.

This former Jewish ghetto area was the most tumbledown of all the structures I saw in Castiglione. Nunzio Valentino, the energetic, forty-two-year-old owner of my hotel, had told me that four hundred houses were standing empty throughout the village—with many in the old Jewish Quarter. A year after my visit, in April 2017, I read a message from Nunzio that his *albergo diffuso* concept was expanding beyond his Borgo Santa Caterina complex. He announced that an additional twelve structures in that falling-down Jewish Quarter, known as the Santa Maria District, would be converted into an *albergo diffuso,* with twenty units and forty-five beds. He told me that the project would take three years, and he was doing it with financial help from the European Union. The EU is expected to provide one hundred million euros to be spent through 2023 toward the recovery of abandoned buildings in Sicilian historic centers. The money certainly is not enough to help all of the thirty-six hundred villages with populations below five thousand residents. But it's a good start.

This past winter, there were problems with buildings in the

Santa Maria District that had been, for decades, "left in abandonment and reduced in very poor condition." In a message to me in January 2017, Nunzio singled out a group of houses "which may present a serious threat to the safety of pedestrians [and] tourists[;] the beams that support the safe houses are now old and in bad condition, and the structure becomes even more to risk when there are heavy rains." Apparently heavy rains hit this northeast corner of the island during the fall and winter of 2016, and loosened stones from some of these abandoned structures tumbled into the street.

He concluded his January message by asking rhetorically, "Who are the owners?" In the spring of 2017, apparently he expected to be the owner—and willing restorer—of some of them.

Many abandoned buildings in Castiglione di Sicilia and elsewhere in remote Sicilian villages are available for purchase by individuals as well as potential hotel or *pensione* buyers—provided the owner or the owner's heirs can be found—usually for very low prices. The catch: Buyers must promise to renovate, usually within two years of purchase. Renovations likely will cost well into the thousands of euros. According to news reports, foreign buyers, including descendants of original residents who emigrated to America during the last century, are showing interest in these small Sicilian villages.

Nunzio said that in the 1960s, twelve thousand residents lived in Castiglione. Now, in the second decade of the twenty-first century, some 3,200 remain in the town and its surrounding neighborhoods, or *frazioni*. One thought is that many of the structures in this quarter first associated with the Jews may have been occupied up until the end of World War II, when many Sicilians, desperate for jobs abandoned in a war-damaged economy, emigrated in the last major Italian diaspora.

"Second- and third-generation Americans come here to stay at my *albergo diffuso* and show me old photographs taken of the homes that were occupied by their ancestors before they emigrated," Nunzio said. "The homes are still there—some occupied, some not. It is emotional for many of these visitors."

I would learn a lot about the *albergo diffuso* concept slowly growing in Sicily and Italy over my time at Borgo Santa Caterina and much later in my trip during a meeting with a member of the Sicilian Parliament in Palermo. Nunzio Valentino claims credit for creating, on the island, one of the first hotels of this type. In late 2016, he opened another *albergo diffuso* in the tiny village of Gallodoro, high in the hills above Taormina, and held discussions with mayors of other area villages.

He lives in Giardini-Naxos, a handful of miles away down on the Ionian Sea coast from Castiglione. He makes the commute to Borgo Santa Caterina several times a week to deal with guests. Nunzio opened the hotel in 2004 with four rooms that drew only a handful of visitors that first year. By the time I got there twelve years later, he had bought neighboring buildings above and to the side of the original cluster, expanding to sixteen rooms, and was drawing six thousand guests a year. His ten-year goal: one hundred units with two hundred beds. Nunzio's property is on the edge of the historic center, next to the ancient and abandoned Jewish Quarter that he will expand into over the next three years. Two traditional hotels are self-contained and higher up on the mountain.

I don't doubt that he will reach his ambitious goal; if all his success depends on his energy, he has a lot to spare. He speaks in short, rapid bursts, and is always moving. He sits down to talk, then jumps up and paces back and forth, constantly praising the *diffuso* concept and making suggestions about other villages I should visit in day trips.

I had two villages on my long list of places to visit while based in Castiglione: Novara di Sicilia and Montalbano Elicona. Valentino recommended another two, Motta Camastra and Gallodoro. All were within an hour's drive, and the eleven days I planned to stay in this part of northeastern Sicily would be ample time for visits. This grouping provided many of my favorite memories of my journey across the island.

Novara had been recommended to me by a couple of Sicilian-American friends. And I must admit I chose Montalbano Elicona because of the first part of its name: Montalbano, the surname of my favorite Sicilian detective, who had come alive for me through a couple dozen books and television shows. I had corresponded with the writer, Andrea Camilleri, over the years and have written about his detective and how the Salvo Montalbano mysteries give the reader a legitimate inside look at the Sicilian mind-set and the island's culture.

For this journey, I emailed Camilleri and asked if his character's name comes from Montalbano Elicona and, if so, why. His assistant wrote back, pleasantly shattering my illusion, saying the detective is named for a close friend of Camilleri, the Spanish writer Manuel Vasquez Montalban. Vasquez Montalban, who died in 2003, was a prolific writer who also wrote mysteries involving a Spanish detective, Pepe Carvalho, who, like Salvo Montalbano, was a gastronome, a lover of food. Interesting irony, but the village high in the Peloritani Mountains north of Castiglione had nothing to do with my Sicilian detective. I would go anyway. On the map it seemed small and isolated, deep in the mountains. But first, I would drive to Novara di Sicilia, a small village of perhaps 1,600 souls.

TWO

A "Friendly, Inquisitive People"

Sicily is best understood as a continent in miniature.

—Franco De Angelis,
Archaic and Classical Greek Sicily:
A Social and Economic History

T HE WORD "nestled" suggests many things. It could mean a small child held close in the warmth of a parent's bosom. Or a precious object tucked away for its protection. In Sicily, many villages can be described as nestled in the mountains, or cradled under a bluff or along a saddle between gentle peaks with views over vast plains, locations chosen by its early peoples, the better to see enemies coming from far off.

Novara di Sicilia meets a couple of these meanings. It sits on the boundary between two mountain ranges, the massive Nebrodi to the west and the smaller coastal Peloritani. It is held in the embrace of a hill with, from near the top, an unobstructed view north to the Tyrrhenian. Due north of Castiglione di Sicilia, along SS185, Novara overlooks a vast area that was, in Roman times, a center for agriculture. The Romans, on the verge of creating an empire, took Sicily from the Carthaginians in the First Punic War, more than two hundred years before the birth of

Christ. Sicily became the then-Republic's first province, and the Romans used its lands and people, along with those of Sardinia and Corsica, to raise grain to feed a quarter million people—Rome's estimated population in the late second century B.C.

Novara was known as Novalia under the Romans, a Latinized word with a general meaning of "lands reclaimed for improvement or agriculture." When the Muslims took Sicily over from the Byzantines a thousand years later, the village was known as Nouah, or garden. Its ancient and medieval agricultural past is marked throughout the year by such events as Gioco del Maiorchino, where large wax-coated wheels of pecorino cheese are rolled down steep cobblestoned streets to see which one remains upright and travels the farthest. There are chestnut fests and events centered on shearing sheep and baking bread.

Twenty miles north along SS185 from Castiglione, Novara pops into view over the top of a heavily forested mountain. From this summit, a long plain slopes down toward the Tyrrhenian Sea and ends at the seashore, twelve miles farther along, at Castroreale Terme. A pair of volcanic Aeolian Islands, lightly made out through the coastal haze of industrial Sicily, rises up dark from the cobalt blue, almost black, of the sea.

From the town, it is obvious that its placement was based on its townspeoples' ability to spot the approach of seaborne invaders as well as on its proximity to the farming of the plain below.

I arrived midmorning, when under cloudless skies villagers are about, shops were open, and the sun's rays, hidden for the past few days by a milky gray cover over this corner of northeast Sicily, bounced off the rain-wet cobblestones of the main street, Via Corso Nazionale. Novara is no different from many small Sicilian villages in that the primary attractions for day-trippers are the churches. This village was well cared for: The unique cobblestone designs in the streets all over the historical center were well maintained, and the medieval buildings were scrubbed clean of the centuries of grime.

As I walked the streets throughout a day there, people passing would smile and nod in greeting at this obvious stranger, softly saying *buongiorno* or *buonasera*. Novara was only the second village where I spent time on this particular journey, and it was clear that the non-Italian-speaking traveler needed to learn basic phrases and carry a well-thumbed phrase book. The people in these villages certainly know Italian and will gladly respond to a traveler's attempts at language, but they speak their own Sicilian dialects to one another.

I found friendly Novaresi sitting at tables in crowded bars along the Via Corso Nazionale. A pair of middle-aged men invited me to join them for coffee, shouting *"Hey, signore,"* as I looked about for a place to sit in the improving February sunshine, and then motioning to an empty chair at their table. Folks this open to strangers have yet to be overwhelmed by tourists and their noisy street-blocking diesel buses.

The affability of most Sicilians I've met in recent years runs counter to the belief many potential visitors cling to, including a handful of travel writers, that islanders are a secretive, somber lot. This likely was true in bygone years when the Mafia's grip was rock solid, and people in isolated pockets of the island looked askance at strangers, trusting only immediate family members. But some two hundred years ago, before the Mafia became a force, one German, traveling by foot from Palermo to Siracusa, wrote that "Sicilians are a very friendly, inquisitive people, who manage in a quarter of an hour to ask the stranger quite ingeniously about everything they want to know."

I could make this same observation today. Visitors who take time to meet and get to know Sicilians beyond those in tourist T-shirt shops know this. My Italian is basic indeed, but even when I have been invited to dinner in a Sicilian home where no one speaks English, we all have managed, somehow, to communicate.

One of my goals in my multi-hour visit was to find that one restaurant that most of the local people would point to. I wanted non-mainstream traditional food found only there or in the rural parts of the province for Messina. Italian and Sicilian food, even if based on similar ingredients, tends to differ from north to south and from deep inland to the Mediterranean coast. Novara is far enough from the sea that meat and vegetable dishes dominate over fish.

Everyone I asked for a recommendation eagerly pointed to Ristorante La Pineta a few dozen feet from my last coffee stop. I found a menu full of traditional food with names I had not seen elsewhere. I asked the *signora* for her advice. Without hesitation she pointed to *contadina sugo di salsiccia*, or peasant sausage sauce. The pasta was *maccheroni* that was *fatti in casa* (made by hand), from semolina wheat. The dough is rolled in strips around a small-diameter stick, each piece about three or four inches long. I knew that this kind of pasta is made fresh each day, but I asked the *signora* anyway, *"Quando è stato fatto?"* (When was this made?) *"Oh, signore. Questa mattina. Ovviamente! Ogni giorno"* (Oh, mister. This morning. Of course! Every day), she said, pushing her index finger into her cheek, indicating "delicious." The *sugo*—"sauce"—was light tomato, not strong and spicy like in other places in the south of Italy, and peppered with chunks of delicious pork sausage. It was a memorable meal that was not strictly local to Novara, but one I regularly found in the mountain villages I visited in Sicily's northeast province. The shape of the pasta might vary from place to place, but the sauce was definitely from the mountains, where pork dominates.

I took my time with this *mezzogiorno* (midday) meal. Spindly, crunchy green beans followed the pasta, then a salad of various greens and herbs that the *signora* told me were plucked from the hillsides—no flat-tasting, mundane iceberg lettuce for me—and then an apple torte with a lightly browned crust that seemed to float off the fork. And last: a double espresso, *caffè doppio*. The bill, I recall, was around twelve dollars for three courses, dessert, and coffee. Over on the east coast at over-the-top touristy Taormina, the kind of village I generally avoid, the final bill would have been twice that or more.

Montalbano Elicona seemed elusive, harder to find. It lies well to the east of SS116, which runs from the Tyrrhenian coast at Capo d'Orlando to Randazzo, at the base of Mount Etna's north slope. Like Novara, its elevated perch is along that middle land where the Nebrodi Mountains slide up against the Peloritani.

My map clearly showed where I was supposed to turn east off of the highway, just south of Floresta, and onto smaller provincial roads, but those lesser *strade* become a mishmash heading in various directions. Some were well paved, others once were but now showed little evidence of asphalt, and still others looked as if they had not evolved significantly from the *mulattiere,* or mule tracks, that, long ago, ran between villages or from pasture to town. Periodic signs pointing to Montalbano Elicona helped, reassuring me that I hadn't wandered, and the drive, really only ten miles long but it seemed much longer, was visually delicious to a traveler with plenty of time.

These hills, deep inland, were slowly turning green in the late winter. The roads weaved in and out among promontories spotted here and there with tiny, mysterious stone structures, and suddenly dropped down through heavily forested ravines and gullies. The drive that first day was a delight in exploration, with new beauty to see around each curve. Occasional white ribbons of sheep flowed up and down knolls turning from tan to green, each chased by pairs of barking dogs in complete control of their flocks. And there were occasional signs that identified the area as a land of *tholoi.* I had never seen that word before. This would require some research.

A pair of subsequent visits allowed me to try more roads or pathways that connected, at different points, to the main roadway into the village. No matter the route, my rental car, moving around a tight curve with me honking to alert potential drivers in the opposite direction, would invariably come out of a dark cluster of pines and hardwoods onto an open hillside. There, across one last valley, Montalbano Elicona's burnt sienna–colored stones of its houses and churches would erupt out of a small bluff dead ahead. The stones gleamed in the light of a sun's ray that had escaped out of a cleft in rain-full clouds. It was February turning into March when I arrived; clouds and rain had dominated each drive. Because I often travel in Sicily during colder-weather months, I recalled a Sicilian phrase for this time of year: *Frivareddu è curtuliddu, ma nun c'è cchiù tintu d'iddu* (February may be short, but it is the worst month). Those occasional blasts of sunlight and the way they bathed the greening land were a cherished sight indeed.

The village is along an ancient route through the mountains that carried the flow of pilgrims journeying to sacred shrines or of armies dating back to the time of the late Roman Republic, just before it became an empire under Augustus. In 1943, the same British and Canadian units that went through Castiglione di Sicilia in pursuit of Germans escaping north to Messina also moved through this countryside. Centuries before, the Arab geographer Idrisi described these pathways when the Normans ruled the island. The origin of Montalbano Elicona, now filled with modernized medieval homes and buildings, is obscure, but the Normans likely built it and the castle that sits at the top, perhaps on the site of an older hamlet now lost to history.

So, where did the name come from? Historians and literary investigators have long argued about this. A possible explanation is that it comes from the painted figure, so prominently displayed on Sicilian carts and presented in Sicilian puppet shows, of Rinaldo di Montalbano, one of the many knights of Charlemagne, the ninth-century king of the Franks and the first Holy Roman Emperor. Such village-naming practices are not unusual in Sicily. Farther to the northwest, on the Tyrrhenian coast, the village of Capo d'Orlando likely was named after another of those knights.

The second part of the name, Elicona, is thought to be of Greek origin; Latin writers wrote it as Heliconius. A nineteenth-century writer named a river there Oliveri. It's another example of how names shift from millennia to millennia, century to century. The Latin name could refer to the ancient name of a river once crossed by Roman armies. The fog of time hides many clues. When the two names were put together and placed on maps is anyone's guess.

Montalbano Elicona's main piazza is wide open with one side flanked by a grand church, Maria Santissima della Provvidenza, which is attached to what was once a convent for Dominican friars. That convent now houses the city hall, or *municipio,* and police station, and at the far end, a tourist information office. On the opposite side of this central piazza, along Via Provinciale, is a line of businesses, including a corner tobacco shop. A main street, Corso Principe Umberto, runs perpendicular along the piazza's edge, dropping sharply downhill to an unadorned residential section of the small village.

Tourists do come here, but the residents I spoke with said the numbers are small. "We remain quiet and undisturbed," a server in a small bar along the Corso told me while I had my second espresso of the morning.

Karen La Rosa, a U.S. friend who organizes tours in Sicily, brings visitors to Montalbano Elicona. When I told her I was coming here, she sent a photo of a Catholic priest posing with a historic manuscript he had restored. She urged me to look him up, saying he had restored dozens of old texts. I left the coffee bar/pastry shop along the Corso and started walking along a gradual incline toward the castle and upper town. A short distance away and moving resolutely downhill, I spotted a black-frocked figure, an elderly priest, with sharpened features and piercing eyes. He saw me, as we drew closer, and Karen's photograph popped into my memory. It was Monsignore Benedetto Rotella, the priest she had photographed. I stopped, introduced myself, and conjured up, on my cellphone, Karen's photo of him with the book.

"*Ah, sì. Ricordo*" (I remember), he said. I asked if I could see his library of restored books. He was all business. No, he told me. He had to open up the large church, dedicated to Mary, along the square, and had other obligations as well. "*Ma vieni*" (but come), he commanded, grabbing me by the arm, turning me around, and marching me off down the street. The *monsignore* instructed me to wait at the front door while he entered from the side, farther down the Corso. A few moments later, a loud click, and the large front door slowly swung open, revealing the priest and a darkened sanctuary slowly waking up to the light from the square.

We walked down the center aisle toward the altar, where he proudly showed me the large carving of a wooden Madonna with Jesus on one arm and holding a sheaf of wheat in the opposite hand. He told me he would be unable to show me the restored books, even if I returned to Montalbano Elicona within the week. I would be leaving the area in a few days, moving on to villages farther south and more in the island's interior. "*Mi dispiace. Non c'è tempo*" (I am sorry. There is no time), he said.

Then, "*Arrivederci. Forse un'altra giorno.*" (Good-bye. Perhaps another day). He grasped my hand in both of his. I thanked him; he turned and disappeared down a short hallway.

I left Mary's shrine and, and in the slight chill of an overcast day, walking on the beautifully paved Corso, headed uphill and along a series of winding streets. The clock showed a couple of hours before *riposo* would begin, but most shops along the way were already closed. This is a small village—perhaps only 2,500 residents, including those living in eight or nine small clusters of houses in *frazioni,* or neighborhoods—and it was still February, well before any kind of tourist season would begin.

Many larger Sicilian and Italian villages are jammed with cars during the morning and late-afternoon hours as people shop and take care of their daily business, but this one was not. A small grocery store was open, as were the tobacco shop and a couple of coffee bars. That was it. A handwritten sign on the door of a clothing shop indicated it would be open only three days a week. Uphill, the castle, a large stone structure built during the mid-thirteenth century under the reign of the enlightened Holy Roman Emperor Frederick II, was closed.

I spent a few hours wandering the walkways and lanes of the upper town, where buildings, most lovingly restored, had been built during the medieval era. Eventually, I headed down, back toward the square where I found the *bar-ristorante* U Sicilianu still open. I ate there twice over my two trips to the village, enjoying the local pasta dish with sausage sauce, a meal I could not seem to get enough of. Typical of the people I met here, none in the restaurant spoke English; my basic Italian served me well enough. Even the friendly folks in a small tourist office located near the *municipio* spoke only Italian and dispensed brochures and maps only in their native language.

Eventually, I made my way back to the upper village, where I discovered that a small *biblioteca,* open late in the afternoon just as *riposo* was ending, had an excellent photo display. The photos showed Montalbano Elicona buildings in various stages of restoration through much of the twentieth century, with most of that work coming after World War II. There was no war damage, the library manager told me. Retreating Germans had stopped in the village, taking food but not harming anyone. The medieval buildings, many constructed in the fifteenth and sixteenth centuries, were showing extreme age with crumbling walls. And the unpaved narrow streets were bumpy with rocks poking through the hardened soil.

These streets were smoothed out and paved with cobblestones set in beautiful designs; gas, water, and sewer lines had been installed, homes were rebuilt, still maintaining their medieval character. All in all, this village had transformed itself into an appealing place to visit. I spent only two days there and would have welcomed a much longer visit, wishing I could watch spring turn into summer deep in these northeast Sicilian mountains.

Midafternoon of my second day, when I had been passing the time waiting for an appointment with a village official, I decided to ask someone in the *municipio* if they had a map showing the location of a series of ancient Greek tombs, those small stone structures with rounded roofs. Signs along the roads into Montalbano Elicona indicated they were called *tholoi*.

La signora did not have a map, but she telephoned the police department and asked for Inspector Bartolone. "He speaks some English," she said, and would be happy to drive me to one of the sites.

Bartolo Bartolone, friendly and with no gun on his hip ("Not necessary," he said, adding with a wink, "Here is peaceful.") met me inside the *municipio*. We walked to his small Fiat Panda patrol car, well dented and rusty in spots, and, eschewing seat belts like most Sicilians I met, he drove perhaps four or five miles. We passed a stone structure, clearly visible from the road but one that I had missed during two trips here. Then, a mile or so farther, a few dozen feet into a wheat field, another rose up. Built with tight-fitting stones and a dome top, it was surrounded on three sides by wheat shoots, barely poking above the ground. I was embarrassed that I had missed these two structures. It was a gentle reminder for me that travelers need to slow down; I had been so focused on getting to this village for a ten o'clock appointment that I failed to see what was around me.

Despite hurrying, that appointment had been changed to two o'clock, the delay opening up the morning with the policeman. When the receptionist told me of the time change, I had struggled not to show irritation and then realized that several people in this village were helping me far beyond what I originally had expected: the priest from the day before; a woman in the *biblioteca*; a young man who had volunteered to show me a few sites; a woman in the restaurant who talked to me, in limited English supplemented by my limited Italian, about her village; now I was with this unarmed, jovial officer who seemed to enjoy our conversation and this break in his routine. I relaxed over the appointment delay; it meant there was time to do something new and have my curiosity met about the *tholoi*.

The inspector parked next to the fenced-in wheat field. Many times traveling around Sicily over the years I had seen numerous abandoned stone structures of various sizes and shapes and assumed they had been cobbled together by sheepherders as a place to wait out winter storms while tending flocks. They also could have been shelters for field-workers who would sleep and eat there during the harvest rather than walk home each evening.

But these particular structures in this part of northeast Sicily, with their rounded domes, were a few thousand years old. Inspector Bartolone waited for me at the fence, pushing down and lifting up the barbed strands so I could crawl through. A handful of decades ago, Sicilian farmers had the legal right to shoot at trespassers, even kill them, with no repercussions. Those laws were dropped in the mid-twentieth century. I knew this during my many trips to Sicily, but I was always nervous when I treaded on someone's land—to eat my lunch in the shade of a five-hundred-year-old olive tree or to get a better view of something. This time, the presence of a uniformed police officer helping me navigate the fence was reassuring.

The almost-white stones of this *tholos* were beautifully and tightly fitted together with no apparent need for any bonding material. It was hard to tell how the dome was pieced together; it could have been made with hardened mud bricks or stones. Each *tholos* would have been here long before the Romans took Sicily over from the Greeks and later invented cement.

The structural form, created in the lands of the Aegean Sea, dates back to the late Bronze Age, or between 1600 and 1100 B.C. I imagine many would have been knocked apart by earthquakes, with some rebuilt either by locals wanting to use them as shelters or by twentieth-century archaeologists eager to give the generations a look into the distant past. These structures, in the original intent of the ancient Greek colonizers arriving on

Sicily three thousand years ago, were not shelters, but tombs. The Sicilian *tholoi* were much smaller than some found in Greece.

In Athens, a large one served as a dining hall. I had, many years before, been in a giant beehive-shaped tomb near Mycenae, Greece. The structure, in this wheat field outside of Montalbano Elicona, was typical of the ones throughout the area—all protected by the government, Inspector Bartolone told me. Most sit on the surface of the land. A few were built into the sides of hills, like the one in Mycenae. Sicilian shepherds certainly used them as shelters. Who knows what happened to the people buried. In the local Sicilian dialect, the structures were referred to as *pagghiaru mpetra,* or stone huts.

The inspector drove me back to the village. I had time for a leisurely lunch, a conversation or two, to sit in the sunlit square, and easily make my two o'clock appointment. Montalbano Elicona, I decided, would someday make a wonderful base to spend a more leisurely few weeks exploring this mountainous part of northeast Sicily. Two others, also in the province of Messina, are on that list as well: Motta Camastra and Gallodoro. They would be next.

THREE

Greeks, Arabs, and *Gebbie*

[H]e was determined to be an attentive traveler. . . . he would observe the customs of the country with the eye of reason, taking time to study them closely and consider their advantages and disadvantages, rather than jumping to conclusions or simply parroting the prejudices of his fellow Frenchmen. He knew he had a lot to learn.

—Jonathan Conlin,
Tales of Two Cities:
Paris, London and the Birth of the Modern City

MOTTA CAMASTRA is like hundreds of really small villages peppered throughout Sicily and hidden in the clefts of rolling hills. Much of the hamlet's older section—its origins are twelfth century—sits on a large ledge that was created millennia ago when the hill sloughed off on one side. Houses slither around the edge of this slough to the backside of the hill; others creep up a slight incline to look over the stone structures below. Houses are built on top of steep drop-offs. I worry that earthquakes, which periodically hit parts of Sicily, will one day send them sliding down into gullies below. This high-up location allows for views of the valley and side valleys carved thousands of years ago by the Alcantara River and its tributaries. The Alcantara survives, and is one of the few year-round, free-flowing rivers left in Sicily. In ancient times, the island had many large rivers, now mostly dry or running with water only in the early spring.

The village was reached at the end of a rough road slightly wider than a single lane. It likely was a mule track or footpath that juts, corkscrew-like, for a handful of miles off the SS185 highway that runs along the bottom edge of Etna's north-slope skirt, between Francavilla di Sicilia and coastal Giardini-Naxos. Driving up from just beyond Francavilla, the small road flowed through stone-fenced fields and groves of olive, orange, almond, and walnut, which thrive in this microclimate. Here and there, small plots of grapes that in the fall would become wine made their way up the sides of slightly sloping hills.

On the last day of February, under cloudy skies and following a day of rain and moderate Mediterranean temperatures, blossoms on the almond trees were barely beginning to peep out. Far below, in the Alcantara River valley, the trees were in full bloom. In the fields sat tiny clusters of abandoned stone huts and houses. This was a common sight, underscoring not only the impact emigration had on Sicily and elsewhere in the South, but on how farmers left their ancestral country homes when the economy failed them and moved into their home villages and towns to try other professions.

This town had barely six hundred residents. I saw only a handful as I walked the streets with Venera De Luca, who told me that before World War II the population exceeded three thousand. And like many other villages in the south of Italy, many people who saw their land and homes destroyed and were unable to rebuild or find work in Italy's devastated postwar economy, emigrated elsewhere. Most of the departing Mottesi (Muttisciani in Sicilian) went to Australia and Argentina; others went to the United States and Canada.

This diaspora left empty the usual number of buildings that held homes and small shops, like those in Castiglione di Sicilia and Montalbano Elicona. Many of them, including farmhouses in fields outside the village, remain empty today. If you look at Motta Camastra from above, the town is much larger than the population warrants. The number of empty buildings must be large.

"The farmers are no more," Venera said. "Young persons go away; except for a few jobs in nearby Francavilla di Sicilia, there is nothing for them here to make a living. A few of the people are still farmers, but on a very small scale. For them, it is like a hobby, something to hold on to their past with. Maybe they have a big garden and sell their results in small carts during market day in the village. The prices from your neighbor are a little higher [than in stores], but you know [the crop] is different, a better taste." Olive oil and wine made locally are sold from one neighbor to the next, she said.

Today, as in Castiglione di Sicilia and Montalbano Elicona, a kind of reverse migration is slowly taking shape. Venera told me that beginning around 2010, people from northern Italy and Catania in Sicily began buying some of those crumbling structures with an eye toward restoring them for summer homes or perhaps bed-and-breakfasts. Sicilians are, after all, beginning to warm up to outsiders and the economic impetus those foreigners and increased tourism in general can provide. Motta Camastra is no different.

"It is very, very quiet here, where you come because you want solitude, where you can reflect on your life," Venera said. "You are in contact with nature; you are in a position to listen to nature. In winter, we are like the bear. We hibernate in our homes. You must come here in the spring and summer when the smells of the mountains come alive."

She was right. It seemed that it was only a few dozen feet or so from pavement to the soft-earth hillsides that cradled the tiny stone village. Since it was almost March when I arrived, I could smell the yellow ginestra and mimosa blossoms opening up on those hillsides. "This is the poetry of the soil," she said. "In the city, you lose this contact."

As we walked along a stone street in the tiny center a blue panel truck pulled up in front of a small market. The deliveryman carried in a low-slung box of bread and rolls, fresh-baked only a few hours before, somewhere along the coast or perhaps in Francavilla. Venera spoke to the man, whom she seemed to know. He reached in the back of the truck and pulled out a small *sacchetto di carta* (paper sack) holding a couple of rolls and handed it to me. The smiling, pleasant man refused payment.

Venera, on our stroll, showed me a spot along an innocuous paved lane between buildings where a scene was shot for the *Godfather* movie. A few moments later, she stopped to talk with an older woman standing high on a balcony overlooking the main street into the town center. I watched the two friends interact— the balcony-street scene is common on this island—and thought of my neighborhood back in the United States, where friends sit on porches and greet their neighbors. Venera rejoined me and continued to wax poetic about life in this quiet, warm-hearted place.

"Sicilian people are completely different" than people in many other countries or even in northern Italy. "They show you hospitality and make you part of their life—you are a brother, a part of the family, no longer a guest—because we communicate with the language of the heart."

Venera was strictly a local resident who, at the request of a friend I had met at the beginning of my trip, had offered to show me around, not as an employee of any tourist association or welcome-wagon committee. I took her sincere words to heart. They were soft-spoken guides over and over as I spent the next three months traveling from village to village.

In more than one place, I was invited into homes for family dinners; a few baristas in small local coffee bars would refuse to take my money when I ordered my usual *caffè doppio* (double espresso). "Welcome," one of them said to me, pointing out that he knew I was only a visitor passing through and asking where I was from. In Racalmuto, Sicily, where I have been perhaps eight or nine times over the years, there is one coffee bar that absolutely refuses my money because one day I told the owner how much I loved her small town. I walk in after a year's absence, and she looks up and shouts, "You have returned!"

Motta Camastra struck me as that kind of village. I was only there for a short while and, after Venera left to get on with her day, I sat in the little square and watched the life of the village move, slowly, around me: in and out of the tiny tobacco shop, the slightly larger grocery shop, a butcher's shop. Venera had told me there is a place there where I could stay if I had time to return at the end of my three-month trip. I wish I had done it.

Months later, I remembered a discussion we had about the history of her island. The Sicilian culture draws from all of what the island's conquering armies left behind, good and bad, and she said that with such a blend of Greek, Roman, Muslim, Norman, German, French, and Spanish, that Sicilians subconsciously chose "to have a noble soul, to become warmer. In the north [of Italy], they are very cool. In a small Sicilian village you can touch this noble reality."

She, like many other Sicilians I have met over the years, acknowledges that these Mediterranean islanders became a closed and suspicious people as they were overwhelmed by organized crime that slowly grew in the late 1800s, then flourished. Now that the Mafia, which got its modern beginnings in the 1860s after Sicily's unification with Italy, operates well underground and hidden from the tourist experience, this aloofness is beginning to melt away. It started as a rural society those islanders, distrustful of the newly established Italian justice system, turned to for protection and as a way to resolve personal conflicts when ineffective state police refused to intervene. In essence, it started out serving rural people; then it devolved into turning those people into its terrified victims.

The island's version of the Mob still exists, of course. Today, unlike the violence that grips such places as Calabria under the 'Ndràngheta or almost daily unleashed by the Neapolitan Camorra, the Sicilian bosses today are more likely to be found in suits and ties, running shell companies that hide a multitude of illegal activities. Mob murders on the island still occasionally happen. In May 2017, a local boss of what Sicilians call Cosa Nostra (Our Thing), was gunned down in Palermo while riding his bicycle. A newspaper reported that Palermo prosecutor Francesco

Lo Voi described the slaying as "a warning to the state that Cosa Nostra . . . may have been lying low, but was far from beaten."

At the beginning of my 2016 visit, I ate in my favorite Paler-mitani restaurant in the heart of the city. It had recently been ex-panded and beautifully remodeled. I commented to its owner, a man I saw trip after trip, how stunning it had become. When I returned three months later, the business was dark and locked up tight. I saw the forlorn owner standing in front. We didn't speak, but he looked at me and shook his head, a grim expression on his face. A friend later told me that the prosecutor had closed it on the suspicion that the thousands of euro it took to remodel it was Mafia money.

True or not in this owner's case, the state continues to crack down on this 150-year-old crime organization. News accounts routinely describe mass arrests and the confiscation of millions of euro of the Mob's assets.

These reports, and my positive experiences with more and more Sicilians who were open to conversation and friendship, un-derscored Venera's words about the changes overtaking the is-land. It is doubtful the Mafia will ever be eradicated, but it seems to be driven further and further out of sight and out of mind.

My four- or five-hour visit to Motta Camastra was too short. De-spite my early optimism, I would not have a chance to return. The list of Sicilian villages kept expanding. Next was an even smaller village: Gallodoro, conveniently translated from mod-ern Italian as "golden cockerel" or rooster; its Sicilian name is Jaddudoro. It is closer to the Ionian Sea than Motta Camastra

and sits on a hillside in the Peloritani foothills nearly thirteen
hundred feet above coastal Taormina.

The origin of Gallodoro's name is a bit more complicated than
simply "golden cockerel." As explained to me by Antonella Siligato, an area resident who works as an interpreter and guide in
Taormina, the valley that the village overlooks is Valle Aurea,
from the Latin vallis aurea (Golden Valley), so named because of
its profusion of wildflowers. The name Gallodoro, she said, actually comes from the Latin *vallis* that evolved into *gallis* "and
so on . . . and then Gallodoro." The idea to make the rooster its
symbol must have come much later when the Italian name could
easily be translated that way. I am sure all the villages I visited
during this journey have similar stories to tell about their naming origins—something that would be most confusing if I allowed
the practice to dominate my notebook.

My Castiglione host, Nunzio Valentino, who earlier recommended Motta Camastra, also had recommended Gallodoro,
pointing out that it had no hotel or centrally located restaurant
other than a large bar and a small *ristorante* across the valley that
offers a short menu of local specialties. The village, he said, had
tourism ambitions with the hope of accommodating visitors seeking a low-cost base for explorations throughout the area around
more-expensive Taormina. The hills above the coast draw a handful of hang gliders each season.

A visit, Nunzio said, would give me a chance to discover a
place long before tourism would begin in earnest. He was right:
Gallodoro, along with the few even smaller villages nearby, is
worth a traveler's time. It fit perfectly into my goal of finding small
places before they are trammeled by mass tourism—something

the region of Sicily and provincial and local governments want to happen on a grand scale. Sicily is economically depressed; unemployment is high. Increased tourism is seen as a savior.

Later, when Nunzio met me in Gallodoro to introduce the mayor and other villagers, I discovered that he and *Sindaco* (Mayor) Alfio Filippo Currenti had been friends since childhood. Also, I discovered that Nunzio was in negotiations to open a new hotel here. He told me he would not own the restored building— the *comune* owns it and had been using it as a recreation center for schoolchildren and town festivities—but he would manage it. Initially, he said, it would be self-contained in only one building. Eventually, if increased tourism demanded it, other abandoned buildings nearby could be bought and renovated, making it a true *albergo diffuso*. Several months after my visit, I read that the one-building hotel had opened.

The townspeople see tourism potential in this high-mountain village of four hundred residents. Like Castiglione and dozens of other places in Sicily, it has its share of abandoned homes. Given the historic size of the village and number of unoccupied structures, the town could handle a population of fifteen hundred. Slowly, some outsiders are buying a few castoffs and restoring them for use as summer homes. During the winter after my visit, I read that a large abandoned structure, one that had stood for centuries through bad weather, wars, and earthquakes, had collapsed under the weight of heavy snow.

During that first day, I met Antonella Siligato, who agreed to serve as interpreter. For our initial walk around the village, Antonella gave me a lesson in its history.

Gallodoro, in ancient times, was a district of Taormina. It started out as a Greek outpost some three thousand years ago, and a modern history I later read indicated its early name was Bocena. It was established in a wider area beyond the medieval village we see today. Evidence of these early colonists, likely offshoots from Naxos seeking protection higher up in the mountain from coastal raiders or warring factions from other colonies, is shown by archaeological finds of a necropolis, or burial place, plus coins and pottery shards, among other treasures.

Romans followed Greeks, then Byzantines from Constantinople took over, followed by Arabs in the ninth century. Eventually, Spain dominated the island for more than three hundred years. In 1634, the king of Spain, in need of some ready cash, sold the village and its surrounding territory to a wealthy family. Given the political upheavals of the times, ownership of Gallodoro went from family to family until the 1860s when the invasion of Sicily by the island's final conqueror—northern Italians—occurred. The municipality was shifted to the town of Letojanni, on the coast just below the village and located fewer than two miles north of Taormina. Gallodoro finally got its independence returned in 1952.

Antonella pointed out examples in these high mountains of an Arabic system to move and store water runoff for drinking and crops. There are several basins, large and small, carved out of stone that today are still called by the Arab name *gebbia*. A Sicilian American friend of mine later told me that his mother, who grew up in the southern Sicilian village of Racalmuto near Agrigento, talked about doing her laundry in *la gebbia*. The phrase for a basin for washing in North Africa is called *al-jabbiyah*. Such traditions easily live on in this Sicilian land of millennia-generated DNA diversity.

"We know we have many Arabic traditions and many Norman ones," Antonella said. "We are Greek, Roman, Arab, Norman, Spanish. We are all this." And, with a hint of pride in her voice: "Now we are people of the world." A pause, then: "We are Arab in the way we live and in the way we eat."

Later, Antonella and a small group of her friends wanted to show some of the various ancient ruins around the village. Before setting out, first by vehicle, then on foot, we ate a quick lunch at the only bar. The chief of police, *il commandante di Vigili*; another officer; a few villagers; and the mayor joined us. It didn't take long until perhaps eight or nine townspeople were sitting at a long table engaged in friendly, boisterous conversation. Occasionally Antonella would interpret for me, but mostly I just sat, eating a bountiful bowl of *pasta con pomodoro,* and listened to this group of friends enjoying one another's company.

Antonella told me she lived in an even smaller village, Melia, just over the mountain and tucked on a hillside above a small valley, the Valle del Ghiodaro. On an opposite hillside, joined to Melia by a bridge, is still another small cluster of houses called Mongiuffi. The combined population in these unique hamlets is fewer than 650. Potholed provincial roads following what once were walking paths, or *muleterre,* connect these three villages. SP13 starts up the mountain from the coastal road at Letojanni. After a few miles, SP11 splits off toward Mongiuffi-Melia, eventually passing through a short tunnel dug by Austrian prisoners during World War I. SP13 continues on to Gallodoro. At Mongiuffi, the single road becomes SP12 and loops around to the north, passing through Roccafiorita and a couple of other tiny villages before heading back down to the coast, landing between Sant'Alessio Siculo and Santa Teresa di Riva.

The valley's name of Ghiodaro evolved from the Greek and means *dono della terra,* or "a gift of land, of nature." It is the name the Greeks gave to the stream that tumbles down the valley between Mongiuffi-Melia. It was used by the Greeks and later the Romans to provide water, through a long aqueduct, down to the coastal town of Taormina. A small stretch of that aqueduct can still be seen near the two opposite villages.

This interconnected complex of villages includes, higher up, a really tiny one (with 250 souls), Roccafiorita (mountain full of flowers).

The drive to the first archaeological site took our small group along a pathway just below the top of the hill opposite the village of Gallodoro. This was a place called Ercia. We parked near the easterly rim of that hillside and trudged through wet underbrush along a trail drawn like a black line across the green of a painter's canvas. It was slippery; I was wishing I had a walking stick. A couple of the younger men kept their eyes on me, ready to leap if I stumbled in the rocky descent.

At the top, my eyes were first drawn out to the east and the Ionian Sea. I tried to spot, well off in the distance, the toe of the Italian mainland boot, but the haze overwhelmed it. I looked down the mountain and slightly to the south, where Antonella was pointing out small grayish dabs, again like paint on a canvas, which were Taormina and Letojanni. I thought of the crowds of tourists drawn to those towns below and was glad I was here with a couple of new friends and only a slight wind rustling through the fresh undergrowth.

I needed to sit and plopped down on a rectangular stone. It was then I saw it: the foundations of various structures, Greek in origin. There would have been a few small buildings here, plus the low walls of an enclosure for quartering animals, likely sheep. And the stone I was sitting on was part of a group of stones encircling a hollowed-out impression into the top of a low boulder. This, Antonella told me, would have been a low and wide stone pool, a *gebbia*, to hold fresh-crushed grapes for winemaking.

The idea of these *gebbie* fascinated me. I would see a monster *gebbia* on the hilltop across the valley later that day, a smaller one in Gallodoro itself, and several in the Sicilian countryside as I made my way from one place to another over the next two months. I could just imagine my Sicilian-American friend's mother, as a young girl in Racalmuto far to the southwest, pouring water into a stone hollowed out in ancient times and washing the family's clothes in it.

This small collection of arranged stones, hidden away by the thick undergrowth in this place called Ercia, were shaped and stacked millennia ago, perhaps by Romans and then Byzantine, Arab, and Norman settlers. Such winemaking sites like this were spread all over the territory of Gallodoro and the three other villages until the end of the nineteenth century. This grouping, and the grouping we saw later that day, is on private land. I suspect Gallodoro is unable to acquire the sites, but the interest they hold for serious travelers cannot be denied. If this first site was interesting, the second was spectacular.

We drove back around the edge of the valley through

Gallodoro, dropping off Antonella because of another commit-
ment, and then we traveled up a ridgeline to the southeast. This
place was called Castiddaci, from the Latin *castorum acies,* which
means "fortified place." It possibly was a camp *(accampamento)*
for one side or the other during a battle in the civil war between
Octavian (the future first emperor of Rome) and Pompey in 36
B.C. This Roman camp could have been built on a site dating
back to the fifth century B.C., when the tyrant of Siracusa destroyed Naxos, driving the Greeks up into these mountains.

The road stopped at a gate, indicating the land beyond
was private, but we could easily enter from the side. Giovanni
Curcuruto, a photographer and historian, led the way, dodging
soft, brown evidence of the cows that graze here in various seasons. We slowly moved around the bluff of the hill—that Austrian POW-built tunnel on SP11 was directly below—and were
rewarded with magnificent views of the Ionian Sea. We encountered a stone structure with its high walls still standing. This was
once a Byzantine church that had been built on top of a Greek and
perhaps Roman temple. Some dispute that the structure and surrounding ruins date back that far. Some say it only goes back as
far as the Middle Ages, or even only the sixteenth or seventeenth
centuries.

But Giovanni, who had been here several times and let his excitement overflow when showing a visitor such ruins, pointed to
the bottom row of wall stones, hand-shaped and age-stained light
yellow, on the empty and unroofed interior. *"Greci,"* he proclaimed. Then he raised his walking stick up to the next row of
stones set in a different style—clusters of smaller, individual
stones fitted together in a somewhat orderly fashion. *"Romano."*

And then up higher to a third row. *"Bizantino,"* he said with authority. These also were small, but haphazardly fitted together.

It was clear in his eyes: This structure, like so many in the Mediterranean world, had started out as a pagan temple and then, over the millennia, evolved into a Christian church. Ironically, Antonella later told me, archaeologists have never explored here. "But hopefully they can do it in the future." If that ever happens, perhaps then Giovanni's interpretations of these distinct collections of stones can be sorted out.

The walled enclosure was surrounded by heavy undergrowth cut through only by the small, tapered animal pathways that were our only way through. If all this greenery could be cut away, ancient foundations of many houses and outbuildings would pop into sight. There was an entire village here, Giovanni said. This would have been a place of retreat—retreat away from the coast and where a beleaguered people could keep watch on the coastline several miles below.

I turned from the large, roofless ruin to look downhill. One hundred feet away stood an impressive circular stone structure perhaps six feet high. It had a rock dome and, beneath it, facing the ancient church and what likely was once that small village, was an opening. Giovanni beat me down the hill and to the opening, impatiently waiting for me to stumble down after him.

He held out an arm, presenting the opening like a host pulling back a curtain to expose something wonderful and unique to a guest. I looked in. Perhaps ten to fifteen feet down was a rocky bottom. *"Che cos'è questo?"* I asked. (What is this?) *"Una gebbia!"* Giovanni said. He pointed to the rock-strewn bottom. It wasn't the real bottom. Over centuries of disuse, rocks from above, trig-

gered by rain and wind, had rolled down and through the opening, filling it to the level we see today. In reality, this *gebbia* was
some sixty feet deep. It originally was built to hold a water supply
for the tiny village. Channels would have been dug on the hillside,
around the stone houses, directing the water to the entrance. A
well fills when dug deep enough to capture groundwater; this
basin is filled from the top, protected by the dome roof, and people
drew water with buckets lowered by ropes.

I saw all this in early March. By summer, Giovanni said, visitors would see something else: the tops and spaces around the
rock jumble inside would be writhing with life. *"Serpenti!"* he
said. They slither around this hillside and, oblivious to the dan-
ger, tumble through the entrance onto the rock just below. They
can't get out, and spend their lives greeting their newly arrived
cousins and start breeding. Who knows how they survive. I know
Sicily has a species of rattlesnake, along with black snakes. There
are also green snakes and a few other species as well. Whatever
was down in *la gebbia* held no interest. Herpetology is not my
strong suit.

A few weeks later, Giuseppe Coslovi rescued me. Nearly drenched
with rain, I was huddled against the stone wall of a small house
just off Gallodoro's main square. He came out of the front door
of his home a few dozen feet away with a spare umbrella in his
hand, offering it to me. I accepted, and we spent the next few
hours on the edge of the square talking about art, my journey
thus far in Sicily, and life in his small village. Fortunately for me,
Giuseppe spoke excellent English. As he shared insights about

history and culture, I couldn't help thinking about all the Sicilians and Italians I've met over the years from whom I could have learned if only I were better at their language.

It had been a few weeks since my last visit to Gallodoro. The mayor, Alfio Filippo Currenti, during a friendly lunch at his house with a group of villagers; his wife, Antonella Strazzeri; and his mother, Santina Bartolotta, had invited me to return for a special ceremony: the unveiling of a new sculpture of the town's modern symbol, the golden rooster. I would be far inland in Mineo at the time, but it was an event I wanted to witness.

Such purely local happenings in small villages are never planned with tourists in mind; because of that, they appeal to me the most. I often have been the only outsider at local religious festivals and other purely civic events that are important to devoted townspeople. Of course I told the mayor that I would return. So I easily handled the two-hour drive from Mineo, being chased by rain during the drive to the northeast. I was way ahead of schedule, so I found myself in the small town square, with the newly formed pedestal and a shrouded sculpture tightly wrapped to stay hidden from prying eyes. Only a few other early arrivers were milling about under personal umbrellas. Two local food stands were being set up beneath portable awnings.

We still had time to spare, so Giuseppe invited me to his house for an espresso. We walked inside to plant-filled rooms—green-leafed golden flowers and small, manicured shrubs in containers. Pots of delicious-looking herbs filled tables; others were arrayed along the tile floor. It seemed a mass of confusion, but looking closer, they were well organized, each pot turned just right to show off the plants' best sides. Art canvases and small mosaics made up of tiny stone flakes covered the walls or were leaning against furniture in between plants. Religious themes, landscapes, and paintings of figures dominated—some framed, others still drying.

Over espresso and mineral water, Giuseppe told me that he worked, for thirty-three years, as a gardener for various hotels in touristy Taormina. On his own time, or when he couldn't work because of rain, he made art. He has religious paintings to his credit, along with mosaics. In Sicily and elsewhere, he is known for his paintings on doorways; people hire him to do this in private homes and in hotels and small *pensione*. And like Sicilian cart painters of old, he fills canvases with mythical figures: Saint George and the dragon, Saint Phillipus, Saint Francesco, Saint Antonio.

"It is not easy for them to find people to do this kind of work," Giuseppe said. "It doesn't pay very much. I do it because I like it."

Giuseppe's creativity didn't stop there. His gardening background created in him a love of plants, particularly cacti large and small. Just off the living room was a smaller room with glass windows on three sides, itself full of succulents, stacked high on shelves. In all, Giuseppe had five hundred plants in this tiny Sicilian house. Among those were three hundred waxy succulents, broken down into 150 varieties. "Many of them are rare," he said, all thriving in Sicily's wintertime humidity, warming the home, and giving the retired gardener joy in his later years. Age sixty-three when I met him, he had been painting since he was a teenager and had been growing succulents for decades, some very old and others being cared for through several generations of plant life.

The few hours inside Giuseppe's home passed quickly. The

rain had paused, just in time for the ceremony of the golden rooster. The crowd had grown, almost filling the tiny piazza. A horse harnessed to a modern, heavily decorated version of a Sicilian cart was sitting at the edge, the horse shuffling from one foot to the next. The cart's paint was fresh and vibrant. Along the back panel, just below a seat big enough to hold two adults, was a series of fantasy paintings of legends from the ninth-century era of Charlemagne. The side panels were adorned with paintings of deep-purple grape clusters. The metalwork was impressive, cut and welded in geometric shapes.

In earlier times, Sicilian cart makers were subspecialists: One craftsman would build the frame. Another would tell, in paint, the stories well beloved by Sicilians. Others would build the wheels and create the metalwork with its own series of designs and shapes. This modern cart with traditional themes was smaller—graceful and loose-limbed—than older Sicilian carts. It was like the difference between a four-wheel western U.S. buckboard and a light, two-wheel harness-racing sulky.

The mayor saw me admiring the rig. With him was a friend from out of town. He pulled the two of us together and invited us to climb aboard the cart. There, we sat side by side as a handful of folks snapped photos. Then the cart's owner grabbed the horse's halter and began leading us up the curving road to the center of the town above. It was a nice respite. I've seen a lot of painted carts throughout Sicily, in processions and festivals and even traveling briskly along a highway near Palermo, but I had never ridden in one. This was a slow walk, and when we reached the upper part of the village, other folks were waiting for the return ride. I jumped down, took photos of the brightly painted images, and headed downhill back to the piazza along a paved footpath with many stairs between stone houses.

The ceremony was about to begin. *Il Sindaco* Currenti was speaking. At his side was the gentleman I had ridden with in the cart, introduced to the crowd as Professor Florencio Vicente Castro of Badajoz, Spain. It appeared the man had the honor of pulling off the covering hiding the sculpture of the golden cockerel. He walked up, gave a brief speech, and yanked the cloth, revealing a stainless steel, gold-colored rooster, created by the Sicilian artist Nino Ucchino. As far as I could tell, Signore Ucchino was not there.

The villagers were delighted, the mayor was beaming, and I was enjoying every minute. Other than the Spanish professor, there were no outsiders here, as far as I could tell. It was not a tourist event, but a small village's gathering of friends and neighbors. Children were playing with tiny umbrellas, running circles around the golden rooster. Everyone seemed to be in groups, laughing, and loud talk was everywhere.

When the crowd started moving up a short street to the town-owned building, where the hotel would open months later, the fun really began. I walked into a room set off by a large stone wheel that once crushed olives for oil. On top of the structure supporting the wheel stood a group of men dressed in red and white and armed with accordions and brass horns, playing raucous Sicilian music. A long food-filled table—chicken, in honor of the rooster outside, was the main course—stretched along one wall. People were eating, the sound of loud talking almost drowning out the music. My friend Giovanni Curcuruto, one of my guides a few weeks earlier to the ancient sites around Gallodoro and with cameras strapped around his neck, yelled my name high above the din, waved his greeting. The beaming mayor stopped by and gave me a Sicilian greeting with kisses on both cheeks. His wife, Antonella Strazzeri, did the same, and a handful of people I had met over two days of visiting this delightful hill town stopped by to shake hands and wish me well.

I left with a full stomach and the lively Sicilian music bouncing around inside my head. Walking toward my car for a return trip to Mineo and then Vizzini, I crossed a small bridge over a tiny stream. Glancing down, I spotted a small grayish tub, carved millennia ago out of solid rock, capturing the stream's water and, overflowing, releasing it downstream. Ah yes. *La gebbia,* a reminder that the far-distant past is still part of life in these tiny Sicilian villages.

FOUR

Literature and Oranges

The oranges of the island are like blazing fire among emerald boughs. And the lemons are like the pale faces of lovers who have spent the night crying.

—Abd ar-Rahman al-Itrabanishi,
twelfth-century Sicilian-Arab poet, quoted by Helena Atlee
in *The Land Where Lemons Grow:
The Story of Italy and Its Citrus Fruit*

MY JOURNEY now shifted more inland and to the south, out of the northeast province of Messina and into the east-central province of Catania. This part of the trip also would be an excursion into what I refer to as "literary" Sicily. Two prominent Sicilian writers were born there and are well remembered, despite having been gone for decades: Giovanni Verga (1840–1922), who was born in the countryside near Vizzini; and Luigi Capuana (1839–1915), a native of nearby Mineo. There are other prominent writers and poets from the island, of course: Leonardo Sciascia (1921–1989), from the tiny village of Racalmuto in Agrigento Province, and Luigi Pirandello (1867–1936) from Kaos, a *contrada,* or neighborhood, of the city of Agrigento. Two Sicilians are Nobel Prize winners for literature. Pirandello won in 1934, and the lyrical poet from Modica in the southeast of Sicily, Salvatore Quasimodo

(1901–1968), won in 1959. Pirandello's most famous work is his play *Six Characters in Search of an Author*. My favorites are his collections of short stories: *Tales of Madness, Tales of Suicide,* and, particularly, *The Oil Jar and Other Stories*. These only scratch the surface of his life's work. Quasimodo's outpouring includes numerous collections of his poems, many in English. The series that grabbed my attention was the English translation of *The Night Fountain,* a collection of some of the poet's earliest work, done during his late teens.

I believe that Sciascia, who died at age sixty-eight in 1989, would have been a strong Nobel candidate had he lived longer. Of course I could not ignore Federico De Roberto (1861–1927), who was born in Naples but lived a long and productive life in Verga's Catania.

My first focus on this part of the trip would be Verga and Capuana and their villages. The two were colleagues who met while both were working in northern Italy and who then carried their lives and their work back to their Mediterranean island.

Then I would briefly dip my toe back into the southern interior of the province of Messina, a short distance to the north, to visit another village that was a home and the final resting place of another great Sicilian writer, Maria Messina (1887–1944): the village of Mistretta, where she lived with her family for six years and where she began writing. Her father was an educator who frequently was transferred to different villages and later onto the mainland.

Some of her biographies say she was born in Palermo, but there are those who believe she was born in the village of Alimena, in the province of Palermo. I knew that village was her father's birthplace and that there is no real evidence, other than hope against hope, that she was ever there except as a visitor. I would also visit.

I include Messina alongside Verga because he became her mentor in the literary art of *verismo,* or the special brand of Italian literary realism that called for portraying society and humanity in the reality of everyday life—good, bad, and tragic. No soft-pedaling, no portraying the lower classes as humble people of the soil but rather in the angst of their poverty and grueling daily lives. His influence on this young woman's career was significant.

Many of the literary giants of that period were not particularly friendly toward women writers. Verga and Capuana especially ignored women's efforts. But a young Messina, who in 1909 had a collection of stories published by a Palermo publisher, sent a copy to Verga, never imagining that he would respond. When he read her first stories, however, he adjusted his attitude about at least this woman writer and became her champion.

Her work dispels the notion that Sicilian literature focusing on the plight of women and their place in society in the late nineteenth and early twentieth centuries had no market. She ranks up there with Sicily's best and brightest. Messina, who became progressively disabled with multiple sclerosis, fell almost into obscurity after publishing numerous books and short stories through the late 1920s. Leonardo Sciascia resurrected her, as it were, four decades after her death. He got publishers to rerelease some of her work. I would learn more about Maria Messina in Mistretta and in a later conversation with one of her English translators, Elise Magistro.

The drive south to Mineo, my first village in the deep interior, briefly followed the coast via SS114. I moved up onto the autostrada for a few miles to avoid the heart of car-crowded Catania. Once past this delightful but confusing city, I dropped back onto SS114, then turned west a few miles later onto SS385, in the direction of Caltagirone. A drive along this road, mile after mile, is through beautiful orange groves—perhaps the largest collection of such *aranci* on the island. Oranges littered the dirt shoulders of the roadway, sad waste that fell from overhanging trees.

A light rain pursued me, and shortly after my turnoff from SS114, I began to see them: beautifully dressed black women sitting on folding chairs at regular intervals, singly and sometimes in twos and threes, among the clutter of fallen oranges. They waved and smiled brightly as I passed. This roadway apparently is a popular trucking route from the coast to Caltagirone and beyond into the interior. Many trucks, as they drove by each seated lady, honked their air horns; the late morning was full of those sounds. I took this highway three times en route to various places on my itinerary; the women were always there, through heat and rain, always beautifully dressed and hair combed to perfection. I seldom saw cars or trucks pulled over to the side. Occasionally a folding chair would be empty.

For years traveling around Italy and Sicily, I would occasionally see women alongside the roads. Friends told me they were mostly Eastern European or from Africa. They were present in the Veneto, outside of Venice; along the Appian Way outside of Rome, sitting on broken pieces of ancient monuments; in Tuscany, in twos and threes, in clearings in the woods next to the road-way that runs alongside a sprawling U.S. Army post. But I had never seen such an extended display as the one along SS385. I suspect all are immigrants who likely are in the grip of local Ma-fia bosses. I couldn't imagine their plight. I kept moving. The morning drive seemed bit heavier on me than the weight caused by humidity and frequent rain.

The lineup of seated women ended just before the village of Palagonia, built on what was once a prehistoric and ancient Greek site. Within moments, the hazy specter of Mineo, high on a pla-teau to the southwest, came into view, giving the village a north-ward view toward towering, snow-crusted Etna. I took the Mineo turnoff and moved upward on a corkscrew-style road. In a few moments, I was on a busy main road to the village center. Out-side the gate that led into the old formerly walled village, a large outdoor market was well under way. The parking lot was full, forcing me to park on the precarious edge of its driveway. I got out and walked through the crowd of shoppers and toward the medieval gate leading into the *centro*. There, around the main piazza with a huge statue of Luigi Capuana looking over his home village, cars plugged every conceivable spot.

I called my host, who would rent me one of his two *pensione* rooms for the next week. Ninni Maglione told me he would meet me in the square next to the only vacant parking spot—a taxi stand with the ominous sign warning against anyone else park-ing there. He told me to get my car from outside the walls, bring it in, and park there, and he would meet me soon. I did—I could see no parking police anywhere despite the confusion—and Ninni was waiting for me.

We briefly discussed our mutual friend Santi Buscemi. Ninni spoke no English, so I made do in basic Italian. Santi had recommended that I go to Mineo, which I had not heard about, and said I should stay in Ninni's small *pensione*. Santi was a speaker at a conference, on Sicily, in Philadelphia that I had attended. He teaches at New Jersey's Middlesex County College and has translated two of Capuana's books, so he knows the village well.

Ninni got into my car and pointed the way: up a small, two-way street, a sharp, almost backward turn up a steep incline, and then to a full four-stall parking spot in front of his building with five cars already squeezed in. "Park over here," he directed, pointing a bit higher up the hill. "These spots will be empty soon." Then, he took me to Il Vecchio Pasticcere (The Old Pastry Chef) a few dozen feet away, bought me a cream-filled *cornetto* and double espresso, and introduced me to his friends. During the next six or seven days, I could not pay for anything in that small bar; I was Ninni's guest. My money was no good.

A young man, a twentysomething wrapped in a white, flour-dusted apron and sporting a well-trimmed goatee, entered the bar through a small interior door. He was carrying trays of small cakes and a variety of cream-filled pastries. As the door swung open, I saw a collection of pots and pans and an oven in the large kitchen. He delivered his newly baked goods to the bar and then walked over to my table. "I am a pastry chef here. I am told you want to see Mineo," he said, in clear English. "Let's go for a ride."

That was my introduction to Salvo Andrea Leggio, on my second day in his native village. After a brief conversation, a young woman joined us, Elsa Maglione. She is Ninni's daughter.

Salvo, who grew up driving curving, potholed Sicilian roads, had no trouble maneuvering through the car-choked village and onto the outer road on the edge of the plateau. Smoothly shifting gears, he tore down the mountainside and across the tops of low-slung hills. Eventually, we started uphill again and stopped alongside a fence cordoning off an upward sloping field. "This is Mount Camuti," he said. "It is the location of the necropolis of Camuti, a very ancient, very old place."

We climbed over the fence and walked up the incline. Gray boulders populated the landscape. Salvo said we were walking through what was once a prehistoric village, dating back to a period in the Bronze Age (2000–1400 B.C.) that saw the rise of small urban centers such as this one. This, archaeologists believe, was part of the Castelluccio culture, which was known to bury their dead in caves and was spread throughout southeast Sicily.

All that is left here are small caves in the larger stone faces of short cliffs. Some are natural, some roughly carved, and some are adorned with fading carvings around their entrances. I read later that there is a "philosopher's stone" in the area where tradition holds that if an expectant mother sits on the stone, her baby will become a poet. I didn't see such a stone, but such traditions, going back centuries, are certainly part of the Sicilian culture.

The view from Mount Camuti is spectacular. From the edge of the incline, the village of Mineo is spread out far below, across the top of its plateau. Farther out is a large valley stretching all the way to the south slope of Mount Etna. Groves of olive and almond trees extend for miles east to west on the slopes of the lower hills below the town. Along the wide valley bottom, for miles in both directions, is a succession of the orange groves I had driven through the day before.

We sat and admired, in the late afternoon, this magnificent sweep of land with Mineo at our feet. Clusters of tiled rooftops popped up here and there, tucked into the clefts of hills across the valley, demonstrating how Sicily is really a land of small, strung-out places—newer stones piled on top of ancient stones. The sun, off to our left, was setting behind the hills beyond Caltagirone, soon to drop into the sea beyond Palermo.

My guided explorations in and around Mineo did not end there. The next day, Ninni took over, and I was able to get a sense of the village that the great writer Luigi Capuana grew up in. We met in the pastry shop, where I was having my usual breakfast of double espresso and *cornetto con crema*. "I am going to the cemetery today to make arrangements to add my brother to the family plot," he told me. "Do you want to go?" Of course I would. Spending extended time with a willing villager is always a good idea. One never knows what he might see, or learn, or finally understand about a place and its culture.

The Mineo cemetery was off the side of the plateau on a bluff that protrudes, like an elbowless forearm to the west. When I had driven into the village two days before, I was stopped with other traffic along Via Roccovè while a funeral procession made its way off the main road and onto the lane leading to the cemetery. The hearse moved slowly to allow the mass of mourners, perhaps a few hundred feet deep and on foot, to keep up. While sitting there, I could see, in the distance, the grayish shape of what looked like a Byzantine church, a familiar structure in the *cuba* style.

At the side of the roadway was a monument shop named M.d. Marmi, where workers carve headstones, stone figures, signs, and plaques for family tombs. Ninni turned onto the lane and pulled into the stone-cluttered parking area of the shop, where workers were sculpting with loud, screaming machinery. Dust filled the air, coating the workers like the marble sculptors I once watched in Pietrasanta, Tuscany, on the Italian mainland. Ninni told me this workshop had been in the same family for a handful of generations. He greeted the owner, and the pair went off to discuss business. I watched the craftsmen for a bit, then strolled across the lane and looked at the gray structure I had seen a few days before. It was indeed a Byzantine church, much like the one I had seen, inside and out, in Castiglione at the beginning of my trip nearly a month earlier. It was behind a high fence with a locked entrance at the front.

Ninni showed up with the shop's owner, and we walked into the cemetery. The two men went to Ninni's family tomb and had a lively discussion about how to incorporate a brother's remains. But first, Ninni pointed out to me the nearby tomb of native son Luigi Capuana. I had seen his giant statue in the town square, and here, on the edge of the cemetery and with an outstanding view of the countryside, was his moderately elaborate tomb.

Ninni finished his business. The craftsman left, and we walked to the cemetery custodian's office to find out whether we could enter the Byzantine *cuba*. The two men conferred in what I presumed was local dialect, and Ninni came out, shrugged his

shoulders, and said in Italian, "It is not possible. It is too dangerous, and there is no money to fix it." Hence the fence and the
locked door. We left—I was disappointed—and Ninni continued
downhill on Via Roccovè. He had another destination in mind,
one that would raise my spirits.

A short distance down from the village, a road veered right
with a sign and arrow proclaiming SANTA MARGHERITA just ahead.
Ninni pulled up along the edge of wide, deep gully. Across, on
the other side and barely standing, were portions of what once
was a large two-story farmhouse. That was all there was of Santa
Margherita, a *contrada*, or neighborhood, of Mineo. The roof was
caved in, walls to what were once rooms were partially collapsed,
sheep were grazing in and around those woeful ruins, and a pair
of dogs was scampering among the sheep.

"This was the country home of Luigi Capuana," Ninni told
me. "Now it is owned by the *comune*, but there is no money to do
anything with it."

We drove around the end of the gully and parked near the ruined house and outbuildings. I wanted to walk down to the complex, but Ninni stopped me, pointing to one of the dogs running
and barking among the sheep. "They might be dangerous," he
said. I've had near misses with feral dogs in southern Italy, where
they are known as *cani libre* (free dogs), so I backed off.

Just then, a man drove up in a small truck, climbed out, and
started down toward the house. Ninni called to him, asking if the
dogs were safe. *Sì, sì,* he said with a laugh. We walked down,
choosing our footsteps carefully among broken stones and thorny
undergrowth, and prowled around the edge of what was once the
main room of the house, now wide open to the elements. It was

a short exploration; the heavens were threatening rain, and Ninni urged me to come back to the car, parked next to the sign that proclaimed this to be a home of Luigi Capuana. We left, and I sadly realized that even if the *comune* could raise the money, this home and its associated buildings likely were too far gone for any kind of restoration. The sheep and, later in the season, cows were making quick work of it, along with rain, wind, and time.

We returned to Mineo. At some point, overlooking the broad valley, I saw far below and to the northwest what appeared to be a well laid-out housing development, much like an American subdivision; there was nothing ancient or medieval about it. I asked Ninni. "It used to be housing for the American military families at Sigonella," he said, referring to the U.S. Naval Station where I, long ago as a navy reservist, had spent two weeks. That housing area, built long after my time at the base, has become a center for immigrants, Ninni said. They live in the houses and get language education and some training before they move on to other places in Italy and Europe.

I drove by that area a few days later, skirting the housing development itself. Along the dusty road on the outskirts sat hundreds of men, apparently from sub-Saharan Africa, waiting for rides or for offers of work from local farmers. The harvest season for the oranges had just ended. Later, in the fall, it would be time for the harvest of olive and almond trees higher up on the slopes. The problem, for Sicily and Italy, of boatloads of immigrants coming ashore must be overwhelming. Based upon what I've seen during several visits, the government seems to handle the seemingly never-ending influx better than surrounding countries. A few days after my conversation with Ninni, I watched uniquely and brilliantly adorned African women walking through Mineo's main square, each with a Sicilian woman at her side. This was part of their orientation and, I suspect, the beginning of language training.

Maria Giovanna Cafiso led the way into a bright, wood-paneled room filled with ancient manuscripts. It was spotless; no dust anywhere, and the books were precisely lined along a few dozen shelves holding some thirteen hundred volumes. These were the work of Jesuits and Capuchin friars from about A.D. 1500 to 1600. White gloved, she removed one from the shelf, opened it carefully and reverently, cradling it in her arms like a beloved infant. She showed me the hand-drawn pages. She returned it to the shelf and walked over to a tabletop, pointing to a large book encased under glass. It was a Latin Bible dating to 1493—the oldest volume in the collection.

These books made a stunning array spread throughout two rooms, and they are part of what is known in Italian as the Ex Biblioteca Dei PP. Cappuccini. The Capuchin books date back to the earliest days of that order, which had split off from the Franciscans in the sixteenth century.

These treasures are diligently cared for by Maria and her associates at this small well-organized library, contained within a larger library of seventeen thousand books. The greater library is dedicated to Luigi Capuana, whose works, along with symbols of his life, are displayed on other floors. The building was once his family home, located, unlike the rural home I saw with Ninni, in the heart of the village. It likely is where the noted Sicilian author was born. Families of means often had a home in town and a home in the country where animals were raised and crops grown. Maria gave me a full tour of this triangular-shaped town house, including the spaces where generations of the family had lived and died.

I had come to this building to learn more about Capuana—a writer and poet whom I first discovered when, a month earlier during a meeting in Philadelphia, my new friend Santi Buscemi handed me a copy of *The Marquis of Roccaverdina*. Santi had just translated it into English. I already knew a lot about Verga, Capuana's friend who was only a year younger, but Capuana was new to me. At the library, I discovered all of Capuana's books and also came across the books of his and Verga's contemporary, Federico De Roberto. De Roberto was born in Naples of a Neapolitan father and Sicilian mother. At age ten, following his father's death, he was sent to his mother's family in Catania for his education.

These three men crossed paths in Milan during the late 1880s, each drawn there by its reputation as Italy's intellectual center and perhaps because many Sicilians of means longed to escape the confines of their island. De Roberto and Verga were fellow townsmen; the much older Verga also grew up in Catania in his family's city home a short distance from their country home in Vizzini. Capuana eventually became part of this circle. Archibald Colquhoun, translator of De Roberto's *The Viceroys*, in his 1962 introduction, imagined their relationship this way: "[I]t is pleasant to think that the meeting of these three Sicilians amid the Lombard mists helped to bring about a renovation of Italian letters."

This renovation became known as *verismo*, or quite literally "truth." Santi Buscemi points out in his introduction to Capuana's novel that the three men were the three major *veristi* who "reacted against the sentimentality of the romantic and mannerist writing that preceded them." Their styles were so powerful in the world of Sicilian letters that it is no wonder, as Buscemi points out, two twentieth-century writers—Luigi Pirandello and Salvatore Quasimodo—who studied their works became Nobel laureates in their own right.

The lives of these people seem interconnected, as if by a literary thread that stretches from the mid-nineteenth to the mid-twentieth centuries. Verga and Capuana, nearly the same age, had a vast correspondence in which they discussed their lives and their work. Capuana, in turn, had a close relationship with Pirandello. In fact, Capuana gets credit for shaking up the much younger man's world by insisting that he stop trying to be a poet and start writing short stories and other fiction. Pirandello listened, and in 1934 was awarded the Nobel Prize in Literature "for his bold and ingenious revival of dramatic and scenic art."

I visited the library a couple of times and gleaned what I could about the life of Luigi Capuana. Often I sat in the sunlight of Mineo's main square, Piazza Buglio, watching kids chase one another around the base of Capuana's statue. The bronze face had darkened considerably over the years, and the man's north-facing features were hard to make out. The sculpted head on his tomb in the cemetery on the village's edge clearly shows his sharp, mustachioed features, a look cultivated by many men of means in those days.

A careful reader of *The Marquis of Roccaverdina*—and one who sits in Piazza Buglio as I did over several days—has to see parallels between Mineo and the book's setting of fictional Ràbbato. As Santi points out in his introduction, the setting, high on a plateau of the fictional place and the real place, is similar; the views of Etna and the sweeping orange grove–filled valley are the same; and the men's club the marquis belonged to and the one Capuana attended occupies the same spot on the square today as described in the book.

As the evening approached, Capuana likely would walk from his home to Via Erice and down its length to the piazza where he would participate in the evening *passeggiata,* or walkabout, and talk with friends about the day's events and catch up on all the village gossip. Such walkabouts still take place today, throughout Sicily and Italy, in villages and towns big and small. I would always try to get into the square at the hour of *passeggiata,* find a spot on a bench across from the earthquake-damaged Church of Saint Thomas, now closed for repairs. Often, Ninni would join me, ask me what I had done that day, share news of the village, and together we would enjoy the growing dusk, listen to the murmuring of the strolling gentry, and appreciate centuries-old traditions.

I was running out of time in Mineo. If I had not been on a tight schedule with several more places to visit, I would have stayed in Ninni's *pensione* for a month or longer and gone on long walks in and around the village. A day or so before leaving, as I sat with my morning espresso in Il Vecchio Pasticcere, Salvo sat at my table and announced that his family was gathering that night for pizza—pizza made in the family's handmade wood-burning oven. Would I like to join them? Of course. We agreed to meet in the late afternoon. He would drive me to the family home on a generous plot of land in the *contrada* Costa Badia, just off the gradually sloping backside of Mineo's plateau.

The family was gathering in a small structure just off the main house. The four-year-old wood-burning oven occupied one corner, a work counter sat along one wall, and a table with rows of freshly risen, round-shaped pizza dough occupied the middle of the room. Salvo immediately donned a white apron and went to move burning logs of hardwood around the oven's interior. It was an art, he said, to shuffle the logs from place to place so the interior bricks would heat uniformly. I watched the fire-making ritual and observed Salvo's father, Franco Leggio, getting the carefully shaped mounds of dough ready. The mother, Agrippina Florulli, and Salvo's wife, Floriana Giammellaro, were preparing the various toppings, ranging from sausage and vegetables to anchovies and salami. Later I met Salvo's sister Veronica Leggio and infant daughter Emma, newly arrived from their home in Catania.

When the time was ready and the oven at the right temperature throughout, Salvo took down from the wall his wooden-handled peel, more often referred to as a pizza "shovel." Italians call it a *buccia di pizza*. The teamwork among family members took over. Franco started shaping the mounds of dough, and Agrippina and daughter-in-law Floriana installed the toppings. Salvo scooped them, one by one, onto the peel's blade and slid them into the oven, its interior bricks showing a bright yellow-orange patina.

Moments later he brought out each pizza, sized individually, perfectly crisp and with slightly blackened edges, and placed them in neat, overlapping rows on another table. This went on for perhaps thirty minutes or more. Three or four dozen pizzas in all came out of that wonderful family oven. We all would eat several of them that evening—I ate two, noting that they were perfect in a Neapolitan sense of the word. The crusts were thin and flexible, as Italians and Sicilians like them, requiring knives to cut and forks to hold the pieces together. The others would be distributed among the families, stored and eaten over the next few weeks.

It was a delightful family evening. Each adult was curious about what I liked best about Sicily and about my work. We exchanged family information: how many kids and grandkids, what our professions were, and who lived where. Salvo, of course, spoke English, as did his mother; the others listened patiently to my attempts at Italian. A lot of laughter was spread around that table that evening. I've been invited into many homes over many trips, but this was the largest gathering—and one of the liveliest—in all my years of travel. I wanted to stay days longer in this village and around all the people I met there, but my schedule was calling. Vizzini, birthplace of Giovanni Verga and the scene of several of his novels and stories, was next.

FIVE

A Knife Fight in the Ruins

The traveler sees what he sees; the tourist sees what he has come to see.

—G. K. Chesterton

Vizzini was high on my list of intended destinations. Not only was it the birthplace—or at least near the birthplace—of Giovanni Verga, but it was the setting of many of his late-nineteenth-century stories and novels. His most famous book, however, was located elsewhere. *I Malavoglia* (in English *The House by the Medlar Tree*) was centered, just fifty miles away, on the Ionian coast, in the even smaller village of Aci Trezza. Its fame was largely derived due to the 1948 Visconti film, *La terra trema (The Earth Trembles)*, which was based on the novel. Over the last few years, I have spent a lot of time in Aci Trezza, where I learned a lot about the novel and the film and met an elderly local who had appeared in the film so long ago. There is a small museum there that shows, through implements and furniture, how the poor fishermen and their families lived; perhaps a better word is, simply, survived.

I like a description, written by translator Archibald Colquhoun in his introduction to a novel by Verga's friend Federico De Roberto, that embraces the realism of life captured in *I Malavoglia*: ". . . the Furies dog Verga's fisherfolk at Acitrezza . . . we glimpse for the first time the southern worker, sober, toiling, undemonstrative, bitter sometimes at hope deferred." This realism, or truth of daily life, as shown earlier in the discussion of the two writers' contemporary, Luigi Capuana and his village of Mineo, is, of course, known in Italian literature as *verismo*. Now, in Vizzini, I could focus on Verga's other works and get a feeling for the place and the nonfisherfolk, the peasantry, he wrote about. In contrast, Capuana and De Roberto primarily wrote about the privileged classes.

Verga's family's connection to Vizzini goes back several generations. The family has a small palazzo next to the village's center. Its name is prominently displayed on the building's façade. It also had land in the countryside and a home in Catania, thirty-eight miles to the northeast.

A check of various sources shows confusion over the place of Verga's 1840 birth. A lot of notations say it was Catania. However, many scholars believe that as the time for his delivery approached, some sort of pandemic was sweeping through Catania and the larger cities of Sicily, perhaps smallpox, influenza, or even cholera. The family is believed to have traveled inland, to their rural home somewhere between Vizzini and Licodia Eubéa, two small villages just four and a half miles apart. Those Catania notations could come because these places are within the province of Catania. It's like saying I was born in Ada County, Idaho, without listing the city.

At any rate, I like it that Colquhoun waxes poetic in guessing that Verga's birth took place in Vizzini itself, writing that it was "one of those remote places in the interior whose roofs lie like leaves around a church, and whose male inhabitants appear to spend their days in the streets, cloaked and silent, staring into space."

I drove into Vizzini late in the afternoon. *Riposo* was over. The streets were filled with automobiles and pedestrians doing their shopping, seeing doctors, or taking care of daily business. I had no idea where the room I had rented was located. I drove into the center, expecting to park and make a call using the one phone number I had. The traffic confusion, typical of most villages in the morning and late afternoon, was overwhelming. There was no place to pull over; I could only keep moving from one section of the village to another. Everywhere I went, nearly all streets were one-way. I drove through the historic center and onto a road that followed the crest of the plateau.

The early evening view from this road, which ended in front of still another church, was spectacular: farmland dotted with stone houses in the distance, the sky turning from blue to light pink and then fading quickly into mellow charcoal. I relaxed as I drove, taking in this scene on one side and medieval buildings, with their warm, honey-colored stones, on the other. Finally, I turned around, drove back down and through the square, and escaped through the town gate I had entered when I arrived, careful to wait for approaching cars to clear it since it was wide enough for only one vehicle at a time. Outside, on the edge of this small village, I parked in a large, nearly empty lot, populated by large trash bins into which it seemed the entire village dumped its daily refuse.

In almost every new place I visit, there is always a brief moment when I am unsettled and wondering whether I made the right decision. Sometimes, in that confused frame of mind, I'll think that a particular village really doesn't seem all that interesting and maybe I should move on. Then I pull over, settle down, and think my way through the confusion. It always gets better, and the next day and the day after that and so on I become like a native, knowing how to seek out an elusive parking spot, which way to turn, where to find a good place to eat, and, of course, where the best bar is for my morning espresso.

But what really sells me on a place after a day or two is the people. The warmth they extend to a stranger who they sense really is interested in them, their culture, and their history changes any misconceptions I felt during that initial foray into the daily hustle and bustle of Sicilian life. They almost always are proud of their village and are eager to share it.

I called the number. Alfredo Giarrusso answered. His English was excellent, and my nerves, already softened by the view I saw from the plateau's edge, immediately relaxed. The house with my rented room was not in the village, but a few miles into the countryside. In fact, I had passed the turnoff to the small, white structure when I first headed toward Vizzini. Go back the way I came, Alfredo advised, and he would drive toward me. Go past the fields filled with tall, succulent cacti, and he would meet me in the middle of the road. I did, and soon he was there, smiling, waving and flashing his headlights. I followed him to the house. There I met his sister, Luciana Giarrusso. They were sitting down to dinner. "Would you please join us," he asked. Certainly.

I was feeling as comfortable in Vizzini as I did in Mineo, just a few miles away through rolling, greening hills in this early

Sicilian spring. Alfredo, as host, had no obligation to me other than providing a place to park, a comfortable room, and internet service so I could work. He and his sister were renting as well from the owner of the country house who was out of town for a long period of time.

Starting with dinner that first night, our relationship quickly turned into friendship. Alfredo and his sister are pharmacists who, with their retired father, own Vizzini's oldest *farmacia*. My host invited me to join a social gathering at their home. Friends had heard that Alfredo and Luciana had a guest who was interested in the village and its history. They wanted to meet and share their knowledge—knowledge gleaned from family stories that went back decades and two or three generations. Alfredo, who was planning on getting married and would soon move from his friend's house in the country to the Giarrusso ancestral home just a few blocks from Vizzini's historic center, wanted to show me the building he and his father had been renovating.

Having my days filled with this kind of attention from friendly Sicilians was invigorating. The gathering included two or three male friends of the brother and sister. I absorbed some cultural lessons as well as historical. Alfredo told me that the owner of the house he and his sister rented—architect Luigi Scalogna—bought the land it sits on. Most interesting was the fact his father, who had died when Luigi was six, had been the *campiere,* or armed range guard. The guards, outfitted with shotguns, kept people from trespassing and stealing fruit or animals. I discovered, a few days later, a photograph in Vizzini's museum that Giovanni Verga took of his *campiere* on his family's land near Licodia Eubéa. These guards, well into the twentieth century, were allowed to shoot intruders. Such laws, along with one that allowed a husband to kill his wife if he found her with another man, have been changed, thankfully. "This was their heritage," one of the young men at the gathering said, adding, with a smile, the younger generations don't subscribe to those traditions.

We shifted subjects. I never asked whether Luigi Scalogna's father was ever involved in shooting a trespasser. A bit of Sicilian history was a better topic, especially when it dealt with how land ownership was handled after Giuseppe Garibaldi, the northern Italian who chased the Bourbon rulers out of Sicily and Naples. He caused the island to become part of Italy, and he promised reforms that would ease restrictions that upper-class, or noble, landowners imposed on peasant workers. He also promised to redistribute land to the lower classes—a promise that never materialized. That broken promise shattered Sicilian illusions that Rome would be a good shepherd of its island folk. A distrust of Rome exists to this very day.

One of Alfredo's friends, Luigi Calmo, said this led to riots in various places around Sicily. In Bronte, on Etna's western slope and today famous for its pistachios, Garibaldi's soldiers massacred a dozen protesters, including a few nobles. For some reason, Vizzini and the surrounding area missed a lot of this unrest. "We always have had common land here," Luigi said, calling it *terre demaniali*. This roughly translates in Italian to "state land" and is supposed to be accessible to all classes. But this, too, didn't work out the way it was intended. Members of the upper class would "rent" the land, taking over major portions. Peasant workers, unable to rent their own land and have farms of their own, would then have to work for the nobles.

Luigi said, however, some of these from the lower classes were able to elevate their status from common laborer to management while in the employ of the nobles, making up a sort of middle class. For example, he talked about how his grandfather was a *massaru*, a Sicilian job title for an overseer, a man who worked for wealthy landowners and managed the estate and its farms, supervising peasant workers. Today, the peasant class is gone.

Through this era and into the twentieth century, the land around Vizzini helped it become a center for leather production, whether rough leather for export or for local craftsmen. Most were shoemakers; others crafted different types of leather goods. What established it as a center was a significant crop that had existed in Sicily since Roman times: Sicilian sumac, or *sommacco*. Parts of the bush could be made into dyes: reds, yellows, blacks, and browns. Oil could be produced from its seeds to make candles.

But this species of sumac, a bush that grows between six feet and nearly ten feet high, was more valuable than all that because the tannic acid in its leaves and branches could be turned into tannin, a product critical for tanning leather. Much of Vizzini's rough leather was shipped to Florence, also well-known for its leather shoes, coats, and purses.

Alfredo's ancestors also had ties to this industry, which at its height had hundreds of workers and several places where the tanning took place. He said, for example, his great-uncle's job was to find workers for the industry. Today, however, that industry is gone. In the mid- to late twentieth century, chemicals were developed that replaced tannin. Large corporations took over leather tanning, pushing out the small producers.

Luigi said his grandfather, the *massaru,* "did not know how to use the modern way, so he grew other products. He diversified." Bigger companies took over the manufacturing end of the leather business, using high-tech machinery to make shoes on a grand scale. That gradually eliminated the craftsmen who made things by hand. In Vizzini, there is only one craftsman left—former *calzolaio,* or shoemaker, and now shoe repairman Francesco Giallo.

The next day, Alfredo and Luigi took me to Francesco's tiny, darkened shop lighted only during daytime through the front-door glass. We three crowded in; Francesco, aged seventy, was warmly wrapped against the shop's chill in a light blue, fleece-lined jacket and wearing wide, black-framed glasses and a charcoal-colored canvas patrol cap. He greeted us and motioned for me to sit in one of the shop's two chairs. The shop smelled richly of leather and polishes. Pieces of tanned leather were scattered here and there, and shoes to be repaired rested on a small bench, next to an ancient machine for sewing leather to soles. Against the wall, a small case held shoes already repaired and awaiting their owners. There were no name tags; it's likely Francesco knew every one of his customers and which pair belonged to whom. He was a warm, engaging man of good humor and delightful dark eyes. Warned by my two friends about my visit, he was well prepared for a conversation about the lost craft of handmade shoes.

He pointed to a photo on the wall, taken, he said, in 1955, showing his father and a group of other craftsmen making shoes. Five years later, at age seventeen, Francesco went to Switzerland to work for a heavily mechanized shoe manufacturing company. He returned fifteen years later and left the machines behind, taking up the hands-on art of his father. However, in the mid-1980s, in an effort to modernize the local industry, he was involved with bringing some of the Swiss machinery to Vizzini, but that did not last long. The larger, more commercialized shoemakers continued to dominate.

"In the end, I surrendered," he said. Around 1990, "I decided to make a living just fixing the shoes."

I looked down at his feet. Francesco was wearing a handsome pair of black wingtip shoes. I had to ask. "Did you make those?" His smile was filled with irony. No, he said. "They have to be machine-made because of the depressions in the leather, the design."

Seeing Francesco in this tiny shop, smaller than most closets in a modern home, brought back a memory from a few years earlier. I was in a small town in Tuscany. The rubber sole on one of my shoes was peeling back. I remembered seeing a shoe-repair shop on small lane a few blocks from where I lived. I went by two or three times, but it was always closed. One afternoon, after *riposo*, I saw a light, and the door was slightly open. I went in and asked the elderly man, sitting on a short stool and wearing a weather-beaten apron tied twice around his slim middle, if he could repair my shoe while I waited. *"Certo che posso,"* (Of course I can), he said, adjusting his half-frame glasses on the tip of his nose. He grabbed a pot, swirled a long-handled brush deep inside, spread the glue, and held the rubber down with gnarled fingers. He held it for perhaps five minutes, quietly whistling a soundless tune under his breath. He took a black-spotted rag off the bench, wiped the sole clean, and handed the shoe back to me. *"Quanto?"*

I asked. *"Niente,"* he replied briskly. I insisted. Shaking his head, he turned to his bench and started work on something there.

The two men, Francesco in Sicily and this man in Tuscany, both about the same age, spent their days in their small shops, greeting the occasional customer, turning out quick, efficient work—when work was to be had—and likely knowing they were among the last of a craft that had lasted for hundreds, if not a few thousand, years. Francesco said that shoes today are not often repaired; they simply are replaced. None are handmade.

I asked him if he could make a pair of shoes for me; I would be in Sicily for another two months and would have plenty of time to come back for them. Oh, no, he said, shaking his head and speaking the dialect of Vizzini while Alfredo translated. "I don't have the right equipment anymore," he said, patting the antique sewing machine next to him. "I just fix."

There was a directional sign at the beginning of a side street off of Vizzini's main square. With an arrow pointing to the right away from the square, it listed a destination: CUNZIRIA. This was within a kilometer or so, perhaps a twenty-minute stroll, and I was told that a modern *agriturismo,* a rural tourist accommodation, was named for nearby Cunziria, a small, abandoned complex of very old stone houses and warehouses. I didn't know anything about either place, but thought it would make a nice walk on a warm spring day.

I started out from Alfredo's pharmacy, on the edge of Piazza Umberto I, and immediately turned left onto Via Masera. The street offers a gradual slope down the edge of the plateau and, within a short block, I passed a building to my right, slightly elevated, and opposite it stood Chiesa di Santa Teresa. A sign on a building said this small piazza was included in a scene from the film *Cavalleria rusticana,* an adaptation of Verga's short story. The building likely was the tavern where the protagonists challenged each other to a duel with knives. The church, across the small square, was where the women went to pray. I knew that many of the scenes in that story were drawn from the author's home village. This also was true of places in his major novel *Mastro-Don Gesualdo* and a couple of other short stories, including "La Lupa" (The She-Wolf). I would spend time, during walks around medieval Vizzini, seeking out some of these spots.

First I wanted to wander down to Cunziria, once a thriving *contrada* of Vizzini. Via Masera turned sharply to the left, but another branch, straight ahead, became a small provincial road, SP147. This onetime mule path flowed gradually down the side of Vizzini's plateau through a tunnel of tall trees just beginning to leaf out in the early spring. Far below, a cluster of buildings emerged, their whitish stones offset with light tan and gray patches. These structures—individual homes and larger warehouses, plus a church building—were abandoned. Snaking its way through this surreal collection was a small stream, the Masera, also the name given to the street. It was this water source, and the fact that this valley floor was exposed to abundant sunshine, that allowed this place to emerge, in the nineteenth century, as a major industrial center for the tanning of leather. It was closed down by the mid-twentieth century.

I walked into the decaying complex. A quick count showed

there were perhaps forty structures, some two stories tall. Many, without doors, offered views of dark, empty interiors. The larger warehouses were open. Just inside the doorway of one were rows of stone tubs for the soaking of raw leather in the tannin derived from the Sicilian sumac and combined with water from the Masera. Again I had found *gebbie*. These particular tubs, of course, were not Arab made as some I had seen earlier in my travels; the word is commonly used today for modern water storage basins and animal watering troughs.

Much later, I read that this deserted, ancient village of Sicilian stone, once home to one hundred workers and family members, was closed about the time of onetime shoemaker Francesco Giallo's youth and in the face of manufactured chemicals replacing the need for nature's tannic acid. The large fields of cacti along the hillside above Cunziria and around Vizzini itself have replaced the Sicilian sumac no longer needed as the area's major crop. This complex is owned by the province of Catania and is on loan to the village of Vizzini. There are great hopes for it. Perhaps it can be partially restored to show tourists a part of Verga's world, or as they refer to it here, the "literary Verghiano heritage."

In the center of this cluster was a low stone wall, a perfect place to lean against and eat a simple lunch. I pulled out a paperback copy of Verga's *Cavalleria Rusticana and Other Stories* and, fighting off a desire to take a quick nap in the comfortable spring sunshine, began to read the title story. I had once seen, back home in Utah, Pietro Mascagni's opera based on the story and later Franco Zeffirelli's film of the opera. The story itself is a quick read, perfect for a lunchtime repast. I was near the tragic conclusion when the name Cunziria leaped off the page. Verga had used this place, a complex of homes and shops for tannery workers, as the scene for the knife fight between the two protagonists, Alfio and Turiddu Macca.

I looked around and imagined seeing such a duel in the open space in front of me, now fenced in and with someone's horse methodically grazing the emerging patches of grass and drinking from the tiny stream. What timing: discovering I was in the midst of Verga's Cunziria while chewing a salami-and-cheese *panino*.

The motion picture of another Verga story, "La Lupa," was actually filmed here. This very short piece also is in the *Cavalleria Rusticana* collection, but I didn't realize the film's tie to Cunziria until my visit to Vizzini's Museo Immaginario Verghiano, which is dedicated to Giovanni Verga, his life, his photographs, and his literary masterpieces. Theatrical posters hang in one small room showing all the films and operas made from his writing. His photographs are stunning. They focus on the everyday people of Verga's time: the farmworkers, the field guards, and the women.

Verga's presence is felt everywhere in this village. The building the museum now occupies was the setting for the home of Mastro-Don Gesualdo in the novel of the same name. And, later, when I walked down the long steps into Piazza Umberto I, near the doorway to Alfredo's *farmacia*, I saw a marker indicating the piazza's name and these words, *Tutt'a un tratto la piazza sembrò avvampare in un vasto incendio* (Suddenly the square seemed to blaze in a huge fire)—a line from the early pages of the novel. Vizzini certainly honors its native son in every way possible.

Palazzo Verga has survived. This huge stone structure, built prominently along the edge of the main square, dates back to the eighteenth century and, according to my new friends, is still in the family. The three-story façade is moderately ornate with two built-in square pillars, one on each side, with ornate capitals. A single round pillar rises up on the left. The pillars support a terrace that hangs out over the sidewalk. One source I looked at said the interior of the palazzo's upper floors was never completed. Why, no one seems to know.

A story that Alfredo told me underscores the durability of such well-built two-hundred-year-old buildings that have survived earthquakes and wars. In the final days of the Allied invasion of Sicily in July and August 1943, a German tank division retreating north toward Messina rolled through the village along SS194, which follows the route through Piazza Umberto I, known locally as Via Roma. Apparently the British and Canadians, fighting their way up along Sicily's eastern third, were close behind. A German tank, hoping to bring down a building and block the roadway, fired a couple of rounds at the Palazzo Verga façade. The exploding shells broke off the ornate capital of the square pillar on the right side, but the building stood fast. The gunner, apparently a man in a hurry, took off along Via Roma. To this day, the large, brown gash at the top of the pillar remains.

I mentioned to Luigi Calmo that I had not seen much of Vizzini beyond the area around Piazza Umberto I. He offered to show me the upper village, where a friend had access to the Basilica di San Vito, located in a part of the village with streets laid out in an Arab format more than a thousand years ago when the Muslims ruled Sicily. En route to the basilica, along the route I took when I arrived lost and confused several days before, Luigi told me that the village's name, in Roman times, was Bidi. Later, for reasons lost to time, it evolved into Bidinini, and from that Vizzini. It arose from prehistoric settlements to a Greek settlement, then Roman, Byzantine, Arab, French, and Spanish. The village we see today developed in the Middle Ages around a castle, now gone, its stones likely incorporated into other structures as the village grew.

We drove along Via Roma and continued on where the name changes to Via Verga. The Basilica of San Vito, with an open square in front, loomed large. Luigi's friend, Giovanni Giarrusso (no relation to Alfredo, I learned later), a retired photographer and now church sexton, was waiting with a key. We walked into a sweeping interior and Luigi said that this was one of the oldest churches in the area, first built over a Christian crypt in the late fourth century and originally named Chiesa dello Spirito Santo (Church of the Holy Spirit). Over the centuries it was home to a confraternity whose members were the village's shoemakers. As a reward for their service, the crypt became their final resting place.

Luigi told me that a second church, Chiesa della Madonna del'Itria (Holy Mary Who Brings Water) was next door. *Itria* comes from the Greek word *idrōs,* meaning sweat, or more loosely defined: water. The massive Sicilian earthquake of 1693 that devastated much of southeastern Sicily nearly leveled both structures, as well as the rest of the village. When time came for rebuilding, both churches were combined into one under the name Basilica of Saint Vito.

Giovanni led us across the small square to the Mother Church, S. Gregorio Magno (Saint Gregory the Great), The massive sanctuary was wide open, dwarfing a cluster of seats for services. Such huge, pure spaces are typical of the larger churches in Italy and Sicily; I often sit in them after a long, hot day of wandering, feeling the coolness of the air and stone surfaces. It's not a religious thing for me, although I often light candles and think of family members. This place struck me the same as many other places I have been in: peaceful, quiet.

Then, in the midst of this contemplation, we heard shouting coming from a side chapel. A group of men—Giovanni said they were church workers—were struggling with a large statue of Saint Gregory, likely used a few days earlier in a procession in his honor. Now it had to be returned to its spot of great distinction in the large sanctuary.

The men, looking almost in uniform in their black clothing, carried the larger-than-life likeness of the saint across the stone floor and, with a lot of shouting and maneuvering, hoisted it into its tight space. Everyone seemed to be shouting orders; no one appeared to be in charge, but I suspected one of the men was. Their grip on the brightly painted figure, representing colorful gold-inlaid saint's clothing, was fierce. Dropping it or letting it bang against the wall was out of the question, something too horrible to contemplate. Soon, the yelling quieted down. The men, now speaking to one another in quiet, reverent voices, inched it back and forth into place upon its platform. They let go a collective sigh of reassurance, smiling and nodding satisfaction to one another. Disaster averted, one more time.

Vizzini citizenry long ago sought permission from Rome to declare Gregory as the town's protector. One source said it was because he had been born there. No one today really thinks he was. Official sources say the future pope had been born in Rome in 540; they also indicated that his father owned vast lands in Sicily. When Gregory was in his early thirties, he reportedly founded six monasteries on his Sicilian estates—hence the likely tie to Vizzini. His giant stone statue in Largo della Matrice overlooking the world beyond fronts his church.

Alfredo and I are sitting in the small *farmacia* late one Sunday morning, just after the Palm Sunday service and short procession in Piazza Umberto I. We had watched, from his front door, the tradition unfold. The priests and altar boys presided from the elevated steps of the *municipio*, the town hall, ministering to the crowd in the square below. There rarely is any separation of church and state in Italy, particularly in the far south. The top of the city hall steps work well for such an event. The square, jammed with the faithful, seemed to hold a majority of the village's six thousand Vizzinesi, most waving palm fronds. As the service from the steps ended, a long line of worshipers, led by a priest resplendent in colorful robes and carrying a processional crucifix, made its way into the square from the opposite direction.

The *farmacia* was quite old. Business was slow on this Sunday morning, and I had time to look at the beautifully crafted cabinets that had been there for a century or longer. Alfredo, thirty-six when we met, was born in Catania, where his pharmacist father, Mario, a native of Vizzini, was working at the time. When he was five, his dad was able to purchase the Vizzini pharmacy from a childless fifth-generation owner with no one to pass the business on to, and the Giarrussos moved back to their ancestral village. Now that Mario has retired, the business is in the hands of his son and daughter.

Given the way Sicilians pass professions, land, and homes from generation to generation, I wouldn't be surprised if this shop goes to someone in the third generation. Mario, who occasionally steps into the pharmacy to work a bit, spends most of his time in retirement remodeling the home that, amazing to me, has been in the family for six or seven generations, dating back to 1774. In fact, an ancient stone cut with that date sits in the middle of the entryway floor, left in place by renovators who worked around it.

Now a seven-minute walk along Via Roma from Piazza Umberto I, the house back then would have been in the countryside. "Two hundred years ago, it was a house in the middle of nowhere," Alfredo said.

"When I was born, my grandmother lived in the house," Alfredo continued. "She died when I was fourteen, and we have been rebuilding it ever since, collapsing the inside. It was my father's dream to live there, but now it will become the home for my wife, and me, and our child."

It was *riposo*, time for lunch and when each day Alfredo or his sister would close the *farmacia* for a few hours and take a break. On one of these afternoons, he invited me on a tour of his ancestor's house where he would live with Stefania Drago and their soon-to-be-born son. We set out in the warm sun, taking in the greetings of passersby who knew Alfredo either as a longtime resident or as their friendly neighborhood pharmacist. Around the area where his three-story home sits on a point of land and two streets form a V shape, a street market was in full swing.

The house smelled of fresh paint, all white, on hallways and walls of the interior rooms. The shocking whiteness was offset slightly by beautiful marble flooring with streaks of white and gray. Here and there were boxes of family treasures, some dating back a hundred years or more. In one corner, under a stairway leading up to the floor above, was a selection of old clay pots in beautiful condition.

Alfredo pointed to boxes of old, musty newspaper clippings and with rusty implements of one kind or another. The few stories he told me that afternoon were fascinating. In the late 1700s, an ancestor named Mariano Giarrusso, who was the brother or son of the builder of the home, Giuseppe Giarrusso, was a monk. "He was very clever," Alfredo said. "He could make things: a cradle that moves quietly, for example. People, very superstitious, were not used to such cleverness and felt he must be associated with the devil. He had to leave being a monk."

Then there is the story of the great-great-great-uncle who designed a windmill to grind grain. In those days, waterwheels drove the large round grinding stones. But tax collectors charged a tax for each revolution of those large waterwheels, "a small amount," Alfredo allowed, "but a tax nonetheless." When the tax collectors discovered the inventor's windmill, they installed a counting device. Alfredo reached into a box and pulled out a metal device that had a row of rotating numbers. "Here it is," he announced proudly. "We still have it."

A year after my visit, I received a message from Alfredo informing me that he and his wife, Stefania, and their infant son, Alberto, were happily ensconced in the nearly 250-year-old, but completely modernized, house. "We sleep in a wrought-iron double bed belonging to my family from four generations," he wrote, adding: "Stefania doesn't appreciate much the bed; they used it [through those generations] to show the deceased family members before the funerals."

It is Easter Week. I had spent Palm Sunday in Vizzini and would leave within a day or so for Piana degli Albanesi, where I hoped to experience another kind of Easter. It would be Eastern Orthodox, a form of Catholicism that split off from Rome in the Great Schism of A.D. 1054. It is now practiced in a few Sicilian villages at the same time of year that the Western church honors the event. And the Eastern churches in Sicily operate with Rome's full approval. But for the day before my last night of lodging in Vizzini, the day before I would drive a long way across the island to the northwest and the province of Palermo to spend nearly a week through Easter Sunday in Piana degli Albanesi, I decided to take a short drive in the Sicilian countryside. This would be an unplanned excursion. The idea would be to stumble across a village, hopefully very small, enjoy a nice meal, walk around in the sunshine, run the palm of my hand along the sun-warmed honeyed stones, and see what there was to see.

In the early morning, I drove from Alfredo and his sister Luciana's rented house into Vizzini, where I could connect with SS124 in the direction of Palazzolo Acreide. I stopped near a coffee shop beyond the historic center and near Alfredo's family house. This was where the street market had been a few days before. I wanted a double espresso and a *cornetto*. The traffic was light and the parking easy in this part of Vizzini. Here, in a small square, was the statue of Giovanni Verga. It showed a tall, angular man, slightly stooped, with both hands reaching out as if to greet an old friend. He was dressed in a frock coat of his time, and, heavily mustachioed, faced the street, his back to the campanile of the Church of Saint John the Baptist.

A threesome of elderly men, *pensionati,* sat in the sunshine. They saw me looking in their direction and one of them waved. Another tipped his Sicilian-style *coppola.* The third, leaning with both hands on his cane, nodded. I'd never met these men; their friendliness touched me. I walked over and asked if I could take their photo. They agreed, laughing, and asked me where I'm from. I told them as best I can. *"Sono degli Stati Uniti, da ovest, l'Intermountain ovest,"* I said. "Oh, Cali-for-nia," one of them responded. *"No, no,"* I said. *"Non la costa ovest. Utah, in montagna. Il vero ovest."* They each nodded, but I don't think they knew what Utah was. We shook hands. I walked back across the street and into the bar for my coffee.

All the outside tables were occupied. I walked over to where a man, probably in his fifties, was sitting alone, and asked if I could join him. He nodded. We talked for the next thirty minutes or so. In good English, he told me his mother was French and he had lived in France for many years. She had married a Sicilian. I wrote his name down: Jean François Jaques Gurrisi. He had been a truck driver until a severe accident put him on disability. He lived off his disability payments and enjoys the Sicilian sunshine in Vizzini, which I suspect was his father's ancestral home.

The morning, despite my early start, was burning away. Jean François was a delightful companion, the kind I suspect I could easily be a friend with if I were to live here. But I needed to be going. We shook hands, wished each other well, and I walked toward my car, passing the three gentlemen in the small square next to the tall, lean statue of Giovanni Verga, his rough-featured face obscured by a deep shadow. They waved as I passed.

SS124 took me toward Palazzolo Acreide. Just a few miles outside of Vizzini, over the crest of a small hill, a magnificent landscape of rich green rolled out ahead. I have no idea what the crop was, or even if it was a crop, but it spread out over several acres before the far edge dropped out of sight down into a small valley. Across that valley and rising higher up on a gradually building ridge-line were delineated pastures with specks of sheep and cows. I pulled over and stopped. Climbing out of the car, I could hear from way across that valley, and carried on a light breeze, the clinking of bells—light, tinkling bells of sheep and deeper, more vibrant bongs of cowbells.

It was a gorgeous sight, and the smells of spring after a few days of rain filled my lungs. But what really caught my attention, in the middle of this sea of green and perhaps 150 feet from the road, was an abandoned farmhouse of dark, broken stone and a roof of irregular, weathered tiles. I saw only the upper two floors of what must have been a three-story structure; it was surrounded by a stone wall with vegetation that had yet to show leaves filling up the interior space between it and the farmhouse. Farther back, where the outer wall was a few feet higher, were the rusted metal roofs of a couple of outbuildings. On the opposite end of this compound was a tall pole with a crossbeam at the top that once likely held wires for electricity. There were no wires, and there was no pathway leading from the highway to the small compound.

I almost never stop to check out the abandoned farmhouses and outbuildings spread across Sicily, but this scene was so beautiful, so serene, that I acted on impulse. For thirty minutes or so I walked along the roadway, this way and that, trying to see the blend of handcrafted stone and green landscape from different angles. A low wire fence bound the property line next to the highway, and I contemplated climbing through it and walking up to the structure. Reason prevailed, however. This was, after all, Sicily, where land ownership is sacred and has to be respected. I saw no evidence of a field guard, or *campiere,* nor would there likely have been one in this remote place even if the profession, so feared in the not-too-distant past, even existed anymore. Still, someone owned it. Perhaps farm equipment was locked up tight behind that wall. With a last, long look at a scene that would have made a magnificent landscape painting, I returned to the car and headed toward Palazzolo Acreide.

I had taken time to read about this larger Sicilian town but had no intention of returning there for a stay. A few hours in the town square, having coffee and perhaps a small lunch, would suffice. From earlier reading, I knew that the Greeks from Siracusa had defeated an Athenian army in a battle here during the late-fifth-century B.C. Peloponnesian War. And the Arabs, in the ninth century A.D. had plundered the town; eight hundred years later, 1693, an earthquake leveled it. Like Noto, to the southeast, which was destroyed in that same quake, Palazzolo Acreide was rebuilt along Baroque lines and both are listed as UNESCO World Heritage Sites for that magnificent architecture. But at nearly ten thousand people, the city was too large for my purposes; for this trip, I preferred the much smaller villages and hamlets. So my visit was less than an hour. I sat in a pleasant square surrounded by those Baroque buildings and caught glimpses of the far away Anapo Valley.

A few miles outside of the city, SS124 stops being a main highway. There's a junction where the dominant road, now SS287, continues straight on to Siracusa, about twenty-five miles away. I stayed on a much narrower SS124, heading in a northeasterly direction. It, too, would end up in Siracusa if I followed it that far, but a sign at a small place called Solarino indicated a turnoff onto a provincial road to the village of Sortino. Checking my map, I saw that I could go there, heading northwest and then loop back onto SS124 at Buccheri, only a few short miles to Vizzini and my last night there.

As soon as I turned onto SP28 and drove a few miles, I knew I had made the right choice. Cresting a low hill, I discovered, laid out in front of me, a small valley filled on both sides and down the middle with an ocean of orange trees. This was March, the end of the growing season, and the harvest should have been finished by now. But the trees were still full of these golden globes, giving this small valley an appealing green-and-light-orange hue like one might find on a painter's canvas. Earlier, it was the panorama of the green field with the abandoned farmhouse;

now, it was a small valley sloping gradually upward, speckled with orange. Sometimes, as I drive around Sicily's rural, wide-open spaces and rolling hills with blankets of fruit trees or of wheat being nudged back and forth by light breezes, I feel I have been dropped into an artist's studio filled with giant landscapes.

Up one side of the valley, through the groves dripping with fruit, up near the curve near the valley's crest, a Madonna loomed large. She was in her own grotto, standing in a crease in the rock on a pedestal with the words AVE MARIA carved across the bottom. Surrounding the small valley's upper edge were steep hills blanketed with rocks. This drive was one of the most beautiful short drives of all my years traveling in Sicily. Among the oranges stood lemon and olive trees, bordered by stone walls fitted together precisely with no mortar, miles of them.

The road carried over the top and away from the valley and dropped down into Sortino—a village that caught me by surprise. At first, I didn't see the hilltop village I had expected. The road widened near the bottom edges of this hamlet of nine thousand people and modernity rose everywhere. There were numerous apartment houses, probably built within the last decade or so, hundreds of small apartments spread among the two- and three-story buildings. I could have been on the outskirts of Cleveland or Denver. Then, a sign popped up ahead: CENTRO it said, with an arrow. This gave me hope. *"Centro"* usually means the historical center. In a few moments, I found myself in a small Sicilian village; all the buildings appeared occupied, unlike other places I'd been on this trip. They had been modernized, but most could date back to medieval times. I drove around a bit. There was a sign pointing to a puppet museum; I read later that Sortino was well known for its puppets, or *pupi*. The museum was closed indefinitely.

It was just before two o'clock. I parked in front of the Mother Church and walked around, looking for a small restaurant. Down a side street, one appeared, its front door wide open. Small tables with heavily starched, stunningly white tablecloths filled a large room. I was the only customer; the lunch hour was almost over; *riposo* would soon begin, and that front door would be shut tight until about eight or nine o'clock that night.

The small menu showed off dishes that I suspected were purely local: there were *maiale* (pig) and boar ragú sauces destined for pasta of all shapes and sizes. The offering that appealed to me was *vitello* (veal). It arrived with a combination of rice and ham sprinkled with chopped pistachios. The *vitello* was drowned in a brown sauce also peppered with pistachios. I asked the young woman server where the chopped nuts were from. "Bronte," she said. *"Dove altro?"* (Where else?)

I had figured that would be her answer. I have yet to meet a Sicilian who is not proud—very proud—of Bronte pistachios, grown in the magnificent volcanic soil on the western slope of Mount Etna. I drove there once and spent an hour or so walking about in an orchard of pistachio bushes, with the landowner's permission, of course. When I was there, many years ago, the pistachios were reddish colored and in large, heavy clumps on the branches. Eventually, by harvest, the bony shell—most split open while on the tree—would turn into the recognizable ivory color.

Ironically, Bronte pistachios are slowly being supplanted by nuts imported from Iran and Iraq, and other Mediterranean countries are slowly developing their own pistachio production.

It takes time. Bushes can take more than a decade to reach their full potential. Bronte's farms are small, averaging two and a half to five acres each. Those groves, with ordered rows of treelike bushes inching up the western slope of Etna, are beautiful in the late afternoon light.

I love pistachios and the way Sicilians use them in a variety of dishes. In fact, the best *cannolo* I ever had was in Noto, where the *pasticciere* (confectioner) handed me one where both ends had been dipped in crushed pistachios. The sweetness of the ricotta and the tang and crunch of the nuts, wrapped in a just-made crust, were sublime.

So, for dessert, what should I order? The young woman ticked off a long list of choices, but I stopped her when she mentioned *gelato al pistacchio*. What other choice was there? It arrived, in a very light green, almost ivory-colored mixture. A friend in Palermo, whom I credit with introducing me to such a gelato, told me to always avoid it if it is heavily green. That means food coloring has been added. "It's not real that way," my friend said. I have followed her good advice all these years.

I was in the restaurant—the only customer during a ninety-minute meal—long after they would normally have closed. No problem, the young woman told me with a smile. "You should never be rushed when you eat." The chef came out, his reddish face under the white brimless cap, and wiping his hands on a small towel, he reached out to shake my hand. "My favorite is the *vitello*," he said. "You have ordered our best dish." The bill for two courses, a bottle of mineral water, and a sublime dessert, was fewer than ten euros.

Sortino and this *ristorante,* I decided, would someday warrant a return visit. I also wanted to visit a massive necropolis outside of Sortino called Pantalica. It was too late in the afternoon, and daylight this early in the spring would fade by five o'clock. All I knew was that this was a prehistoric series of cemeteries created by the Sikelian people, predecessors to the Greeks. Individual tombs were carved out of rocks, and the place functioned from the thirteenth to the seventh centuries B.C. I drove by it along a road that dead-ended at the now-closed entrance to the preserve. Exploration would have to wait for another trip. My calendar told me it was time to move on. Easter Week was next.

SIX

An Orthodox Easter and a Bandit

There is an uncertainty about travel that affects even seasoned travelers.
For us it's mostly exciting, but there's always a feeling of anxiety in aban-
doning (even for a short time) what we know (even if it's tedium). To travel
is to make yourself vulnerable—leaving, with your papers and plastic, the
high-tech security of your home and wandering sumptuously among im-
perfect strangers. Couples by definition take the familiar with them; for solo
travelers, the apprehension is greater.

—Thomas Swick,
The Joys of Travel: And Stories That Illuminate Them

Easter is Sicily's biggest celebration, bigger than Christmas or
any particular saint's festival. Events in most villages last a full
week and are meaningful to people whether they are true believers or are there simply for the cultural memories of their child-
hoods. The two most emotional events I ever attended were held
in Enna, one of the most highly publicized Easters in the Mediterranean world. On Good Friday, hooded and robed, members
of various confraternities carry large statues of the crucified Jesus and the sorrowful Mary with the symbolic sword through her
breast through the streets in a six-hour silent procession. Two days
later, in sharp contrast, joy abounds on Easter Sunday. The risen

Christ and an ecstatic Mary "run" toward each other on the shoulders of hundreds of men. Thousands of spectators cheer as mother and son are reunited and are carried, side by side, up the steep steps into the Cathedral of Enna. It is a remarkable spectacle, meaningful to the faithful and casually religious observer alike.

I once spent a week in Enna observing Easter in a Sicilian city famous for the way the event is honored. Later, I heard about another Easter conducted in a much different way. Ironically, in a country dominated by the Roman Catholic Church, the Italo-Albanian Greek Catholic Church celebrates Easter according to the Byzantine rite in a couple of southern Italian and western Sicilian villages. Such churches are subject to Rome but follow the Eastern Orthodox rituals and traditions. These Eastern Catholic churches honor Easter at the same time of year as the Western Church. The Greek Orthodox Easter elsewhere is usually a few weeks later. Sometimes, the differences in the calendars of east and west align, and the two Easters fall on the same day, as they did in 2017.

The biggest Eastern Orthodox Easter in Sicily happens in a small place known as Piana degli Albanesi. There, those churches stand just down the street from Roman churches. Another Orthodox Easter is celebrated near Piana in the much smaller village of Mezzojuso, twenty-four miles away but more than an hour's drive over winding roads. There, two giant churches—one Eastern, one Western—are arrayed side by side in the town square.

For my next Sicilian Easter a few years after I saw Enna's version, I chose Piana degli Albanesi. I also visited Mezzojuso. First, though, I had to learn why the Eastern Orthodox religion, which split from Rome in the Great Schism of A.D. 1054, is allowed to exist in a land dominated by the Roman Catholic Church and its Rome-based pope.

Rome, under Constantine in the early fourth century, moved its new Christian empire east to Byzantium, located on the Bosporus, and renamed that Greek city Constantinople (today's Istanbul, Turkey). There were three presiding bishops running the Christian Church throughout the Mediterranean, from Rome, Constantinople, and Antioch in south-central Turkey. Over the ensuing centuries the Roman popes began to assert their primacy, and this began, from the fifth to eleventh centuries, to drive East and West apart. Eastern theology evolved with a heavy Greek influence; Roman law influenced Western theology. By 1500, following the expulsion of the Jews in 1492, Sicily was nearly 100 percent Roman Catholic. The Albanians, while absorbed in the Roman church as a condition of allowing them to stay, were allowed to practice the Byzantine rite.

There were major differences in the two theologies, differences that became clear to me as I witnessed events that week in Piana degli Albanesi. Orthodox priests can marry, while Roman Catholic priests cannot. I spoke with Papās Giorgio Caruso, an English speaker, and his young son in Mezzojuso, and my Piana degli Albanesi host pointed me out to an Orthodox priest, garbed in traditional black robes and a square black hat, and his wife, who were strolling the streets late one night just before Good Friday. Neither my host nor the priest nor his wife spoke any English— the Albanian language is generally spoken by the six thousand residents—so we never were able to have a full conversation other than to simply say, *"Ciao. Il mio piacere."* (Hello. My pleasure).

In the Roman church, the altar is front and center; the priest does his work in full view of the parishioners. In the Orthodox church, the altar is behind a screen, with a slight opening, and the priest usually works and chants with his back to the congregation, coming out occasionally, singing and swinging incense. The Orthodox services Thursday night and Good Friday, while long and with nearly everyone standing much of the time, involve chanting by various priests and the congregation.

I once read that these churches and their Sicilian and Italian congregations represent a "Byzantine oasis in the Latin West." It was extraordinary for me, a Westerner, to witness a rite that dates back to the sixth century when Justinian ruled from Constantinople deep in the Eastern Roman world.

With rare exceptions, there are no statues in an Orthodox church. There might be a Madonna, perhaps, and a prone crucified Christ that are used in the Good Friday procession. These churches have icons, images typically painted on wood, woven into cloth, or painted in frescoes. One writer called them "windows into heaven." They are usually images featuring Christ, Mary, saints, or angels. Western churches have numerous paintings showing scenes of earthly events along with many three-dimensional statues. Many of the icons I saw in both villages were fairly recent or beautifully restored and showed a remarkable craftsmanship. Art, in whatever form, certainly is revered by both theologies.

The Great Schism caused much discord and violence over the centuries. Each side excommunicated the other. But, in Jerusalem in 1964, Pope Paul VI and Patriarch Athenagoras revoked their religions' decrees. In recent times, the two churches, which certainly will always remain separate, have settled the waters. I was surprised to see, in front of the congregation at the main

Greek Orthodox church in Piana degli Albanesi, a large photograph of Pope Francis, visible all the way to the back of the sanctuary. It was a reminder that Rome, while spiritually obliging to
Eastern traditions, still controls things.

Albanians started coming to Sicily and southern Italy in the
late fifteenth century after attacks in Anatolia and the Balkans by
the Ottoman Empire. They escaped in Venetian ships and were
allowed to stay in areas around Palermo, probably in places similar in concept to today's refugee camps. Within a few years, they
were granted permission to build villages in the hills to the southeast of Palermo on land originally known as the "Plain of the
Archbishop." King John II of Spain and Sicily allowed them to
practice their Orthodox faith, and the village became known as
Piana dei Greci, or Plain of the Greeks. It retained that name until
1941, when Mussolini's government changed it to today's Piana
degli Albanesi, or Hora e Arbëreshëvet in Albanian. This was
done to reduce the sting felt by members of this ethnic minority
when Italy's fascist army attacked Greece and showed imperial-
ist aggression toward Albania.

Mezzojuso, with three thousand residents—half the population of Piana degli Albanesi—was another of these communities
settled by Albanians escaping from the Ottomans. Originally,
Muslims had settled it during their domination of the island in
the ninth and tenth centuries and it was taken over, in the late
eleventh century, by the new conquerors, the Normans. Its name
can mean a couple of things, including "Hamlet of Joseph" or,
in Italian, with *giù* substituting for *juso*, "halfway down" because
of its location on a hill. Conveniently for the immigrating Alba-

nians, Mezzojuso was nearly abandoned by the late fifteenth century.

On this journey, I spent nearly a week in Piana degli Albanesi with plans at some point during Easter Week to go to Mezzojuso. I wanted also to see Campofelice di Fitalia, just a few miles south of Mezzojuso and with only five hundred residents. It likely wasn't an Albanian settlement since it is relatively new, being organized in the early 1800s. But it was close by.

I got a lot of information about Piana degli Albanesi from reading Norman Lewis's book *The Honoured Society: The Sicilian Mafia Observed*. Lewis had a few pages about the town that were not necessarily Mafia related, unfortunately describing it as "a wretched little township." I found the modern village to be the opposite of that description given that I was there several decades after Lewis. He did touch on the Mafia's influence by telling stories about the mayor, Don Ciccio Cuccia, in the 1920s.

The don presided over a visit to the village by King Vittorio Emanuele and a few years later by Benito Mussolini. Ciccio apparently tricked the king into becoming godfather to his "bawling infant," Lewis tells us. And when Mussolini visited on his anti-Mafia campaign through Sicily, Don Ciccio, who felt the dictator had disrespected him, arranged to have the town square empty of regular citizens when Mussolini made his speech. The don then arranged to have a photographer sneak a photo of him with his arm on Il Duce's shoulder, and Mussolini "found himself addressing a group of about twenty village idiots, one-legged beggars, bootblacks, and lottery-ticket sellers specially picked by Don Ciccio to form an audience." The don should have listened to Mussolini's harangue. In it, he declared war on the Mafia, and the don found himself, weeks later, in prison.

Lewis's book was originally published in 1964, long after the town's name had been changed from Piana dei Greci to Piana degli Albanesi, but for reasons unknown to me he kept referring to it with the "Greci" name. Since his description of the town was significantly different from my experience, I suspect he wrote those pages long before the writings were collected and published.

I was settled in a small apartment in Piana degli Albanesi, on a village lane for pedestrians only. To get to it, I had to walk up a steep hill from my parking spot, then up an even steeper set of steps, reaching a gradual incline to my front door. Later, after unpacking, I took a short walk. Along the way, I passed open doorways and windows with sounds of families inside preparing for dinner, televisions blaring, kids talking loudly. I was listening to voices speaking Albanian, or perhaps a dialect combining Albanian with Italian or, maybe, Sicilian. It was a cacophony of sounds like I had never heard before.

It was late afternoon. There was still a chill in the air as I walked down the gray stone steps flanking the outer wall of the Cathedral of Saint Demetrius Megalomartire of Thessalonica. I stood at street level and saw several people doing business in the few shops along Corso Giorgio Kastriota, kids riding bicycles, old men standing in groups smoking, talking loudly, gesticulating. *Riposo* had ended. This was my first overnight visit here, and it was early in the week. I had spent Palm Sunday in Vizzini and its surroundings, and now, on Monday, I was getting my bearings in this new place.

Monday is the third day of Holy Week in Eastern Christianity, after Lazarus Saturday and Palm Sunday. It is the second day of the Roman Easter. On that Saturday, at vespers in the Eastern church, congregants honor the miracle of Christ raising Lazarus from the dead, and this officially ends forty days of Lent. The faithful, perhaps even the not so faithful, eat traditional foods, including spiced breads. I had seen several Roman Catholic Palm Sunday traditions; if I had known that the Orthodox week began on Saturday, I would have left Vizzini sooner.

Once, many years before, I had driven straight through Piana degli Albanesi, along the Corso, on my way to a wide-open field, known as Portella della Ginestra, or Portelja e Gijinestrës in the local Albanian dialect. It is fewer than two miles away, on the road to San Giuseppe Jato. I knew nothing about the village itself. But I did know a lot about Portella and about the deaths there, on May 1, 1947. Eleven, perhaps fourteen, Piana degli Albanesi townspeople, including three children, were shot to death, and twenty-seven were wounded during a May Day celebration honoring the Communist Party's victory in the new Sicilian Parliament. It is a tragedy cloaked in mystery.

Before it got too dark, I decided to drive out to Portella. I had been there a few years earlier while working on another book, and I could never shake the emotions I felt while I sat there among stones now carved with names of the dead, imagining the terror.

There is controversy over who conducted the massacre. A local bandit, Salvatore Giuliano, and his men joined with some Mafia hit men on behalf of wealthy landowners who feared the Communists would redistribute land to the peasant farmers. The men used machine guns left by the U.S. Army at the end of World War II to fire upon the celebrants. During trials three years later on the mainland in Viterbo, Italy, Giuliano's men maintained they fired over the heads of the May Day crowd, intending simply to intimidate them. They claimed it was the Mafia gunmen who fired *into* the crowd.

Giuliano was never captured alive; one of his most trusted lieutenants killed him in June 1950 after agreeing to work with authorities searching for the bandit, who was hiding fifty miles to the south, in Castelvetrano. The lieutenant, Gaspare Pisciotta, had hoped to win amnesty for his role in the 1947 massacre but was sentenced to life. While he was in prison, the Mafia ridded itself of Pisciotta, who apparently was negotiating with prosecutors to name names, by having someone poison his morning coffee, and he died an excruciating death. Salvatore Giuliano meanwhile was buried in his family plot in the village of his birth, Montelepre, not too far west of Piana degli Albanesi.

Portella, at the bottom of towering Monte Cumeta, is much more developed today as a historical site than when I first visited in 2010. There is a large parking lot across the local road capable of handling hundreds of vehicles and buses that show up every May 1. The walkways among the rocks that bear names of victims have been paved, and benches and low stone boundary walls are new. The marker, carved into one of the granite rocks, quickly summarizes in just a few words the events of that day; there is no mention of Giuliano or the Mafia. Carved into another upright stone is a statement from Sicilian writer Ignazio Buttitta:

> *Cu camina calatu*
> *torci a schina,*
> *s' è un populu*
> *torci a storia*
> (Who walks bent over
> twists his spine;
> if it's a people
> it twists history)

I stayed for perhaps an hour, sitting under a sky that was shifting from cloudy blue to looking like marbleized ice cream, and listening to the light breeze whisper down along the face of Monte Cumeta, which looks southeast across this valley whose name roughly translates to "door of the broom," with "broom" referring to the yellow ginestra plant that blankets this area. The lower slopes of this singular peak looking over this stretch of tragedy were turning green. Above hung a sweep of nearly vertical broken granite that stretched out in a shape like an Australian boomerang cradling the lower slopes where Salvatore Giuliano and his men had lain hidden, their fingers on machine gun triggers.

I knew there were people, elderly by now, still living in Piana degli Albanesi who were there as children on that awful day. Plus, there was a museum I wanted to visit. Soon, the emotion I felt in this sorrowful place became too heavy, and it was time to leave. A few minutes later I parked in my spot by the post office and walked up the street, past the Orthodox cathedral.

I saw the sign. It is between the cathedral and Antico Bar Sport with its friendly staff that happily dispenses excellent espresso. The sign, hanging above a doorway to a clean, well-lighted room, said simply: CASA DEL POPOLO (House of the People). I had been headed to the bar to get coffee and a cream-filled pastry, but I stopped and looked in. There was a collection of six elderly men, sitting around tables, some just talking, others quietly playing cards.

It wasn't the usual card-playing crowd I always saw in Sicily with their shouting and slamming cards down hard on the table, gloating triumphantly at beating and loudly arguing with an opponent who was probably a dear friend since childhood. These men were somber. The game didn't seem important, but the comradeship did.

The Casa del Popolo is a communist club. I had seen these meeting halls throughout small villages—and, of course, there were clubs in other places for the political centrists and the far-righters as well. But here were this village's last surviving members of the Italian Communist Party, the party that won control, along with the Socialist Party, of the Sicilian parliament in elections less than two weeks before the May 1, 1947, attack.

The men, sitting inside the unheated room in their heavy coats, saw me looking through the glass. One jumped up, crossed the room, and opened the door. *"Prego,"* he said. (Please.) And he motioned me in. I was delighted to be invited into a private space by men who likely figured that with my white hair and beard I might be one of them. I nodded, said *buonasera* (good evening), and looked at each one of their grizzled faces, their Sicilian-style hats, the *coppole,* firmly in place. I said, in Italian, that I could only speak their language *solo un po'* (just a little). They smiled, nodding acceptance of my inability to communicate. I suspect, listening to their subdued conversations, that even if my Italian were better, I would have had difficulty with the mixture of Albanesi and Italian words that make up their purely local dialect.

There were posters with the names and symbols of the Communist Party in Italy and one that might have been exclusively Sicilian. Ironically, there was a communist plaque on the wall next to a cross with the crucified Jesus. Dozens of photographs of people attending local meetings and rallies were stuck on a bulletin board. Then, hanging on the back wall, a painting caught my attention. It was done with liberal use of oils, dark and red in color, depicting death and destruction on an ugly yellow plain punctuated by sharp granite rocks poking out of the ground. Seven men, in peasant clothing and Sicilian caps, were either running from something awful, red, green, and white flags in their hands, or they were wild-eyed and shouting. Two bodies were facedown on the yellow ground, blood pooling around them. In the midst of all this confusion and death was a wounded black horse down on its side, its head raised up and its face in agony. The painting is graphic, powerful. Its roughness might lead some folks to discount it as a poor piece of art. To me, it was that very roughness and its profound message that raised it in my eyes.

I turned to the men, their eyes on me, watching as I looked around the room. "Portella?" I said, nodding toward the painting. They nodded slightly in unison, not saying anything. *"Eravate la?"* I asked, hesitating a bit as I struggled to find the proper way to ask the question, hoping to use the plural "you" ("Were you there?"). A couple of the men nodded silently; the others did not. I knew asking more questions was beyond my ability, and I did not want probe old wounds, emotional or otherwise. Children, beyond the three who were killed, were among the wounded. I couldn't know if they would have been willing to talk about it even if I had had an interpreter with me.

No one I encountered in the village so far could speak English. So, I went up to each man and shook hands, thanking them for their invitation into their small club room where they spent their days with each other, retelling stories and commenting on daily events in the village and the rest of the world they read about in the short stack of newspapers on a table. I waved as I headed out the door and, to a man, they broke out in big smiles and waved back. Every time I passed by during that week I would look in and a few would always return my nods.

Tuesday of Easter Week was like every other nonholiday day, except in the evening when there would be special church services. I decided to make the short drive to the northwest, just twenty miles, to Montelepre, the birthplace of that bandit, Salvatore Giuliano. I couldn't get him out of my mind, as well as the events surrounding Portella della Ginestra. It took me less than an hour to get there, following the usual winding roads over and across hills with stony tops and land wide open as far as I could see. Montelepre is on the backside of the mountains that surround Palermo and is small, with only six thousand Monteleprini. In the fourteenth and fifteenth centuries, rich landowners planted large groves of olive trees in the fields around this village to supply oil to Palermo, which otherwise had to rely on oil imported into Palermo from growers in Gaeta, located near Naples on the Italian mainland, and from Tunisia in North Africa.

I wanted to find Giuliano's home. I didn't know if it would be preserved or even exist anymore. I had seen Francesco Rosi's remarkable film *Salvatore Giuliano* (1962), which presented a rough, unvarnished recounting of the massacre that had happened just fifteen years earlier. Much of it was filmed in Montelepre. In 1947, troops from the mainland and members of the Italian news media occupied it as investigators probed the massacre and looked for the men involved. Scenes of local life in that tiny town were truthfully portrayed—I particularly remember the scene of the town drummer, the *tammurinara*, Sicily's version of a town crier, who walked the streets, proclaiming the news of the day, pounding on his drum to get the people's attention. The film was realistic to the point of Rosi using Piana degli Albanesi residents, many of them survivors of the actual event, to re-create the horror of the massacre in the midst of those granite boulders at the site where the tragedy occurred.

The birthplace of the bandit is also the ancestral village of singer and politician Sonny Bono, whose father came from there. It was busy with cars and people shopping in an outdoor market along Via Castrenze di Bella, beginning at Piazza Ventimiglia. Despite the confusion, I found a parking spot along the street, near the square, and walked its length, enjoying once again the humming life of a small village. I drank espresso, sitting at a tiny table on a sidewalk, ate a pastry, and soaked in my environment for perhaps an hour. It would soon be noon, time for lunch, and later *riposo*, so I didn't want to linger too long. The outdoor market, which likely had been going since just after dawn, was, in fact, closing down.

I stopped at a fruit stall and purchased a half-kilo of *mandarini* (tangerines). I asked the vendor where Salvatore Giuliano's home would be. He pulled a small map off the shelf, the kind printed for visitors, and marked the spot where the house was. He said a *nipote* (nephew) of Giuliano's operated it as a small museum, but it was always closed. The nephew could be contacted at his nearby restaurant, Castle Giuliano. Perhaps he would give me a tour.

It was lunchtime, so I went directly to the restaurant. The server said it was possible to see the house. She would call the nephew and ask him to show me, once I had eaten. A plate of delicious spaghetti and a side dish of spinach later, Daniele Sciortino walked in. He said he would meet me in front of the house, just a few hundred feet away around a curve. Fifteen minutes later, he was waiting at the front door. The house, with a brick front, was narrow, perhaps only thirty feet wide. A sign was attached next to the door, telling of its former occupant. No one was living there now; the family, two or three generations later, was maintaining it as a historical site.

"I am the great-great-nephew," he told me, turning a large brass key in a battered, ancient lock. We walked up three flights of stairs to the top floor and into the only room, at that level, which he said was Salvatore's. Its furnishings were meager, probably set up to show visitors rather than present the room as it was when Salvatore lived in it. There were no clothes on hooks, simply a bed and a small table holding an ancient typewriter and a very old film camera. Pictures on the walls were of Salvatore in various poses, many of which I had already seen in books and on internet sites. Everything in this room and elsewhere in the house was covered with a layer of dust.

I wanted to take a photograph. "No photos," said Daniele in a kind but firm voice. We walked down a flight to the room that had been Salvatore's sister's. It also was sparsely furnished. The next flight down led to the parents' room, again standard and spartan. We reached the larger ground floor. The kitchen was tucked under the stairway, and the larger room doubled as the family's dining area and living space. It was like stepping back into the early 1900s. The small cooking stove was a wood-burner. The tiles on the counter were cracked, and, as in the bedrooms, dust was everywhere. A few pots and pans hung on the wall of that tiny corner. A couple of chairs, a small table. That was it. It seemed untouched since Salvatore's mother passed away. Salvatore was twenty-seven when his trusted friend killed him in 1950 in Castelvetrano. He likely lived in hideouts through most of his twenties while he and his fellow bandits robbed from the rich to give to the poor, occasionally visiting his mother while dodging authorities. This is what made him a hero among western Sicilians who later refused to accept that he could have been behind the massacre of the kinds of people he had helped over the years. I doubt that many folks who grew up with the legend of the bandit would believe he was evil, even if irrefutable proof were found that he indeed did spearhead the killings at Portella della Ginestra. Daniele allowed me to take his photograph standing outside, next to the front door. That was it. Simple, plain, not well maintained, its family mementos limited. But it satisfied my long-held curiosity and cost just a few euro.

I do not know whether Giuliano was the Robin Hood character many people believe he was; how much is myth, how much is reality. I have Sicilian-American friends who believe he was a hero and wrongly blamed for Portella della Ginestra. Other books, particularly the one written by travel writer and historian Norman Lewis, look at him critically.

I asked the docent at the Portella della Ginestra section of Piana degli Albanesi's museum about the differences of opinion, particularly in the village where so much pain resulted from that May Day event. All she would say when I asked if he was a hero like Robin Hood or a villain: "People are divided." Like any good journalist, or docent, should do, she kept her opinion to herself. I can understand why. If the massacre at Portella were not an issue, some folks consider him a man of the common people. Lewis quotes the bandit as saying, "A rich man no more misses a million lire than he would his hat, but if you take a sack of wheat from a peasant, you leave him in misery."

The next day, Wednesday of Easter Week, again had few events during the daylight hours. This would give me time to head south to Mezzojuso to see the side-by-side churches, Roman and Greek Orthodox. This would be a quick visit. I needed to spend more time in Piana degli Albanesi to watch as the Easter fever began to rise. But here, in Mezzojuso, I found a small place that appealed to me on many levels. The people walking the streets, the old men on benches, the kids kicking soccer balls against solid-stone walls, the beautiful cobblestones in the historic center all came together for me. I almost was wishing I had chosen this tiny place to spend Easter Week. It, too, celebrated it in the Greek Orthodox style.

I parked and walked toward Piazza Umberto I, where the two churches sat next to each other: The sixteenth-century Greek Orthodox Church San Nicolò di Mira is the village's mother church, fully restored in 1934. It sat on the square itself. Up a flight of stone steps, stood the twelfth-century Roman Catholic Church of Maria S.S. Annunziata. I learned later there is a nearby Orthodox monastery whose monks preserve documents.

San Nicolò's interior is similar in many ways to the cathedral on Piana degli Albanesi: The higher floor at the end apse is where the sub-priests work the screen, the iconostasis, which is covered with brilliantly painted icons. Some, I was told, date back to the sixteenth century. This icon screen has a small opening for the main priest to come and go around the altar, mostly hidden from worshipers. It is behind this screen where the priest celebrates the "Holy Mysteries."

A woman came up to me and asked if I had any questions. She spoke a bit of English, and with my bit of Italian we communicated just fine. She showed me some icons, beautifully arrayed on the walls. Then a man walked up with a small boy in tow. He was the new head priest, she said, introducing me to Papās Giorgio Caruso. The boy, nine years old, was his son. The family had been in this village only a few months. He was the one who hurriedly explained why the altar is behind the screen. "It is for the priest, not for the people," he said. He was busy. There was no time for further questions. He shook my hand; the boy came up and shook my hand, and they left.

There were several workers in the church getting it ready for services that night and through Easter weekend. I began to feel I was in the way. I stood next to a large prone statue, the kind used in processions, in a glassed-in coffin. It was Jesus, with a crown of thorns and ragged red wounds on his hands and body. I felt a touch at my shoulder. A man motioned me to get closer to the casket that would on Good Friday be carried through the streets of this tiny village. I did, and he flipped a switch. The coffin lit up brightly, inside and out. The man was pleased and grinned happily. He was the one who was in charge of the lights. "They all work perfectly. Yes?" he said in Italian. *"Sì,"* I said. *"È bella."* He said he turned on the lights so I could get better photographs. After a few minutes, he shut the lights off. Workers opened the end of the casket and carefully, lovingly, removed the statue of the dead Jesus. They went over the body with cloths and cleaned the glass inside and out. The whole thing would be carried on the shoulders of these men Friday evening, the priest chanting and offering homilies, speaking through a portable loudspeaker to the townspeople lining the streets or following in procession behind the prone statue. That kind man's lights would dramatically show it all. An upright statue of a sorrowful Mary was nearby. She, too, would be carried Friday night.

I went to the Roman church next door, climbing those steps. It was empty; no workers and no apparent preparations. I knew there would be services here for the Roman Catholic congregations, but it would be the Greek Orthodox priests who would conduct the Easter procession. Roman Catholics certainly would participate, and when the Good Friday procession reached a Roman church, it would pause, and the Roman Catholic priest would deliver the homily. It was a blending of the rites that has gone on in these small villages since the sixteenth century.

The Roman church was not as colorful inside as its Orthodox neighbor. The few paintings, showing the usual religious scenes one finds in all of these churches, lacked the impact of the dozens of icon paintings next door. It certainly had a comfortable feeling that I often seek out in Sicilian churches when I want to sit and relax after a long day of walking. I listen to the services and enjoy trying to understand what the priest is saying. Once, when I was faced with a family tragedy and was making arrangements to go home several days early, I sat in one of these Roman churches in a small Tuscan village, watched priests conducting confession with parishioners, and sat through the Mass. It was comforting to me, a nonbeliever. Here, in this Roman Catholic church in a tiny village called Mezzojuso, I sat down in a rear pew and luxuriated in self-indulgent solitude.

Eventually, and much relaxed, I left, heading for Campofelice di Fitalia. Unfortunately, when I got within a few miles, the tiny track of a road was closed. Ahead, I could see that it had slipped all the way down a hillside; a long section of road was completely gone. There probably was a roundabout way in, but there wasn't enough time left for me to find it. It was disappointing. All I knew is that Campofelice di Fitalia—*fitalia* is a Greek word that means plantation—was an agricultural village whose residents produced a wide variety of crops including corn, fruit, olives, various nuts, and grapes for wine.

Once it was under the control of Mezzojuso; in the early 1950s, it became self-governing. I walked beyond the ROAD CLOSED sign about fifty feet and surveyed the damage. Only a thin ribbon of asphalt clung to the edge of the hill. The rest was several feet below. It had been a rainy spring, and single lanes of Sicilian roads between villages in the hilly countryside would often slough off the hillside, still allowing traffic to use the remaining edge. Not so here. This was the only place on my list that I could not get to in the time I had. I would have to content myself with just reading about it.

Thursday morning found me back in Piana degli Albanesi at Antico Bar Sport, near the Casa del Popolo and the cathedral. I decided, after espresso and a *cornetto,* I would do some shopping. I had found an excellent restaurant within walking distance on the edge of the village, along the main road to Portella della Ginestra. But for a late lunch/early dinner on this day before Good Friday, I wanted to fix my own spaghetti *al pomodoro* with crusty bread and bottled water. My tiny apartment had what passed for a kitchen. There were shops along the Corso and just off it on Via Gaetano Petrotta.

The first was a bakery, Balola Forno A Legna S. Rita. It's a long name, but the translation of the Italian describes what it does: Balola is a person's name, *forno a legna* means "wood oven" and Saint Rita was an Augustinian nun in the fifteenth century who had an abusive husband. He was killed, and she joined a nunnery and became the saint for abused women. I walked in, said the customary *buongiorno* one says in greeting when entering a store, and was overwhelmed with the selection of breads on one side of the room and a long row of pizza squares on the other side.

A young woman behind the counter handed me a doughnut. This was a surprise because doughnuts as Americans know them are not plentiful in Sicily. But this one was the best I had ever eaten. It was round, of course, but no hole, crusty with a light sprinkling of sugar and a filling of cream that almost exploded out of my mouth with the first bite. I was hooked. This young woman was a marvelous salesperson. I bought a half dozen.

Then, she showed me the bread. I asked for something that was typical of Piana degli Albanesi. There were two types: *panini di rimacino,* which was a short loaf with a light sprinkling of sesame seeds on top, and *farina di rimacino siciliani,* a round loaf made with a type of flour usually used in cereal. I opted for the first one and also passed over the two varieties of breads made in the Palermo style: *panini bianchi* and *farina bianco tenero.* There also were rolls of various shapes and sizes. I didn't even look at the squares of pizzas since my big meal was going to be home-made spaghetti *al pomodoro.*

I thanked the helpful clerk for her quick lesson in bread types and moved on to a shop that sold me dried spaghetti, a stick of butter, an onion, a few sprigs of basil, and a hefty can of peeled tomatoes. After dropping my purchases at the apartment, I walked back into the village center and spent time in the *centro* and the museum, which had an excellent display, with many early photographs I had never seen before, that was dedicated to Portella della Ginestra.

That afternoon I made the spaghetti from an incredibly simple recipe I learned from watching a video of the Italian American cook Marcella Hazan. The peeled tomatoes and their juice go into a large skillet, where they get crushed. Five chunks of butter are added, and an onion with the outer skin removed is cut and each half is placed facedown in the sauce. This combination is cooked for about forty-five minutes and ends up slightly thickened. In the last ten minutes, I cooked the spaghetti al dente, which means literally "to the tooth"—firm to the bite. When both were done, I removed the onion halves and put the pasta into the skillet. This meal and its several servings lasted me until I left on Monday after Easter Sunday.

Afterward, I honored the ritual of the *riposo*. When I awoke, it was time for the evening service at the cathedral. From the side, I watched the ritual unfold with the chants and the readings by the priests and the congregation in a language I could not follow. The church was nearly full; this is something one does not often see in Italy but is more common in Sicily. I have sat through Mass many times all over Italy and usually there are only a few people in the unheated, un-air-conditioned sanctuaries. But this was Sicily, where religious fervor seems to run higher than on the mainland. And it was Easter Week, another reason why the churches here would fill up. It was a long service, but I enjoyed the human rhythm of it all: the ritualized standing and sitting; the singing of certain texts at specific times by a young man with a beautiful tenor voice; the readings by the priests, dressed in their black robes and square hats; the periodic appearance of the head priest, clothed in white, from behind the iconostasis, spreading wonderful-smelling incense around the apse.

It was far more ritualized than anything I had experienced in the Roman church. I could understand why the congregation participated with rapt attention for more than an hour, right down to young people standing with their parents and grandparents. I don't know the theology behind it all, but one certainly has to honor the culture in which these true believers are immersed.

Shops were open on Good Friday, and the streets were busier with cars and pedestrians than on most weekdays. Not much other than good old-fashioned commerce was going on through the daylight hours, before and after *riposo*. I walked around the village, exploring small lanes between houses I hadn't seen before, and crossing a long bridge for Via Viadotto Tozia that traversed a small valley just off the historic center. On the other side was Trattoria San Giovanni, where I had an excellent lunch. Then I crossed the street to Bar Elena Dolce and sat at a small table on the sidewalk, enjoying espresso and, well, *dolce,* the Italian word meaning "sweet" but commonly known as dessert. I suspect the bar was named for someone referred to as Sweet Elena. It was a friendly place, and I spent a few hours there enjoying the afternoon, still chilly in this early spring, and threatening a bit of rain that never came. People-watching in Sicily is a favorite pastime. I eventually returned to the apartment and did my best to again support the grand tradition of *riposo* and, before it was time for the evening Good Friday services, I got some nagging work out of the way.

I am sure the church services in this Eastern rite were different from the night before, but to the uninitiated nonnative speaker, it is difficult to see any change. The chanting and singing by that tenor with the lovely voice, the spreading of incense, the devoted readings by the priests, and the fact that the sanctuary was crowded front to back and side to side kept my interest. This is a working-class village. Folks attending these services are dressed comfortably, but fanciness is nearly nonexistent. The children are quiet; parents are very much in control. The only sounds are from the front, where the priests and lay speakers are following the ritual.

There are no church bells sounding before or after services, something a traveler usually hears all over Sicily and Italy. Each village, no matter how small, always has more than one church; Piana degli Albanesi, with only six thousand residents, has at least six major churches and one monastery. One would think with all those bell towers there could be an overload of chimes.

I didn't even hear bells during the procession of the Madonna and her son through the streets that evening—the sad Madonna, similar to the one I saw a few years earlier in Enna. Each village's statues, or *simulacri,* in its Good Friday procession differ from the next in the way they are dressed or in the design of the platform on which they are carried. One is the crucified Christ in a glassed-in coffin, which always leads the procession, followed by his mother.

The service was winding down. I left the sanctuary and went out to the street to await the men carrying the two statues on their platforms through the double doors, down the stone steps, and into the small area at street level in front. It was dark. People bundled in heavy coats were beginning to gather. Here, I saw children finally being children, running and shouting to one another, and some of the older ones had devices in their hands that, when spun around using cranklike handles, made a loud ratcheting noise. My first reaction was irritation at the noise and wondering why parents would allow such a noisemaker on Good Friday. No one, adult or otherwise, seemed a bit bothered by the hubbub.

It soon became clear. First Christ, then the Madonna, cleared the doorway; the men, with the long platform poles firmly on their shoulders, made it down the steps. Once they were in the middle of the street and positioned for the long walk down to the next church on the route, those noisemakers burst forth in unison. The men stopped, someone placed wooden-leg supports under the platform, and the men set it down, giving them a few moments of rest. Minutes passed. The ratchets started up again on some prearranged signal, the men hoisted the poles onto their shoulders, and the procession moved on. So, those noisemakers were part of the program, and the kids were in charge.

Every fifty feet or so, the ratchets would start up, the men would stop and rest, and a priest would speak through a portable loudspeaker to the hundreds following behind. This happened throughout the rest of the evening. It took a long time, perhaps more than two hours, for the procession to make its circuit. Despite being cold, those in the procession stayed throughout, and everything went off without a hitch. I always wondered what if the unthinkable—the dropping of a saint off a platform—happened. The horror of it was too much to contemplate.

I did notice the differences from village to village. In Enna, there were hundreds of confraternity members, robed and most wearing hoods. It was very stylized, with the men rocking in a certain rhythm to stay together. Except for the small-town band that played dirgelike music throughout the six hours of the procession, the whole event took place in near silence. Here in Piana degli Albanesi, there were no fancy costumes on Good Friday—those would be brought out on Easter Sunday. The only unique clothing was the robes and hats worn by the clergy. The men carrying the *simulacri* were dressed in everyday clothes and warm coats. There was no band playing somber music. The great differences in the styles of the two villages' celebrations aren't an aberration; Easter Week festivities vary tremendously in tone and content throughout Sicily.

But why were there no bells? It finally became clear on Saturday evening when I relaxed in front of the television in my apartment. I saw a British program on Easter traditions around the world. There it was: altar boys in Italy shown turning handles on loud noisemakers, devices much bigger than the small handheld ones in Piana degli Albanesi. Those devices have different names: *crotalum,* a rattle or a kind of castanet, or known onomatopoetically as a *raganella,* or even a *tric-troc.* The shaking was done to make signals, in the *absence* of bells. I discovered that sounding bells on Friday and Saturday of Easter Week is considered too cheery given the tragedy of Jesus's death. The last ringing of a bell or the playing of an organ in the village before Easter Sunday is during the church service during the first words of the "Gloria" on Holy Thursday. Then, they are silenced for the next two days.

All this newfound information explained, then, another custom I had observed earlier on Saturday. Just before the 10:30 A.M. service at the cathedral, I watched a black-hatted priest come out the front door, holding a wooden board, perhaps three or four feet long. He held it in the middle with one hand and repeatedly rapped it with a small wooden mallet in the other hand. It made a distinctive loud, hollow sound, and his labors went on for two or three minutes as he paced back and forth in front of the church. He walked down the steps and up the building's south side, never letting up the pounding. Then he walked to the front, across, and to the other side of the large stone structure. There he finally stopped the pounding and disappeared through a side door.

He was replacing, with the raps on wood, the normal pealing of bells that would announce the beginning of services. This might be common in some areas of the Roman and Orthodox world, but I had never seen it before.

Easter Sunday was cool with a suggestion of rain. Fortunately, that didn't happen. I was on the main street in front of the cathedral early enough to sit on a nearby bench and watch the morning unfold. It started out small. Cars were blocked at both ends but a few were still parked along the edges. A couple of traffic officers were standing by them, on their cell phones. Someone in the bar across the street where I went later for espresso told me those traffic cops almost never give tickets. They were trying to call the owners, whom they obviously knew in this small town, to come and get them. The calls must have been successful. Within an hour, the cars were gone without a tow truck in sight, and the street started filling with people, including large clusters of tourists. Asians, Germans, and French seem to make up the largest groups. They were fresh off of huge buses parked on the outskirts, all anxious to see the traditional Easter costumes this village is famous for.

Norman Lewis, writing several decades ago when tourism was virtually unknown in Sicily, mentioned that Piana degli Albanesi was Sicily's only tourist town, and only at Easter when visitors showed up. He wrote: "After these brief eruptions of organized gaiety, Piana degli [Albanesi] relapses into the brooding calm of its everyday existence." A careful reader cannot always count on Lewis for total accuracy in his descriptions. At one point, he says the village is the only one in Sicily or even Italy with a Greek Orthodox church. He is wrong. There are two or three such towns in Sicily and a handful in southern Italy.

Then as now, the attraction that draws such crowds once a year involves residents wearing native Albanian clothing of vivid colors: full skirts, heavily embroidered blouses, and unique swaths of embroidered cloth placed in the hair for the women, young and older; white shirts and vests, usually red, for the men and boys, with strong embroidery front and back, along with white pants and sashes for belts. Many of these outfits have been handed down from generation to generation. A young woman passing out red-colored eggs told me that her costume—a long dark green dress, black blouse, and a green length of cloth embroidered with symbols of nature—went back at least three generations; she was not entirely sure how far back.

Some of the women carried baskets of those eggs dyed a rich, deep red. In Greek Orthodox belief, the red symbolizes the blood of Christ, the hard shell represents his tomb, and the cracking of the egg symbolizes his resurrection. In Western culture we have colorful Easter eggs for reasons long lost to our celebrants. And, for some strange and mysterious reason, bunny rabbits, chocolate and otherwise.

The crowd continued to grow to a few thousand. The main street was full its entire length through the center, and from sidewalk to sidewalk. I headed to Piazza Vittorio Emanuele, at the end of the Corso, where a grandstand had been set up for the locals in their native dress. I ran into a man I had met when I first arrived seven days earlier who told me he was setting up the sound system. With a wink, he motioned me to follow him. He led me through the throng into the town hall, the *municipio,* up some stairs, and out onto a balcony looking over the piazza and all the confusion it contained. This would have been the balcony from which Mussolini, ninety-two years earlier, had harangued that sparse gathering with his anti-Mafia rant.

There were chairs, and perhaps a dozen other folks who knew somebody were already gathered. I got a front-row seat, thanked my benefactor, and settled in to watch, from above, the procession of wonderfully dressed townspeople, young and old. Small children, their costumed arms through the straps of traditional accordions, played round after round of folk music. Red eggs were passed out to anyone who wanted one. I envisioned many people spending the night before hard-boiling hundreds, maybe a thousand, of those eggs and dying them that brilliant red.

The early afternoon involved music, dances, singing, and speeches from the *sindaco* (mayor), and other prominent officials. Piana degli Albanesi is only an hour drive from Palermo, and I suspect many on dais and in the crowd were from Sicily's capital.

Then it all ended. The costumed women, men, and children climbed down from the grandstand, the crowd started moseying down the Corso, and within an hour everything was back to normal. The festivities suddenly morphed into a regular Sunday afternoon. A couple of men in the square were dismantling the grandstand and loading its sections onto a truck, a few village sweepers were picking up trash, and cars once again were let onto the street.

I walked down to the bar, ordered an espresso, double this time, and looked through my photos of the day's events. Colorful kids with their instruments; beautiful women, their hair in traditional styles; men and boys in more subdued costumes—the women were the focus of this celebration—all flowed through the camera view screen. It was lovely. What a contrast to the Roman Catholic Easter in Enna with its somber Spanish influence. This was Sicilian Albanian, an event foreign to the Western eye, rare and delightful.

SEVEN

Lives Among the Stone

Perhaps travel cannot prevent bigotry, but by demonstrating that all peoples cry, laugh, eat, worry, and die, it can introduce the idea that if we try and understand each other, we may even become friends.

—Maya Angelou,
Wouldn't Take Nothing for My Journey Now

OFTEN, WHEN looking north from high atop Enna's plateau, usually while standing just beyond the Palermo Gate, one of the remaining ancient gates into the once-walled city in the island's center, I would gaze down to a much lower plateau and marvel at the old village I saw crawling up a slight geologic incline. Years ago, I looked up its name on my map: Calascibetta. The name was familiar; the German literary giant Johann Wolfgang von Goethe mentioned its name once in the Sicily chapter in the classic book on his travels around Italy in the late eighteenth century. He described it in relation to Enna, which at that time was called Castrogiovanni. Mussolini, who ordered a lot of name changes for villages during his reign and had illusions of re-creating the Roman Empire, changed it to Enna in 1927, to approximate the early Roman name of Henna.

Goethe, for his part, didn't think too much of this part of

Sicily. He described it as "an even more fertile and even more uninhabited region." The crest of Enna and Calascibetta "gives the whole landscape a curiously somber character." Well, more than two hundred years later, I have been to Enna several times and never, during my many walks there in the historic center, saw the town or its people as somber.

Now it was time to finally see Calascibetta. The autostrada along the valley floor had a turnoff to the north with signs pointing to the village. The road up was just as circuitous as the road on the opposite side of the valley to Enna, perched on that much higher plateau. By this time, after several journeys into and through Sicilian and Italian mountains, handling such roads in a sturdy car had become second nature.

The entrance to the village was a one-lane, one-way street that carried me alongside the main square. It was midmorning and the town was bustling with cars and people. Again, as in so many other Sicilian villages, parking was dodgy. I saw empty slots directly ahead, at the edge of a giant square, but signs indicated parking there was somehow restricted, loading and unloading only. Out of desperation and not knowing where my *pensione* was located, I pulled into one of those stalls and parked, hoping for the best. The "best" arrived in the form of a woman dressed in blue with badges and patches indicating she was a traffic warden. She saw me and smiled. I smiled back. I approached and asked if it was okay to park there until I could find my quarters and discover a more permanent parking spot. She agreed without hesitation.

"Non si preoccupi. Siamo generosi con i nostri visitori." (Don't worry. We are generous with our visitors.) Then she asked where

I was staying. I gave her the name. She pointed across the square to a building perhaps two hundred feet away. She asked if I had baggage. I pointed to the car's trunk. Open, she demanded kindly. I thought maybe she was a customs inspector in addition to being a traffic cop. I opened. She grabbed the large bag; I grabbed the smaller one. Let's go, she said. And off she went, across the square toward the front door of the *pensione,* dragging my wheeled bag behind her, me hustling behind her, trying to keep up. She deposited it at the doorway, rang the doorbell, and said, *"Ciao!"* She was off, clipboard in hand, seeking out parking violators and ignoring my car parked in that five-minute zone for the rest of the day. Ah, Sicily, I thought to myself.

I also thought about Goethe, who wrote about the weather, the miserable time he had sleeping in a dirty, windowless room in Castrogiovanni, the geology and types of soil, but who never cared to describe any of the people on this island, their culture, or their daily lives. Once he referred to peasants, working in the distance. He saw a lot and missed even more.

Calascibetta is a pleasant place in which to spend time. I took some drives around the nearby countryside and spent a few hours each day sitting in Piazza Umberto I, enjoying the warming spring weather and the views around the square of its medieval buildings packed together and strung along the sloping plateau. The parish church of Saint Peter sits on the square, attached to a bank. Other churches dominate the heights of the village and are reached by a circuitous one-way street that takes you up, around the top, and then back down again to the square where you started. It passes alleyways and really small streets not meant for automobiles. Except for a few wide places along this route and the small square in front of the churches high above, I have no idea where people could park their cars. Motor scooters were everywhere, leaning against the sides of clustered-together homes. I drove the route once and walked it once. Walking was preferable. Some of the curves were tight, sometimes requiring backing up once or twice and cranking hard on the steering wheel to clear the front step of someone's house; SUVs and Jeeps would not do well here.

The medieval village was built near where prehistoric burial sites have been discovered. The town itself is built where Muslims created, in the ninth century A.D., a town called Kalat Shibat. That name—Kalat refers to "fortified place" and Shibat likely is the name of the warrior in charge (it also is the Arab name for the dill plant)—evolved over time into the more modern Calascibetta. When the Normans finally displaced the Muslims as Sicily's rulers in the late eleventh century, Count Roger built a castle and put walls around it. Some of those walls show up here and there at the plateau's summit.

The restaurant I ate in at least once a day—Ristorante-Pizzeria Vecchia Lecce di Carmelo Librizzi—sits high on my list. The name mystified me. What is *vecchia lecce*? I knew *vecchia* was the feminine form of "old." Friends more familiar with Italian had no idea what the combination was. Then it occurred to me, one evening while looking at a map of Italy, that Lecce is a town in Puglia, on the heel of the Italian boot. The restaurant offered dishes typical of the Leccesi tradition. Carmelo was the owner.

I was served throughout the five-day visit not by Carmelo but by his brother, Ugo. Sicilians have their favorite places to go when they want to eat outside the home; some go out many times a week and they rarely change restaurants. When staying in a village for several days, I find a place with good food and friendly owners and go back day after day.

Ugo remembered me and always seated me at the same table, just as he would do with his regulars. He asked my name that first day, and always called me by the Italian version, Giovanni. I ate a new dish each day: broad ribbons of pasta with chickpeas; *orecchiette* (pasta shaped like small ears) with a light tomato sauce infused with strong ricotta, once with sausage and once without; and some twisted noodles I had never seen before with ricotta and tomato sauce. The Leccesi style relies on a lot of spices, and some of those combinations gave a different flavor to some dishes than I had become used to in Sicily. Not overly adventurous, I skipped the deep-fried lamb entrails. I looked up the name for that one: *turcinieddi*. I had once eaten grilled pork intestines in Palermo's open-air market, the Vucciria. Not bad, but I had decided long ago that once was enough.

Over time, caves have served a lot of functions for various people who come, spend a brief moment along time's continuum, and then move on. I thought I was going to see a historical village from the time when Byzantium ruled Sicily. The signs, placed strategically along a main street leading out of Calascibetta, suggested as much: VILLAGIO BIZANTINO, with arrows pointing toward the countryside. A helpful clerk in Calascibetta's tourist office suggested I go there, and she called ahead to make sure a guide,

Gianluca Rosso, would be there to show me around. It wasn't far, less than three miles along SS290.

The drive, down the gentle northern edge of the plateau, was through farmland with olive groves and fruit trees. Occasional stands of timber spread out here and there along the edges of unfarmable gullies. It was easy to see how heavily forested Sicily once was, before conquerors harvested old growth for ships and Sicilians cleared the land for crops, incorporating the downed trees with stone to build houses, castles, and defensive walls.

With less than a mile to go, the road moved up a slight incline and into some woods. There was a sign, an open gate, and a small dirt parking lot empty except for one vehicle. A few dozen feet away was a small shack. Two young men stood outside the open doorway, watching my approach. One was Gianluca, a thirty-something in gray cargo pants and a black T-shirt, with a full, neatly trimmed beard, holding a pair of sunglasses in one hand and, in the other, the most beautiful walking stick I had ever seen, slender and straight and obviously harvested directly from the woods.

We met and introduced ourselves, and Gianluca and I immediately set off slightly downhill, along a thin ribbon of pathway, for the "village." This place, he told me, is full of caves, perhaps as many as three hundred, that had served as tombs for the prehistoric people known as Sicels, who were here when the Greeks arrived. The earliest tombs have been dated from around the sixteenth century to the fourth century B.C. The genetic lineage of those early people was eventually absorbed into Greek DNA, but their ancestors had been placed into tombs of various sizes—from small niches as big as a large shoebox to bigger tombs with hand-carved platforms. They remained there through Roman rule of Sicily from about 227 B.C. to the fifth century A.D. After a brief period when Sicily was overrun first by Vandals then by Ostrogoths, the Byzantines, ruled out of Constantinople, took control of the island in 536.

Gianluca delivered his history lesson in nearly flawless English as we made our way down the trail. When it curved along a streambed, we paused for a breather. He continued, saying he believed that the first Byzantines who settled here were from Cappadocia in Turkey. Those long-ago immigrants had lived in caves, natural and man-made, in that land and, when they arrived in Sicily at this location, saw a place like the home they left.

While the Romans had respect for the early tombs of others, the Byzantines did not; they removed those remains and created their own living spaces, churches, and meeting places. These were carved out of the soft *arenaria* (sandstone), of this old river valley.

As history shows, one invader always displaces another, and by the ninth century the Arabs/Muslims had arrived. These followers of Islam eventually settled in Calascibetta and in the area around these caves. Here, they built terraces on which they grew fruit and vegetables. They irrigated the land with a unique system of waterworks that is still in use in some parts of Sicily. Those terraces are now gone, however; the river that fed them and likely drew those Muslim farmers here in the first place, Vallone Canalotto, no longer exists.

These Arabs and Muslims were magnificent engineers. In this valley, they created a *qanat*, a system of subterranean galleries to run water. These water engineers, or *muganni*, created sloped floors or pathways to direct the water flow. Here is that word again: *gebbia*. These containers carved out of solid rock held water that the cave dwellers used for drinking and for their animals, and, I suspect, to wash clothes. The system today is mostly lost, but there is enough evidence to show how it must have been. Today, there are no people, just nature, and abandoned evidence of long-ago civilizations.

The area, Gianluca said, is home to a variety of small owls known as *assiolo*. They nest in hollowed-out parts of trees or in caves. I did not see any, but I saw large numbers of a type we know as shrikes, a bird that looks innocuous but has a brutal way of killing its prey. This "butcher bird" grabs insects like grasshoppers and impales them on sharp thorns. In more modern times, the barbs on wire fences do nicely.

A grisly thought, certainly. But it was time to move on, and a short distance away we walked into an open area, like a grand stone amphitheater. The back wall, a few hundred feet away, curved in a semicircle and was pocked with dozens of caves, large and small. In the foreground were hillocks of dirt that, I suspect, were washed down from the hill above the stone face. This washing down had occurred through the centuries. I wondered what lay beneath it—stone foundations for small houses, garden areas for crops or perhaps places where some of the Arab terraces were constructed?

I found it humorous that this place was billed as a village. Gianluca chuckled when he told me about all the tourists who come here expecting to see stone houses, streets, and perhaps a church or two.

I used Gianluca's magnificent walking stick to head up a side trail toward this cave-ridden stone face. We reached a cave with carved-out areas for the production of wine. There was a small basin—*un vasca di pigiatura*—where the press would have crushed the grapes. These particular stones had a whitish trace of lime, *calce,* which the ancients used to keep the stone from flaking into the product. I learned that the discovery of this space for pressing grapes into wine was recent. As late as 1999, area farmers used the cave, which had a deep earthen floor, to house animals. When archaeologists removed the dirt, they discovered the small basin below. Also here was evidence that the cave was used as a tomb for Roman children whose remains were likely removed by the Byzantines. Across one opening were the remnants of a stone wall, indicating this may at one time have been a house, perhaps long before it was filled in to hold animals.

It was here that Gianluca told me about his earliest visits to Villagio Bizantino. His first memory of being here was when he was three. Throughout his childhood, he was allowed to scramble around these caves. His family lived within a mile of the place because his father worked here, in much the same job Gianluca has today, for the region's forestry agency. He has walked these trails hundreds of times, on his own and leading groups large and small.

Some of these caves have carvings in the rocks, like the powerful cross with three arms, *un croce trilobata.* Nearby is the carving of a star, which represents, Gianluca said, the entire nighttime sky. These crudely done carvings are rough and badly worn over time, but they can clearly be seen once Gianluca points them out. In some of the caves in Calascibetta, he said, there are faint remains of fresco paintings; here there are no such hints of frescoes, just the carvings in the sandstone.

At one point in the walk, there was a fracture in the rock, possibly an airshaft to a subterranean area created by the Byzantines. We were above a spot where Gianluca believed they created living spaces underground, much as they had done in Cappadocia. Someday, perhaps this theory will be explored. Nearly all of Sicily and much of the Italian peninsula have thousands of sites, some yet to be discovered and others discovered but unexplored—a monumental task for archaeologists and historians—past, present, and future.

Gianluca doesn't spend all his time studying these rocks and owl nests. He also is an expert on the flora of this place. Most are herbal plants; he seems to know them all. There, next to the trail, was the heart-shaped flower, the *cicuta*. This water hemlock plant is close to, and just as dangerous as, the hemlock plant used to create the poison that killed the Greek philosopher Socrates. It is a small, beautiful bush with clusters of tiny white flowers fully engaged in the warm spring air. Nearby was a plant called *nepitella*, a minty plant very familiar to Italian cooks. In ancient times, and perhaps well into modern times too, this plant was scattered around entrances to these caves and doorways of buildings to keep insects out, particularly scorpions. A short distance away we saw the holly-like *pungitopo,* or butcher's-broom plant. This has sharp spines that the ancients used around their grain storage to keep out mice. Farther along was the broad-leafed *acanto,* acanthus in English, which resembles the leaves on top of Greek columns carved in the Corinthian style. These symbols, based on this plant, represent purity for Greeks and Christians.

We moved on, across the stream at the bottom of the little valley, and trudged up a trail to another series of caves, these formed from a sandstone wall almost directly across from the larger natural stone amphitheater. In front of us was a large cave that started out naturally but was expanded dramatically by humans. Outside the opening, sitting on the edge of the trail, was a stone-carved baptismal font, a spot for children, who were not allowed inside, to congregate. This complex—the font and the space inside the cave—was a Byzantine church, likely one of the first churches in the area, said Gianluca.

We stepped inside. While it was not on a grand scale, I was impressed by the scope of the interior, which was divided in half by a ceiling-to-floor wall. An opening connected the two sides. The Byzantines often built churches in tombs. So this cave had been a tomb and was already sacred to the Greeks. The ceiling was unique in that it was shaped like the inside pitch of a roof on a house, a feature common in tombs, with the idea being that the dead could "feel" like they were still alive. When it was converted into a church, the pitched roof remained even though churches were supposed to have a curved ceiling over the altar area.

The side with the pitched roof was for the priest and his altar. The other side was for the people. Its size indicated that it could hold maybe fifty adults at a time. When this site was discovered, long after the Byzantines, the walls were black from the smoke of fires built to warm former residents and their animals.

Even more interesting to me was the discovery that Romans, here before the Byzantines, used these soon-to-become sacred rooms and a space above the ceiling as a *columbarium*, or a place for doves, and there are spaces below the room that would have been reached by a ladder. There, the Romans deposited in niches the cremated remains of people of the lower classes—slaves most likely. The doves above were kept for their meat and their eggs, plus another product: guano, or droppings. This was used as fertilizer for the crops on the terraces. Not only that, the Romans transformed the guano into a kind of glue that was used to hold frescoes to walls.

Gianluca and I sat in a shady area to rest after walking up steep trails, climbing in and out of caves, brushing against thorny *pungitopo,* and smelling the tiny flowers of the beautiful but deadly *cicuta* while thinking of Socrates. Then he pointed to still another plant, the *asfodelo,* or asphodelus. Some call it Saint Joseph's Stick, referring to the myth that when the Virgin Mary was looking for a husband, potential suitors carried sticks of this plant, each hoping theirs would bloom first and, thereby making them Mary's choice for a husband. Saint Joseph's was the first to bloom. The plant also is part of a limited culinary tradition in the mainland region of Puglia. In Sardinia bees visit fields of it, creating a unique honey.

It is still spring, but the temperatures are warming, and the day is hot. "In the summer, when many tourist groups come here, the heat can be unbearable," Gianluca said. "This, after all, is Sicily. We might as well be in Africa."

He pointed with his walking stick to the amphitheater of caves. "This place was occupied for thousands of years, people living in caves, until 1923. Then, it was known as *Mannari.* Farmers from Calascibetta would come here and stay with their animals." That space in front of the semicircular stone face had been set up with walls enclosing pens for the animals, mostly sheep and some cattle.

During World War II, in the early 1940s, when the Allies were bombing Sicilian cities to get at the Italian and German units billeted there, people from Calascibetta came here to wait out the war. Gianluca knows people in the village whose grandparents and great-grandparents lived here during those terrible years.

A cave, home to a prehistoric family, one day becomes a chamber to raise doves for food and a century or two later becomes a sacred space for a church. Still later, it becomes a home for a family needing to stay safe from the modern terror of mechanized war.

"Every people who arrived here transformed this place," Gianluca said. "They transformed the rock. They transformed the rooms to adapt them to their needs. And they transformed the land."

EIGHT

A Day with the Leopard

Be flexible in your plans, because a rigid itinerary is lethal to a good time.

—Anthony Bourdain

T HERE ARE a handful of villages, where I only spent a single day, that stand out in my memory. Sutera is one. It sits wrapped around the base of a high stone-faced monolith, Monte San Paolino. The summit is about 820 feet straight above the highest part of the village, and the 183 steps, religiously followed by nearly every Suteresi to honor their patron saints, Paul, Onofrio, and Archileone, connect the two. I must confess I never made the imposing walk, on either this day or the first time I visited the village five years earlier.

Sutera is located several miles from the southern coast in the midst of Sicily's hilly interior, with villages sprinkled here and there in a land of rolling landscapes. Shafts of stone, like monoliths, seem to spring out of the ground at random. There are castles, or ruins of castles, at the tops of these monoliths. Some are beautifully restored, like the one in Mussomeli. These villages are interconnected by tiny roads, some paved, others dirt, that underscore their origins as paths followed by a people who once walked everywhere, using their beasts of burden only to carry harvested crops to markets.

Driving through land like this is a remarkable experience. There are vast fields, some fallow, others with young, green wheat resembling the visual effect of modern dancers with wind-driven flowing sheets of silk, using them to mimic rolling seas. These seas are sporadically topped with unoccupied, crumbling, stone buildings, not ships. Occasionally, flocks of clustered sheep, looking like whitecaps breaking here and there on this springtime sea, wander across fields of early wildflowers following their *tratturi* (sheep tracks) over the tops of natural earthen mounds heaped up like sand at the bottom of an hourglass.

In this early spring, fed abundantly by more rain than usual after a winter of snow found even at lower elevations, the beauty of the land was overwhelming. It was the time of year when Persephone, the Greek queen of the underworld, was thought to emerge for her annual visit with her mother, Demeter, the goddess of agriculture.

I grew up in the midst of Idaho farmland and experienced springs like this, captivated by the smells of wheat and corn pushing out of the ground and wildflowers around the edges of fields darkened by moisture. Here, this kind of scene is much grander than my Idaho memories. Wildflowers are not just along the roadside or the edges of fields; they spread across the land in huge swaths, either as crops to be harvested for herbs or perfumes, or simply growing wild across fields long abandoned by absent farmers. It's emotional in a way that is difficult to describe.

I came across a line in *Earthly Remains,* a mystery by the American

writer Donna Leon, that quickly expresses my inability to con-
jure up and describe the feelings I sometimes experience in these
periodic drives around this island: "Brunetti knew that, no matter
how much he babbled, he was incapable of conveying the magic
of the scene." Brunetti, as mystery aficionados know, is a Venetian
detective. He was marveling at the beauty of the lagoon around
him. Those same emotions can be felt no matter where one is in
some of Italy or in most of Sicily: land or sea, it is beauty that
makes one forget the sometimes awfulness of history and wars
that were fought here, year after year, century after century.

Now I was in Sutera, a tiny spot rich with its own history. Byzantines who ruled after the Romans likely founded it, followed
by Arabs and Muslims who much improved it. The buildings remained medieval looking, strung together in many places with
few tiny alleyways between large chunks of homes that lined irregular streets still wide enough only for a cart pulled by a mule.

There was a lull between rainstorms. From the small road
snaking its way up from the countryside to the village I could see
for miles across the plain of south-central Sicily the slow-moving
low, gray clouds delivering obvious sheets of rain here and there.
I knew about those 183 steps to the top of the monolith and
dreaded the thought of being caught in the middle of them when a
deluge hit.

Five years earlier, a friend and I had parked near the base, hoping to catch a ride to the top on a new elevator the European Union
had paid for. The elevator, surrounded on the ground by construction fences and seemingly abandoned, had never opened.
While my friend explored the area with his camera, I kicked a
soccer ball with a group of kids who had only the rough cobble-

stoned street as their field. Half a decade later, that elevator still stood unfinished, a tall tower of steel pushing skyward, completely incongruous with the ancient stone houses around its base. The stairs were the only way up, but the few drops of moisture I felt, with my face tilted sharply upward while I tried to make out the summit socked in by low-lying clouds, convinced me to remain on the street.

A break in the rain brought out crowds of people for their morning coffee and shopping trips. I returned to the main square and found a tight parking spot, repeatedly inching back and forth until two elderly men positioned themselves front and back and guided me safely into place. I knew instantly I would like the place. Sutera has a population of only around fifteen hundred, down significantly from the five thousand or so recorded in the 1960s. In a town so small, everyone knew when a stranger was walking among them. Their smiles and nods of hello were warm. Many said *buongiorno* as they passed. I read in a news article long after I left that Sutera, in 2013, had opened itself up to North African immigrants who regularly wash up in overcrowded, flimsy boats on the southern shores. Here they were temporarily moved into many of the abandoned homes in the historic center where workers taught them Italian and helped them go through the two-year process of applying for residency or who prepared them to move farther north into Western Europe. Many work in Sutera's small shops. Some became close family friends with those shop owners. This was a bold move. Usually, migrants are clustered together on the outskirts of villages around Sicily, like that complex far outside of Mineo I had seen earlier in my travels. Sutera gets 263,000 euro in regional European Union funds for this, of course, which helps its flagging economy by paying rent for the homes, paying salaries of locals who work with the migrants, and, hopefully, drawing new business to the area because of its potentially larger workforce.

I asked one man, perhaps in his fifties and wearing his Sicilian cap tilted askew, where the tourist office was. He started to give directions, pointing this way and that, then threw up his hands and said, *"Ti prenderò."* (I will take you.)

We walked a few blocks onto a parallel street and found the office. Despite a sign indicating it was open, it was closed. My guide shrugged his shoulders and said something like, "Perhaps later," shook my hand and left. Another man, walking by, saw that I was waiting. He stopped, pulled out a cell phone, and made a call. *"Aspetta qua,"* he said. Wait here. Five minutes later a woman showed up, smiling, apologetic. She took out a large bronze key, opened the heavy wooden door, and waved me inside. She went to a large cabinet, selecting brochures, maps, and a book about the town. She directed me to the Arab Quarter, pointing out that I had to drive out of the medieval section of the village, follow the road around to the other side of the mountain, and turn at a sign marked RABATO. I thanked her, we shook hands, and I headed back up to the main square and toward my car. But first, I stopped at a friendly-looking bar for my inaugural double espresso. The day was still young; I wanted to do some research about this place, and the tiny bar with a few tables in its warm interior and an internet signal seemed the place to do it.

Borgo Rabato was a pleasant surprise, given the beautiful restoration of many of its buildings and the fine surfacing in various shapes and designs of its cobblestoned streets. It was obvious,

from looking at a map and from glancing up the hillside laid out
in the Arab fashion of narrow pathways with steep stairs, small
stone arches over pathways tying structures together for added
strength, assorted terraces with wonderful views, and no roads
wide enough for cars. I had to use a parking area just below
Sutera's mother church, Chiesa Maria S. S. Assunta. An information sign told me that this church, looking rather plain from the
exterior, had been built in the fourteenth century on a site that
had been occupied by an Arab mosque since A.D. 861.

A small piazza in front of the church offered stone benches
next to planters full of yellow and red spring flowers, along with
Easter lilies still in full bloom. The view of the rolling, bumpy
plain below with its fields of wildflowers and grain was spectacular. I walked up and into the old Arab casbah filled with houses
that were built on one floor in a style called *dammuso*. These one-
room houses usually had a stone loft. Some of the homes I saw
were obviously occupied, perhaps by Suteresi and migrant families. Others were empty, with weathered, reddish signs indicating they were for sale. Walking up into this collection of unique
structures with their stone paths, comfortable stone steps, arch-
ways, and terraces, was a delight. I caught views of another village, Campofranco, in the distance. The well-ordered rows of
vineyards stood out through the light, moist haze, as did the
groves of olive trees and fruit orchards around the edges of the
town below. The potential of this remarkably fertile land has
certainly not been diminished by the passage of millennia.

At one point, near the end of my circuitous route through
Rabato, I passed a large, three-side enclosure with small animal
pens and straw spread liberally across the stone floor. This was

the site of Sutera's famed live nativity scene that draws fifteen thousand to twenty thousand visitors every Christmas season. It is staffed by townspeople in the various roles, along with a few animals and a doll representing the infant Jesus. The show begins with Mary and Joseph walking to different spots around the village seeking a room for the night and being turned away before settling in the manger. There they are surrounded by many gifts, usually of food and large baskets of fruit, nuts, special sweet breads, and even *cassata* cakes. I missed the event by three months, but plenty of photographs abound to show the mystical delight of the performance.

I returned to the village's historic center. It was about one o'clock. I found a likely-looking place, a small restaurant called I Sapori della Piazzetta di Carmelina Lombardo. Roughly translated, that meant "the flavors of Carmelina Lombardo on the small piazza." Inside, food of the day was laid out in a glass case. The selection was bountiful, offering a range of cooked meat and vegetables. I chose chicken fillets and potatoes, and the smiling woman behind the counter handmade a wonderful *cannolo* with the ricotta ends dipped in crushed pistachios.

A man whose job it was to serve the food stopped, after setting my order before me, and asked if he could join me at the table. We talked. I understood his questions just fine and my Italian, growing better each day on this journey, came through. He seemed fascinated that I, with no Sicilian heritage, would find my way to Sutera all the way from America. *"Non hai genatori da qui?"* (No parents from here?), he asked, sounding a bit incredulous. No, I assured him. I just happen to like coming to Sicily. Don't you get tourists here? I asked him. He shrugged. Sometimes, but not often, except at Christmas.

This next story is more about food than it is about a village. The village is Ciminna, in Palermo Province. It is near Caccamo, where I was spending several days. A couple of friends, independent of each other, had suggested I visit Ciminna, so early one morning I made a snap decision to take a day off from wandering the streets of Caccamo and the ramparts of its beautifully restored castle to make the drive.

Caccamo is on one hillside. Across a broad plain to the southwest, Ciminna sits against another, its main streets sloping down toward a tiny square ringed by three churches. Each village, from its highest point, is in full view of the other. The drive is only seventeen miles, but it takes more than fifty minutes to make it, given the roughness of the two state highways and the tightness of their turns.

I had read that there were some Greek ruins higher up on the hill above Ciminna, possibly a temple to Demeter, one of my favorite goddesses. The village itself dates back to the Roman period and likely was a farmstead for the grain crops the Roman Republic, which had won the island from the Carthaginians in the First Punic War, used to supply its armies then working to unite the Italian peninsula. I looked for signs pointing the way to these ruins, but couldn't find any. It didn't matter. I was here for another reason: Ciminna was the setting for a few scenes from one of my favorite films, Luchino Visconti's *Il Gattopardo* (*The Leopard*).

The scenes, which take up just a few minutes in the 1964 film, are exterior shots that required major Hollywood-style renovations of building fronts. Set designers put an entirely new façade complete with balconies—fake, of course—on the front of a large building at the bottom of the village's tiny piazza. This façade represented the exterior of the palazzo owned by the fictional prince of Salina, played by the American actor Burt Lancaster. Then tons of dirt were spread over the asphalt streets to capture what the square would have looked like in the 1860s, the time of northern Italy's invasion of Sicily.

It took awhile for me to figure out where all this took place in this small village of five thousand residents. I entered the town from above and parked along a street with a nice outdoor bar facing a small roundabout. I had no local map and, since the day trip was a last-minute decision, I hadn't had time to lay any groundwork. I often just stumble into a place and hope for the best. That's what happened here.

I saw a man carrying supplies from a truck into a small store. I asked him if he knew where the scenes from *The Leopard* were made. *"Il palazzo Donnafugata,"* I said, naming the fictional grand summer home of the prince. He looked surprised, thought a moment, shrugged his shoulders, and, shaking his head, replied, *"Non lo so."* (I don't know.)

I walked around the edge of the roundabout and started down one of the long, stone-paved streets, Via Dottore Vito Graziano, and then onto the one-way Via Roma. There were portable NO PARKING signs propped up along the entire length. Ahead, a mechanized street sweeper was blowing bits and pieces of trash ahead of it while spraying water out of a tank on the back. About halfway down, I passed a small building with a sign indicating it was a museum. It was an ethnological museum named for a Catholic *monsignore,* and it was closed. For a moment, I had hoped there would be a display inside that could tell me about the Greek ruins. There was no indication when it would open.

The mild springtime temperature was rising. Via Roma gave off a light mist from the quickly drying water left by the street sweeper. There was no bar along this street where I could ask directions, and the small shops that lined it were closed. It was too early in the day. I walked back up to the main intersection with its roundabout and made my way to a tobacco shop/bar—the one with the outdoor tables. There was a worn city map pasted onto a wooden sign. It showed nothing relating to the film or the Greek ruins.

I sat outside in the shade, with my double espresso, the usual *cornetto,* and a short Tuscan cigar. Here it was cool. A light breeze was blowing its way up the walkway lined with tables. Two middle-aged men were sitting a few feet away, glancing occasionally in my direction.

One of the men nodded. That gave me an opening. After we exchanged pleasantries, I asked him if he knew about Donnafugata. The reaction was an instant and explosive *"Sì!"* He got up and came over to my table and plopped down into a chair. He was called Salvatore. He launched into a rambling story about the film. He described it, saying he had seen it many times. Of course I knew the story, having read Giuseppe di Lampedusa's book at least twice and having seen the movie three or four times. But I wasn't going to interrupt this wonderful man who obviously enjoyed telling the story as much as I enjoyed hearing it. I caught about a third of what he said in a mixture of Italian and dialect. Then he offered to show me where the filming took place.

We ended up on Via Roma, walking its entire length downhill to the small square at the bottom. It wasn't much of a square, just a wider part of the village's main Corso Umberto I, but it was opposite the long, modern-fronted building that had been temporarily recast by the scenery magicians and transformed into the façade of a seventeenth-century palazzo. There, next to it, was the Mother Church that also appeared in the film, with its rose-colored exterior nearly untouched by the set designers.

My new friend, sixty-four when we met, pointed to a banner attached high up on the front of the building that had served as Donnafugata's backdrop. It identified it as the place where the exterior scenes were shot, showing a photograph of actors, including Lancaster, in full costumes, standing on those balconies crafted by the movie crews. Costumed extras, many of them locals, filled the square below. That was it: Ciminna's claim to fame as part of film history. All the interior shots for *The Leopard*— the lavish dinner scene in Donnafugata and the grand ball in Palermo—were made in real *palazzi* in and around the capital city. Some additional scenes, likely the ones where the prince was on a hunting trip with his land manager, were filmed in the countryside around Ciminna.

"I was very little," he said, holding his hand knee high, when the movie came to the village. "I remember everything. It was big, big here!"

Salvatore shook my hand, wished me well, and started back uphill. I sat on a bench for a while, watching a few shops start to come alive as owners unlocked steel grates protecting front doors and rolled them upward. There was a small bar. Now it was late morning, approaching the noon hour. I crossed the Corso and went inside the bar, where two men were talking. They paused, and I asked where I could find a good place to eat. They talked between themselves for a few moments, then one of the men, the one visiting the owner, told me there was one just on the outskirts, above the village. He started to describe, in rapid-fire Italian, how to get there, and then he stopped when he saw my confusion. Wait, he said. Where is your car? Up at the other bar, I told him. Come with me. We walked out, got into his small truck, and drove back up the hill on the Corso. He dropped me off at my car and told me to follow him.

A few minutes later, on a ridgeline overlooking the yellowish roof tiles of Ciminna, he pointed to a parking spot in front of a large, modern building with the name Ristorante San Vito in front. He led me indoors and greeted the owner, pointed to me, and proclaimed that he was recommending his restaurant to me, a tourist. Then he waved and left.

I was seated in the middle of a large dining room, the only customer in a sea of tables. It was still early for lunch since most southerners eat closer to one or two o'clock. A waiter, a young man who identified himself as Stefano, the owner's son, appeared. There is no menu, he said. It is not necessary. He only asked what I wanted to drink. *"Aqua minerale con gas,"* I said. He brought a large bottle and took away the bottles of red and white wine that had been sitting on the table.

Then began one of the finest eating experiences I have ever had anywhere. First up, an appetizer plate of sliced pancetta and crudo, green olives, small local mushrooms, caponata of eggplant, ricotta, and a most amazing pecorino cheese. There also were boiled chunks of meat and another variety of meat with a light celery and tomato sauce. In all, there were four plates full of *antipasti*. Maybe this is the complete meal, I thought, a daily special of some kind.

Another plate came out with a variety of mixed cold cuts and thinly sliced french fries. Then another: rolled-up *melanzane,* or eggplant. Still more: a first course of *funghi ripieni,* or stuffed mushrooms, along with a little-ears pasta, *orecchiette,* with *carciofi* (artichokes). These are all grown here, Stefano told me proudly. Then, there was a sample of another pasta. This one I knew: *pasta alla Norma,* made with eggplant in tomato sauce and served on rigatoni.

That was the first course. But I was done. Stefano seemed disappointed when I begged off the *secondo,* which would have been a small steak or perhaps a veal cutlet. I just couldn't do it. I did manage a small dish of gelato, but that was it. Stefano cleared the table. By this time, other diners had come in. Two or three families arrived, plus a couple of tables of businessmen in suits. I watched. Again, no menus, and the plates started coming out with the same dishes I had eaten.

I wondered what my bill would be. Food like this in Rome or Milan would be *molto caro,* very dear cost-wise. I got Stefano's attention and asked for *il conto,* the count. He went over to his father, motioned toward me, and they whispered to each other. He returned and wrote in pen on the paper tablecloth: 23. That was it: twenty-three euro, or about twenty-six dollars. I paid, walked outside, and sat on a bench out front, letting everything digest.

A man from one of the other tables came out and sat next to me, lighting his cigarette. We talked about the food. He said he had to take a break, or maybe two breaks, to get through it all. It is worth going slowly, he added. I agreed and wished I had taken that break. Then maybe I could have had that *secondo* and a bigger, more unique dessert.

NINE

Friendship and Tobacco

The charm of traveling is enjoying innumerable glorious scenes, knowing that we could make any one of them our own, and passing on to the next like some great lord.

—Cesare Pavese,
This Business of Living: Diaries 1935–1950

THE LONG, tapering street that should have been one-way but allowed for two-way traffic was maddening at first. Unfortunately, I was in a medium-size car, one larger than I wanted to rent but got stuck with at the beginning of my journey. In Caccamo in the province of Palermo, I was arriving in the midst of a busy market day, and there were plenty of smaller cars about, plus pedestrians hugging the edges where medieval road builders long, long ago felt no need to provide for people on foot. The road curved, and immediately to my right was a thirty-minute parking spot. I grabbed it. I needed to dismount, find a bar, and see if anyone knew how to get in touch with my host for the next five days in what appeared to be a lovely village, one of the larger I'd visited, with eight thousand residents. I had only the host's first name, and no phone number.

I adjusted the timing card, pasted in the right-hand corner of the car's windshield, to show my arrival time. If a traffic officer were to wander by and see that I had been there longer than thirty minutes, I could get a ticket. So far, in several villages, I'd avoided that ding, which would require going to the nearest post office, standing in what could easily be a long, confusing line, and paying the fine. Knock on wood.

It was a twisty, gradual uphill climb along the street's edge. I was seeking a bar where I could order a coffee and see if anyone knew Giuseppe, the *pensione* owner. I had a choice between staying in his countryside apartment a few miles away from the historic center or in a small apartment in the village. The posted addresses did not get a rise from my rental car's navigation system.

A bar popped into view. It was a small place with a handful of outside tables occupied, as usual, by men, and a few tables toward the back of the dark, poorly lit interior. A couple of customers stood against the long bar, drinking beer from tall, skinny, frosted glasses. Being a teetotaler, I ordered a double espresso and asked the barman if he knew my host, whom I identified in Italian as "a man named Giuseppe who has an apartment in the village." Before he could answer, a tall, lean man, dressed smartly in a three-piece suit and tie and with a well-trimmed goatee and large round eyeglasses, spoke up. He stood at the end of the bar. "I know him," he said in English. "He is a good friend." He set down his drink—it looked like scotch, neat—took out a cell phone, punched in a few numbers, spoke in Italian, and snapped the phone cover shut. "He'll be here in a few minutes."

This was my introduction to George Giannone, a native of Toronto, Canada, who told me he had visited Caccamo thirty years earlier to see his adoptive parents' ancestral village and never went back to Canada. Within minutes, Giuseppe showed up, asked me where my car was, drove George and me to it, and directed me to follow.

The country apartment never came up; it was clear he wanted me to stay in the village apartment. We stopped in front of the castle for which Caccamo is famous, near the base of where state highway 285 continues in its winding course through the village, carrying the additional name of Corso Umberto I. Its dual role as a state highway explains why traffic has to be two-way. There is no room in this densely packed village for two through streets. With the exception of one intersection, there are no turnoffs to the town above or below, just steep steps for pedestrians.

I parked in a free lot in front of the castle, and Giuseppe and George grabbed my bags. We headed up a series of stone steps, up, up, up, along a steep incline with houses on each side, most interconnected. Eventually, we reached the front door of my place. Giuseppe unlocked it, handed over the key, and motioned me inside. It was small with a living room, bedroom, and a tiny efficiency kitchen along one wall. Perfect. "All I ask," Giuseppe said with George translating, "is if you use the kitchen, that you clean everything." Agreed. He shook my hand, gave me his phone number, and left. George and I agreed to meet for dinner at A Castellana, a restaurant down those steps, across the street, and in a building that once was part of the castle. Giuseppe had given me a handful of coupons offering discounts for the food there. My breakfast of espresso and *cornetto* would have to be taken at a small bar a few dozen feet down the street. Just mention Giuseppe's name and breakfast would be on him.

Again, it was all a remarkable set of experiences that regularly happens to me in Sicily. I come into a village unannounced, ask questions, usually at a bar, where someone almost always knows the answer or knows somebody who knows, and it takes off from there. I gain people to talk to, who teach me the history of places I visit, and share perspectives on Sicilian culture, and who are willing to spend time to show me places and things. It was through conversations with George over my handful of days there, for example, that I learned about his village and the castle, Sicily's largest and one of its most restored; about Ciminna and its ties to *The Leopard*; and about Cerda, a smaller village over some hills in another direction, which I would visit later. George Giannone became a good friend.

It was dinnertime, probably around nine o'clock, late by American standards. George and I, he with a pizza and I with a large bowl of pasta, were talking. I told him that I had seen changes in Sicilians I had met over the years. When I started regularly visiting in the early 2000s, many of the people were not approachable. They seemed to fit that stereotype of being mysterious and closed to outsiders. Over the years, I told him, new ones that I met appeared more open, friendlier, willing to say hello to a stranger passing them on the street. The older men on their benches in the square or in a park would engage me in conversation rather than the other way around. I had always blamed their earlier silence on the belief that the Mafia made them cautious about opening up to strangers. I didn't like making that stereotypical judgment, but older books I read always raised that reality.

"The myth that Sicily is only made of the Mafia is gone, finally," he told me in between bites of a pizza with its chunks of baked cauliflower. "Tourism is coming back, and it has been just

over the past three years." He repeated what I had been told elsewhere: Sicilians and their elected officials see increased tourism
as a way out of the economic morass Sicily and southern Italy have
found themselves in. The unemployment rate in the south of Italy, particularly among young people, had, at times, topped
20 percent.

He then said something surprising, something I did not necessarily agree with, but I could see his point. "Compared to the
northern part of Italy, people here are more open-minded." I never
got clear on what he meant by that, but I suspect he felt that some
northerners were dismissive of southerners, thinking them only
as good for domestic work in their northern homes or helping to
harvest northern crops. I recalled the northern Italian legislator
who said dismissively, when he found out his northern team was
going to play soccer in Palermo that they were "going to Africa."

George continued. "Twenty years ago, anyone from somewhere else who was sitting here"—he motioned with his hand
around the room—"would have been stared at. Now they will nod
when you enter and make eye contact." I knew that to be true.
And it also made me think about a man I had met six years earlier in a tiny village near Agrigento, in the far south of Sicily. We
passed on the street. He stopped me and asked my name. We
talked for a few minutes, me answering a few questions about
who I was and why I had chosen his village to visit. I didn't think
about it again. Four or five years later, I returned to that village
and walked into a restaurant for lunch. That man was sitting,
alone, at a table. He looked up when the tiny bell hanging over
the door jingled and, with maybe a second's thought, he called
out my name, first and last. I joined him, he introduced me to the

restaurant owner, and we had a nice meal and good conversation together. I could not begin to remember *his* name.

George nodded, saying that didn't surprise him. "In any large city, people step over you. If you fall down here, everyone will help." I didn't know it then, but that reality would be made clear a month later, when I was nearing the end of my trip. I wish now I had sent a message to George about the experience I had in Santo Stefano di Camastra just a few days before I returned to Milan and my flight home. I'll save that story for later.

He talked about how long it took for him to become acquainted in Caccamo when he had arrived thirty years earlier. It took a few years, but he soon became well known in the village, developed a lot of long-term friendships, and participated, as if he had lived there his entire life, in the town's political and social life.

He had worked as a tour guide at the castle. He was an amateur historian who wrote a lot about Caccamo and its colorful past. He was an expert on the churches, and he told me stories about the statues and paintings in each one. Legend has it, he said, that the ruins of an Arab mosque are beneath the Mother Church. I wondered why that has never been explored. George shrugged. "There are many things underground that have yet to be discovered."

What he told me about the churches surprised me. I had counted seven in a long walk I took in the twilight just before dinner. That is a number not unusual in a Sicilian village of eight thousand. I'd been in some small places where there were three or four within a block of one another, each devoted to a different saint. He said there were thirty-three over time in Caccamo, including chapels and convents; many had closed or were used only during certain church holidays and festivals. I needed to keep in mind that the population was half of what it had been before the 1950s diaspora—the second large wave of emigration from Sicily in the twentieth century—led to thousands of Sicilians leaving for the Americas and Australia.

Caccamo's beginnings are obscured by the passage of time and touch on legend. Some historians have speculated that the name comes from a Carthaginian word, *caccabe,* or horse heads. George told me that some believe the remnants of the Carthaginian army, limping south from Himera on the Tyrrhenian coast after a humiliating defeat in 480 B.C. at the hands of the Sicilian Greeks from Siracusa, stopped on this spot to rest and recuperate. What that has to do with horse heads, no one knows. There is no historical evidence of the event, but the symbol of the city is a horse's head facing the three-legged Sicilian *trinacria.*

The Carthaginian story may be nothing more than an oft-repeated urban legend. What is known about its earliest beginnings is that the Arabs, in the ninth century A.D.—more than one thousand years after Himera—started a community here, naming it Qaqabus. When the Normans took over the island a few hundred years later, they laid the foundations for the castle that now dominates Caccamo and is one of the largest and most completely restored in Sicily.

During the early Greek period, more than a thousand years before Caccamo became a village, Sicily was, according to historian Franco De Angelis, "thinly populated and had much available land to clear and work." This village arose in the middle of a major grain-producing area of the kind that had captured Rome's attention. Rome took over the island, except for the kingdom of Siracusa, from Carthage after the First Punic War (264–241 B.C.). The island became Republican Rome's first province in 227 B.C. Siracusa finally fell thirteen years later.

Caccamo farmers provided grain throughout the Middle Ages to Palermo markets, long after the Romans left as their empire crashed and Byzantium, followed by the Arabs and then Normans, took over. As noted, many medieval buildings in Sicilian villages are joined together, like modern condominiums, on one, two, or three levels. Caccamo's structures are an example. Along that tapered main street through the village's older section beginning at the castle, there rarely is a break between buildings, perhaps only stairways here and there to the sections above or below, but there are almost no streets for a donkey cart or a modern car to turn onto from the main drag. Vehicles have to go a circuitous way to get to the upper or lower town.

Farmers, through the medieval and into the modern periods, lived in these homes, leaving before sunrise to walk with their donkeys and mules to the fields on the outskirts, far down on the plain, and then returning late, long after sunset, putting their creatures of burden in their ground-floor stalls and heading upstairs to their one-room living quarters.

The harvested grain, bundled on the backs of animals, would then be carried to Palermo to the northwest along a narrow track and over a stone bridge, built in 1307, which crossed a stream in the valley below. Other modern roads now lead to Palermo, of course. An artificial lake, created in 1993, covers the stream that feeds it and, regrettably, that ancient bridge.

The castle figures heavily in village history. After it got its start as a much smaller Arab fortification on a protrusion of land overlooking the valley and plain far below, the Normans, in 1094, developed it further, building walls that soar above a sheer, white cliff. That's when its known history begins. Ruling families took it over in subsequent centuries and expanded it even more. The castle was never defeated in battle. Once it lost its military function in the seventeenth century, the various dukes of Caccamo used it as their home well into the twentieth century.

My notebook filled rapidly while George spoke. He pointed out something I had never realized about Sicilian castles, at least from the thirteenth century onward. If you look at a map of where many of them, either now in ruins or restored tourist attractions, are located, it is clear that signals warning of invaders could have been transferred from castle to castle.

It was the lighting of a huge *falò,* or bonfire, blazing at night from high atop each castle, that could be seen from one to another, from sea to sea. Standing high on Caccamo's ramparts, I could easily see the Tyrrhenian coast just seven miles to the north at Termini Imerese. The modern nighttime lights of that port city are evidence that Caccamesi defenders would have had no trouble seeing smoke from a *falò* from one of the many coastal towers along that area. Perhaps fifteen miles to the southwest of where I stood, those manning the Castello di Vicari would be able to see the smoke from Caccamo's castle. They would light their fire, and so on.

Some interesting events took place in the castle that had a significant impact on Sicilian history. One that George mentioned involved a twelfth-century figure, Matthew Bonellus, Second Lord of Caccamo. During that time, the Norman ruler of Sicily, William I, was not considered a good friend of the barons. Because of this, he was known as "William the Bad." He never expected to rule, but three older brothers had died, and the task fell to him. Over time, "William's interest in the affairs of his kingdom was desultory," according to historian Louis Mendola.

It was in the Caccamo castle where Bonellus plotted a revolt. Upon returning to Palermo in 1160, he killed a particularly hated key official of the king, and, strangely, William pardoned him. But this leader of the barons then plotted to assassinate the ruler. After a bloody battle that spilled into the streets of the capital, Mendola writes, "Bonellus was arrested, mutilated and cast into the dungeons where he died soon afterward. . . . and the pompous baron spent his last days as a moribund pariah."

William I was not mourned upon his death in 1166, my friend George said. "The only ones who mourned were the women in his harem." Harems were a holdover, during Norman rule, from the Arab days in Sicily, as were headscarves traditionally worn by non-Muslim Palermitani women.

Ironically, William's son, William II, was known as "William the Good"; he got along just fine with the nobles. The son, who commissioned the construction of the abbey in Monreale, was so highly regarded he was placed by Dante in *The Divine Comedy* and memorialized as "the mourned one" who was able to spend eternity in the celestial sphere of just rulers. Unfortunately, he had no heirs and ended up being the last of Sicily's full-blooded Norman rulers. Perhaps the greatest ruler of this era, Frederick the Great (1194–1250), was only 50 percent Norman. (The other 50 percent was German.)

I wandered up the steep, stony incline to a long ramp leading to the entrance. It is easy to see why this castle was never overtaken in battle: the long ramp makes a turn back upon itself and then takes a sharp left into the entrance. With soldiers raining death and destruction from above onto the clustered invaders who had no straight shot through those heavy doors, it is doubtful anyone would even try. The town itself in those early days was contained entirely within the lower walls along what is now street level. The Mother Church, joined at an angle by two other churches, side by side, is directly below the castle and would have been within those walls.

Throughout my visit, when George and I met for coffee, he told me ghost stories simply as a way to underscore the culture of his beloved village. They were stories using real-life circumstances, such as a young woman who was not allowed to live her life as she wished, and who, after death, came back to the place she wants to be—the castle. I was taken by them into a world of legend and make-believe, of course, but was also stirred by their underlying cultural message.

People have said that at night they hear the ghost of Matthew Bonellus dragging chains around the castle he once was lord of. Then there was the reality-based story of a young girl, a child, in the late eighteenth century who fell down the stairs and died. Some have said they can hear her crying. I walked down those stairs and sat down on one of them and listened carefully. There were no sounds. I was the only visitor at the castle that day.

Etna, Europe's most active volcano, looms in the distance from the view of the upper portion of Castiglione di Sicilia.

Castiglione resident Cettina Cacciola views a portion of the abandoned Jewish quarter in her village, located along the narrow Via Pagana. Restoration is planned for some of these buildings with their conversion into an *albergo diffuso*.

The small village of Gallodoro, high on the slopes of the Peloritani and overlooking the Ionian sea. Its proximity to the village of Taormina, seen in the far upper right, gives Gallodoro hopes for its own tourism awakening.

Above Gallodoro, and on an isolated promontory that projects out toward the sea, are the ruins of a village some believe began with the Greeks escaping attacks on Taormina three thousand years ago. The domed structure is a large *gebbia* for water storage. It got its name from the Arabs who invaded Sicily in the ninth century.

Decorated steps lead up from Vizzini's main square to a street where the museum dedicated to Giovanni Verga is located.

Sitting on Vizzini's outskirts is the abandoned village of Cunziria, once homes and working areas of leather tanners, now a long-lost profession. It is here that Verga, in his short story *Cavalleria rusticana,* set the scene for the knife fight between two men in love with the same woman.

An Orthodox priest ascends the steps of the mother church in Piana degli Albanese, one of the few Italian villages where Rome allows Eastern Orthodox churches.

It is Easter Sunday in Piana degli Albanese, a day of Eastern Orthodox celebration featuring hundreds of townspeople in their traditional dress. A mother and daughter get ready to plunge into the crowd of celebrators.

These men are in the confraternity Ecce Homo, based in the *Convento* in the small, nondescript village of Alimena. They sing a cappella in deep resonant tones in tribute to their faith. They are part of a larger group famous for singing *i lamentatore,* or laments.

From Caccamo, the view across the valley that hundreds of years ago looks over a narrow, dusty road leading to Sicily's capital, Palermo. The man-made lake was built in the early 1960s. It now hides a medieval stone bridge that was part of that road.

Maria Giovanna Cafiso shows a medieval-era book hand-illustrated by monks and now kept in the Ex Biblioteca Dei PP. Cappuccini. This smaller library is in the former family house of Sicilian writer Luigi Capuana, beloved son of the village of Mineo. Capuana was the contemporary and close friend of another well-known Sicilian writer, Giovanni Verga.

A tiny privately owned church sits along a narrow road connecting the village of Racalmuto with the Agrigento-Caltanisetta highway. Owner Alberto Alessi, left, along with a mutual friend Giuseppi Andini, right, gave a brief tour to a curious traveler. Alberto's family estate extends behind the church where he nurtures organically raised olives in his grove of one thousand trees.

Stored in a workshop of a beautiful home on the outskirts of Sambuca di Sicilia are Vito Savelli's puppet creations. The home he shares with his wife, Elisabetta Giacone, is rich with gardens and fruit trees. It overlooks the village and the stunning Belice Valley's array of vineyards and olive groves.

These men remember the massacre on May 1, 1947, when Mafiosi and a bandit band led by Salvatore Giuliano murdered eleven of their fellow citizens. This group of men, natives of the western Sicily village of Piana degli Albanese, spend their days playing cards, reading newspapers, and talking to one another at the Casa del Popolo, or House of the People.

Tucked away deep in the mountains of northeast Sicily, near the village of Montalbano Elicona, is a tholos, an ancient Greek tomb that, over the millennia, was used as a sheepherder hut. These structures, sprinkled throughout the area and beyond, are now protected archaeological sites.

Gianluca Rosso, a naturalist guide at the Villagio Bizantino archaeological site near Calascibetta, stands in what was once a Byzantine church carved out of a series of caves. This space started out as a Roman tomb and later was taken over by the Byzantines after the Roman Empire collapsed. Later Sicilian generations used both this cave and other caves in the large complex for homes, to house cattle and sheep, and to store grain.

Salvo Andrea Leggio, a master pastry chef by profession, lays out a variety of pizzas prepared by his family and baked in a wood-fired pizza oven in their home on the outskirts of Mineo.

Maria Messina began her writing career in the village of Mistretta during the late nineteenth century. As a teenager, Messina lived in the old part of town where many of her stories take place. The ruins of a once-towering castle overlook the village.

Venera De Luca, right, a resident of the tiny village of Motta Camastra, shares her day with a friend.

The one that really meant something to me was when I was standing in a former bedroom in front of the fireplace. This story was told in a plaque on the wall. If a visitor were to come on a night with a full moon, a young girl dressed in white would approach. She is holding a pomegranate, a Greek symbol of love and fertility, and offers a test. Some say only the pure at heart can see her. The test involves trying to eat the pomegranate without touching it with hands and not allowing a single seed to fall to the floor. If the visitor succeeds, a great treasure awaits; if they fail, they have to take the young woman's place.

The young woman is based on a real person, the second daughter of a seventeenth-century Caccamo noble, Don Alfonzo Henríquez de Cabrera. A second daughter would usually become a nun—and that was his daughter's wish—but the family wanted her to marry. The union likely was to make a political alliance. She fled and joined a convent of Saint Benedict. Because she disobeyed her family, she was dead to them. She lost her birth name and became Sister Felicia. Later, she became ill and died very young. It is her ghost that appears, with the pomegranate, before the "pure at heart."

I did not go to the castle at night during a full moon, nor do I think my heart was pure enough. And whenever I try to eat a pomegranate, seeds spill everywhere. I like the image of a young girl in white. I would make a poor replacement, treasure or no treasure.

George told me these stories, which I later supplemented with information at the castle, while we were eating a traditional springtime meal. The dish was called *fritella,* not to be confused with *frittelle,* a sweet, fried doughnut-like pastry served in the Puglia region during Christmas.

The Caccamese *fritella* is peasant food. It is heavily dominated by spring vegetables, including a thorny Sicilian artichoke that is grown throughout the area of north-central Sicily and in fields between Caccamo and Cerda. The dish uses beans, peas, and wild fennel. Small bits of salted pig meat are scattered throughout. The pasta used, in the shape of short, small tubes, is called *ditalini*. The name literally means "fingering," but Sicilians use the word as meaning "small thimbles." This concoction is mixed together like a hearty soup.

"You need only one course," said George. "Forget the *antipasti*, the *secundo*, the *contorni*, the *insalate*," he said. "Of course, dessert is possible and espresso certainly. But this meal is all you need. Everything is in it." I must admit that eating such a meal was fulfilling to the point that I eschewed the dessert, something I almost never do. I couldn't even bring myself to look at the dessert menu. Espresso? Now that is another matter. *Certamente!*

This was our final meal together. I wanted to visit Cerda, a small village about twenty miles to the east. That would be the next day, and then I would leave for somewhere else. I would miss my new friend, George Giannone. A few months after I returned home, he sent some pictures via email of the inside of some of his favorite churches, and we talked a bit on social media. I had questions for him, which he promptly answered. He encouraged me to join the Caccamo social media site, which I did.

Then, one day in January 2017, as I took a break from writing about his beloved village, I saw a post on the site announcing George's death. Something about a health problem, which he never mentioned during our many conversations. His friends from the village posted sentiments and tributes to George. I did, too, after I figured out what to say and how to do it in proper Italian.

At one point, I went to our messages. Many of his were in imperfect English, for which he apologized, saying that he had spoken English so little over the last thirty years that he often confused the English spelling with Italian. The last message was an answer to one of my many questions. I replied by thanking him for his help and his friendship. His response started with a Spanish phrase that is likely part of the Caccamesi dialect, for "you're welcome": "Da nada." Then in English, he continued, "I only do this for the love of where I live."

Before my last night in Caccamo, I headed for Cerda, a much smaller village fewer than twenty miles to the east. My interest? Tobacco.

At some point in the year before I started my visits to Sicilian villages, I came across a newspaper article about an experiment to grow tobacco in Sicily. The fields were on the outskirts of Cerda, a village of approximately five thousand. Growing tobacco was something that had not been done since Sicily became part of Italy, 150 years earlier. A lot of tobacco had been grown on the island in the days of the Bourbon rulers. Giuseppe Garibaldi and his Redshirts eventually kicked those rulers off the island in 1860, bringing Sicily under Rome. Over the next decade, Rome sent its tax collectors south, and they tromped through the tobacco fields, counting the leaves on every plant and levying a tax based on those numbers. Farmers, either not able to pay such a tax or seeing their profits cut to the bone, said, *"Basta!"* (Enough!) They plowed their crop under and started growing something else, something without a tax tag attached.

A lot of tobacco has been raised on the mainland, principally in the north, accounting for 10 percent of world production, or about fifty thousand tons over nearly forty thousand acres, according to an article in the newspaper *Giornale di Sicilia*. The plants are a mixture of Kentucky and Burley strains. But there have been state-mandated cuts in subsidies for the crop, and tobacco production in northern Italy was declining. That opened the market for the crop to be raised in Sicily, which has a lot of unfarmed land available.

Enter Federico Marino, a Palermo tobacco shop proprietor who sought partnerships to seek regional support, along with recruiting entrepreneurs to help fund the project. The idea clicked. The *Giornale di Sicilia* article, published on August 21, 2015, stated that a small group of entrepreneurs, "supported by manufacturers and other tobacco farmers in northern Italy started this new business that has now paid off."

Their first crop, grown on nearly twenty acres outside of Cerda, yielded thirty tons of Kentucky and Burley tobacco. It was all sold to Italian cigar makers principally from the Italian Veneto region. "We gave work to ten farmers," Marino told the newspaper. A grower from the Veneto who supported the Sicilian project is Giancarlo Guzzo. He produces tobacco over nearly fifty-five acres near the village of Albaredo d'Adige. Guzzo is quoted in *Giornale di Sicilia*: "The Sicilian land is excellent. The climate enviable. There are all the conditions to continue this initiative and produce a good tobacco."

Marino expects the number of acres to expand, provided

enough water can be found. For those first twenty acres, he and his partners found two small reservoirs on their leased land that held enough water for the first two crops, the one in 2015 and the one that was beginning to poke out of the Sicilian earth when I visited Marino and his wife, Roberta Cirrincione, in Palermo during the final days of my time in Sicily.

First, though, I had to find them. Cerda is fewer than ten miles due east of Caccamo. My GPS navigation system recommended taking the twenty-mile route down to the coast, heading along the autostrada for a few miles, and then turning south on SS120. These are major roads, and the drive probably would have taken thirty-six minutes. But there was a way, on small country roads, to make the trip by heading directly east and avoiding the autostrada along the coast. George had told me about it during dinner the night before. I took that route and traveled through some beautiful country. I did not see tobacco fields—the plants would have been barely above the dirt—but I saw huge fields of thorny artichokes, their vegetable stalks with those classic artichoke heads poking high above the green undergrowth and stretching for acre after acre. It was a pleasant, cloudless day. The brutal Sicilian summer heat was still a month or two away. I turned off the air-conditioning, rolled down the car window, and enjoyed every minute of the drive.

In Cerda, I went to my usual place—a bar—for information. I asked the fellow who served my espresso if he knew where the tobacco fields were. He gave me a quizzical look, paused a minute, and shrugged his shoulders. *"Non lo so"* (I don't know), he said. I finished the espresso, looked around, and walked down a few doors and into the tobacco shop. They would know, I thought.

But the man behind the counter didn't. Same look, same pause, same shrug of the shoulders. I bought a package of Toscanello cigars, the short ones, went outside, sat on a bench, and smoked one. Delightful. But I was running out of ideas.

After a while, I decided to walk around the village. Within a few minutes I found myself in Piazza La Mantia staring at a pasty green statue, perhaps thirty feet tall. It wasn't of any person; it was a giant artichoke. The bottom was the narrowest, with the leafy stems rising up from a V and widening out at the top with a huge artichoke head in the middle. It was overwhelming. Later, I did some research. It honors the crop that has been grown around this area since Roman times, more than two thousand years. In Sicilian, it is called *cacuocciula*. The Italian word for artichokes is *carciofi*.

I took a photo and thought to myself that Minnesota's giant statue of Paul Bunyan and Babe the blue ox had nothing on Cedra's giant artichoke. Across the square, I saw a building with the word MUNICIPIO across the front. City hall! They would know whom to contact about the tobacco fields.

The receptionist had difficulty with my attempts at Italian, so she called a man over to help. He spoke a little English, and between our two languages he knew what it was that I was asking. He wanted to know who I was. I told him I was a writer and wanted to find Federico Marino and ask him about his tobacco farm. The man went to a computer, asked me to spell my name, and he looked me up on the internet. He saw that I was legit.

A few other city office workers started to take interest. The receptionist knew somebody who knew somebody. She called. A few minutes later, she got ahold of the man who oversaw the crop for Marino. He told her Marino and his wife were in Palermo. He had a phone number.

I thanked everyone who had become involved in my quest. There were perhaps six or seven of those good folks. They wanted a photograph with me. We clustered together and someone took a photo, first with their camera and then with mine. The man who spoke a little English asked me questions about my work and translated my answers back to his colleagues. I spent perhaps an hour there, among some of the friendliest people I have met in my many travels. The men patted me on the back, the women hugged me, and I bid farewell. A long series of *"Ciao, Ciao, Ciao!"* rang across the large room as we waved good-bye. I seemed to float above the small one-lane road on the drive back to Caccamo, the brilliantly green artichoke fields on both sides stretching far to the horizon, those thorny twisted heads nodding in my direction. Such people!

More than a month later, Federico Marino and Roberta Cirrincione met me in a small, outdoor trattoria near Palermo's small-boat harbor, La Cala. We ordered a light dinner of fruit salads. Roberta spoke English; Federico did not. I understood most of what he told me, in between bites of orange and kiwi, about growing tobacco in Sicily. I had discovered, in the various tobacco shops I frequented, a slender hand-wrapped cigar different from the Tuscan cigars I was used to. It was called Italico, and they were similar in shape and size.

Federico told me that the Italico was made in the Veneto and was superior to the traditional Tuscan cigars made in Lucca,

Tuscany. I agreed. I liked the ones I had tried. It was this cigar, made with tobacco grown inland from Venice, which the farmer Giancarlo Guzzo supported.

Proudly, Federico told me that the first two Sicilian crops—2015 and 2016—would be used in the Italico. It would be dried in special facilities near Cerda and transported north for more processing. The Kentucky plants would go through a smoking process with special wood and then dried.

I asked him if there were taxes on growing the crop in Sicily, like Rome had imposed in the 1860s when it sent tax collectors south. He smiled, and said, "Thankfully no. There is no tax on growing the crop. But if the cigar is produced on this island, there are taxes." It would be like tobacco taxes in the United States with those stamps attached to cigarette and cigar packages.

He handed me a cigar. It was like a traditional corona and not at all like the long, skinny Italicos we had been talking about. The cigar had a ring showing his name.

"This is my blend," he said, again proudly. "Your Sicily tobacco?" I asked. He shook his head. This was Nicaraguan tobacco that he blended—"a medium blend, easy smoking, a hint of chocolate"—while visiting a cigar-making friend in that South American country.

"We are not ready to use our tobacco in cigars made in Sicily," he said. "That will take time."

Eventually, instead of selling his tobacco to the cigar makers in the Veneto, Marino's main goal is to establish a production facility in Palermo, employing women as cigar rollers. "Women's hands have a more refined touch," he said. "Women from Treviso, in the Veneto, will come to Sicily and train Sicilian women in the art of cigar making."

Federico said his family had been selling tobacco products in their store since 1968. But he said he wants to do something more. "Something special. I want to give Sicily more life."

It's an ambitious project. From what I could tell, it was possible. The Palermo cigar factory would take time; everything in Sicily takes time. But Federico was confident. His excitement in telling the story was obvious. Together, we smoked the Nicaraguan cigars with the rings that bear his name. It was a pleasant smoke. Well worth the time and the moment.

As Roberta and Federico said good-bye, he invited me to his shop, located in a neighborhood a short cab ride from my *pensione* in the ancient Palermo market, the Vucciria. I went the next day. The shop was quite large, a distinct difference from the usually tiny tobacco shops that can be found in nearly every street in every village. Federico sold pipes as well as one of the largest varieties of cigars I have seen anywhere in Sicily, including a case full of Cuban cigars. We walked into the humidor. I had seen only two of those temperature- and humidity-controlled rooms in Italy before, in Rome and in a shop in Lucca that specialized in Tuscan cigars.

Federico handed me a handmade wooden box with his name carved on the front. Inside were six of his personal Nicaraguan coronas. I accepted the gift and purchased a box of Italico Superiore, the long, skinny cigars hand-wrapped with Kentucky tobacco. They made the journey home in fine shape.

TEN

Maria Messina and the Journey Home

It was a repetition of those sad, faraway days, an eternal nightmare that hung in the air and that ended very slowly.

One evening the pungent odor of fresh flowers and lighted candles veiled the scent of turpentine, and through the open windows one could hear the mournful ringing of funeral bells. . . . Like that, little by little, Marietta slipped away.

—Maria Messina,
"Caterina's Loom"
Behind Closed Doors: Her Father's
House and Other Stories (2007)

SICILIAN WRITER Maria Messina likely lived in two, maybe three places in Sicily, following her educator father from village to village before moving with the family to the Italian peninsula, living in places in Le Marche, Umbria, Naples, Arezzo, Florence, and finally Pistoia. Some biographical statements—all of them are too brief—name Palermo as her place of birth, on March 14, 1887. A few individuals believe she was born in her father's home village, Alimena, today about a ninety-minute drive from Palermo. It is a small village, almost hidden in the folds of rolling foothills that seem to go on forever, like the billowing surface of a great sea. Today, it is home to small merchants and farmers who raise wheat, almonds, olives, and grapes.

I had planned on driving to Alimena at some point. I had no idea what I would find there that had anything to do with Maria Messina. I had no contacts and knew no one who did. The village of barely two thousand people would have to be a day trip; there didn't seem to be any place to stay overnight. Alimena, on the eastern fringe of Palermo Province, was easily accessible from Mistretta, located on the western edge of adjoining Messina Province, a forty-mile drive. Going there and back in one day would not be an ordeal. The west–east route was along small roads that meandered through gorgeous countryside, which meant that once again, I could avoid the autostrada. Seeing new land, rapidly greening in the midst of a moist spring, would be part of the enjoyment.

First, I wanted to get acquainted with Mistretta, where Maria lived with her family from age sixteen to twenty-two. The folks who want to tie her to Alimena aside, there is no evidence she spent her younger days there. She could have lived in Palermo during those earliest years. There is no record found that shows where they lived before Mistretta. It was here that she wrote her first work—a collection of stories entitled *Fine Combs and Other Short Stories*—that ultimately would be published, in 1909, six years after the family's arrival. Some of those early short stories, set in an anonymous neighborhood in a small village, match places in this little town.

I settled in my room in a restored building next to the home of the owners, Nello Turco and Enza Constantino. Their property is up a steep street, Via Santa Caterina, and is directly across from a church of that name. I walked down to Via Libertà, which took me through the center of the village and past the Mother Church. From there I walked up a narrowing street and weaved in and out of the village's oldest section, the Arab Quarter, which had its beginning with the Greeks. Romans were here, too, followed by Byzantines and then Arabs. High above, on a bluff overlooking this original village, are the remnants of a castle. This quarter was where the village began, spreading out in medieval times and then getting bigger as the twentieth century dawned. Mistretta's population is about 4,500, and records show it is declining year by year. Young people can't get jobs here, so they go elsewhere.

It was a quick walk, and I headed back along Via Libertà, where I found a friendly, modern bar with lots of pastries and excellent coffee. I was looking forward to the next day. Neither Nello nor Enza spoke English, but we communicated just fine. I had asked him about Maria Messina, and he promised to take me to where she was interred, in the local cemetery. Maria and her mother had died in northern Italy, in Pistoia, and I didn't know how they ended up in a small crypt in Mistretta, but within a few days, it all would become clear.

After breakfast, Nello and I walked down to the city museum, housed in a former convent next to the Church of San Sebastian. We met Claudio Bartolotta, who showed me a handful of exhibits. On the floor, tucked in a corner, were the broken remains, in stone, of a carving of a skeleton from a church just up the street in the old town, Chiesa del Purgatorio. It had been mounted high up on the church's front exterior and fell, crashing to the ground during the earthquake that spread across Sicily in 1968. Claudio says it is awaiting restoration. When that will happen is anyone's guess.

It was here that I learned about the giants. Two of the original five are housed in this small museum. Every September, during the *feste* of La Madonna della Luce (The Madonna of the Light), copies of the papier-mâché giants, complete with armor, helmets, and swords, are strapped to the backs of two men who march in the procession featuring a large statue of the Madonna, carried high on the shoulders of the faithful. The procession travels a mile or so out of town to the Chiesa del Cimitero. Then, the two giants turn, look at the Madonna, and break out in a dance. They even have names: Cronos and Mitia. Every village has its own way of doing things. Mistrettesi certainly do it differently, combining myth with religion.

Nino Dolcemaschio joined us for what became a two-hour tour of the old town. He spoke rapid-fire Italian; Claudio Bartolotta translated. Our small group, which included my *pensione* host Nello, wandered through twisting lanes that, thankfully, were too small for cars. It was a hilly walk up and down lanes paved with stones. We saw the onetime Jewish Quarter, set apart from the Arab Quarter. It had been abandoned in 1492 when Jews were banished from Sicily during the early days of the Spanish Inquisition.

Arabs defended the castle when the Normans arrived to take control. They were forced out and escaped to a point below the hill that also had stone walls and fought on until defeated.

Physical evidence of that lower fort is now gone, Nello said. Many of the buildings in this ancient quarter were transformed during the medieval period, but according to Nello, some of the lower structures are still the original Arab houses. Many here are abandoned, hoping for buyers to come in and transform them once again into occupied homes.

We passed a small church, Chiesa del Santissimo Salvatore, or Church of the Most Holy Savior. It remains opens twenty-four hours a day, every day. It is strictly for people who want to have a quiet, protected place to pray, no matter the hour. There is a wonderfully crafted mosaic behind the altar of Christ with the Bible. A nun sits at the door, greeting parishioners and ensuring that the solitude is not broken.

Next stop was the bar I had visited the afternoon before. Coffee all around. I discovered that my money was no good there. My two guides refused to be paid; the young woman behind the counter shook her head when I tried to pay for our group. I discovered I was friends with the bar owner's friends. This lasted for two days, or every time that the bartender who first served me was working. When I ate lunch or dinner there, I insisted on paying. An espresso for no charge? OK. But no charge for a full meal was going too far. She resisted, shook her head. I insisted. The dance lasted a few moments. She gave in, grudgingly. Then, with a smile, she finally accepted my handful of euro.

Late one afternoon, after a walk through the old town and a steady climb up to the ruins of the castle, I sat on a rampart overlooking the village. The Arab Quarter was directly below;

the Jewish Quarter was off to the right. The village stretched far ahead, the older buildings giving way to medieval structures, then to more modern, nineteenth-century *palazzi* built in more affluent times. There was a beautiful park with busts of prominent Mistrettesi. Beyond and near the top of a distant hill I could see the church across from the house where I was staying.

Off to my left, in the distance, were green fields and olive groves and rows of trees that likely produced almonds. I noticed a white wall of low fog slowly moving its way across those fields and groves. It took perhaps ten minutes for it to creep up to the edge of the village and slowly overtake the houses. It moved across the town, and then it was gone, and the early evening light returned.

I had, in my back pocket, an English-language copy of Maria Messina's novel *A House in the Shadows*. I was well into it, but I started reading again, looking up every now and then to contemplate a sentence or simply look, one more time, at the village below. I came across this passage: "The twilight reddened the sky, the roofs, and the narrow street. Then suddenly the vivid light vanished in the violet air." I looked up and realized I was seeing what Messina had described. The sun was setting, ever so slowly, and the tiles on the roofs of the ancient quarter below me were turning a reddish hue. In a moment, that light would be gone, the night would turn pink and then violet, and darkness would settle in. I waited, and it happened just as she had written it.

The moon offered me enough light to make my way through the tall grass that covered stones, rubble from the collapsed castle that had only a couple of walls rebuilt by archaeologists. Small lights embedded in the asphalt lighted the pathway down.

The walk through the old town was easy and free as I passed open doors with people inside cooking dinner, and kids, still in the lanes outside, shouting and kicking soccer balls against stone walls.

Again I thought of Maria Messina. I paused in a lane where houses on either side had first- and second-floor balconies. Those on opposite sides of the cobblestoned lane were so close it seemed someone could leap from one to the other. I leaned against a wall, near a light from a curtained window. I took out the book and reread, perhaps for the nth time, part of the first paragraph of *A House in the Shadows*:

> Nicolina was sewing on the balcony, hastening to make the last stitches in the dim twilight. The view offered by the high balcony was enclosed, almost smothered, between the little street, which at that hour looked as dark and deep as an empty well, and the broad expanse of reddish, moss-covered roofs over which a wan sky hung low. . . . [Nicolina] felt the monotony of the constricted landscape as though it were part of the air she breathed.

Again, I was seeing what she described so cleanly, so elegantly. I put the book away and moved on. It was still a bit chilly for April, but I felt warm enough to stay outside all evening. I was hungry, though. I walked out of the old town, past the Mother Church where people were inside for their evening prayer service, and onto a side street and the restaurant my host had recommended. A large plate of spaghetti *al pomodoro* was there for me, along with a piece of wonderfully cooked veal, and a *cannolo* tipped with crushed pistachios. Then an espresso. What a day this had been.

Lucio Amato, age eighty-four, spent nearly every morning on a bench on the sidewalk in front of the Church of Saint Sebastian, directly across from my new favorite bar. Always alone, he sat there because it was warm lounging in the early morning sun. The benches on the cooler shady side of Via Libertà were empty. Other older men, the *pensionati,* were clustered here and there along the sunny side, in small tight groups, milling about the stone steps of the church or in the little park across the street from the museum. They would offer a friendly nod and a smile as they passed Lucio, and he would nod back, but they knew to honor his desire to sit alone.

One morning early in my time in Mistretta, I came out of the bar after a quick breakfast and looked around for a place to sit. The only vacant spot in the sun was Lucio's bench. There were the church steps, but the elderly men had those occupied. I walked across the street, stood in front of the bench, and asked the white-haired gentleman if I could sit there. He gave me a stern look. I thought, Uh-oh, the answer will be no. But then that look shifted into a quick smile.

We sat in silence that first day. By the second morning we exchanged a few pleasantries. The third morning, I asked him his name. I told him mine, using the Italian equivalent, Giovanni. Then I asked him about the building across the street and to the left of the bar, on Piazza San Sebastiano. It had a large sign over the doorway, CIRCOLO UNIONE 1859. The building was wonderfully restored. Earlier I had looked through the windows and saw rooms filled with modern furniture. It definitely looked like a private club, as the name *circolo* implied.

"It is for the nobles," he said, using the Italian word *"nobilità."* "It is not for me, and maybe not for you, but I do not know you. Are you a noble?" I assured him I wasn't, the ice was broken, and we spent the next hour working on understanding each other. I told him who I was and what I was doing in Mistretta. He told me about his family members who had left in that migration to America after World War II. He was a retired cheese maker, a *casaro.* In all my years of traveling in Italy I had never met one. He ticked off for me the kinds of cheese he had specialized in: *provola,* made with cow's milk, a deep yellow cheese that is shaped to look like a pear. "You know pear?" Lucio asked, saying the Italian word *pera* and using his hands to make the shape. *"Sì,"* I assured him. He told me that *provola* is a specialty in the mountains of Messina Province. He also listed *ricotta fresca,* or fresh ricotta, and *ricotta salata,* a cheese made with sheep's milk, salted and aged. And then he added to my list *primo sale,* literally translated as "first salt." Again, sheep's milk is used, he said, and the cheese is a young cheese. He used the word *giovane,* Italian for young, to emphasize that it is a soft white cheese. Sometimes, he said, peppercorns are added.

We sat, again in comfortable silence. A man walked up and greeted Lucio. He was from Basilicata, a region in southern Italy, along the Ionian Sea, and was retired Carabinieri, one of the militarized federal police officers who wears distinctive uniforms designed to show they are above local cops and can appear, and act, a bit intimidating. But this fellow seemed quite mellow and friendly.

That prompted me to tell him about my encounter four days earlier with two Carabinieri assigned to Mistretta. They visited me at my *pensione* and wanted to see my passport and airline receipts. They spoke no English. They were convinced I had overstayed my tourist visa, but I told them I had been in Italy only for two months; I was allowed three. They were somber and unsmiling. They seemed convinced the limit was two months. The senior one went outside and made a phone call. Twenty minutes later he came in and motioned, with a quick jerk of his head, at his companion. The two officers left with no good-byes, no comments. The next day, driving out of Mistretta, I saw them at the opposite end of a tunnel, waving over cars whose drivers had forgotten to turn on the headlights, a requirement when one is driving in the countryside. My headlights were on. From bumptious, intimidating policemen one day to traffic cops the next.

The retired national policeman chuckled knowingly as I told him the two officers were very serious, no smiles. I asked if he was always that serious. He smiled broadly. "But I am friendly now," he said with a wink.

It was obvious the two men wanted to visit. I excused myself and headed down the street. There was a tiny cheese shop tucked away down some steps below a historic *palazzo*. I dropped in, purchased a small bit of *primo sale* with small black peppercorns, and devoured it delightedly as I walked up the steep hill to my car. I spent the day exploring the fields and hills, stopping at a tiny restaurant seemingly alone in the countryside and ate a three-course

meal of pasta and swordfish and salad, washed down with bub-
bly mineral water. I wouldn't have any need for dinner.

The following morning, I was back on the bench well before
the time Lucio would arrive. The sun had yet to hit our side of the
street. None of the pensioners were out this early. I read one of
Maria Messina's short stories, the one entitled "La Mèrica," about
a young mother whose husband leaves for America alone—she
had a vision problem that would bar her from being admitted on
board the steamship departing from Palermo—essentially aban-
doning her and his son with no intention of returning. The title
in English is "America 1911," giving a sense of when the story
takes place. The woman, forced to rely on her family for support,
begins to lose her mind, spending whole days on the front stoop
of her house, her chin cupped in her hands, waiting for a steamship from America that never comes.

For a while, I watched people and cars going by along Via Libertà. Two or three times in the space of an hour I saw the same
woman drive by the Church of Saint Sebastian. Each time she
would slow down as she passed the front door and cross herself,
holding tight to the steering wheel with her left hand. This was
something I would see bus drivers do when they drove past
churches; even a few pedestrians walking by a church or chapel,
anything with a cross on top, would do it.

Given that it was still early, deliveries were being made to the
storefronts along the street. A large truck loaded with artichokes
roared by, followed a few minutes later by a small three-wheeled
Ape, pronounced *ah-pay*, chugging past with a load of freshly harvested basil piled in its small bed, some already bagged in brown
paper sacks for a quick sale. The produce, harvested in the early

morning, as the sun broke over the top of the low inland hills, likely was destined for restaurants and small markets. Everything I encountered while glancing through stalls of outdoor markets and seeing these trucks, large and small, unloading outside restaurants, was local and delivered fresh daily.

Then, for offerings to individual shoppers, a small truck piled high almost to overflowing with vegetables of all kinds moved slowly down the street, the driver blaring his daily spiel through a crackly loudspeaker. He stopped midblock, and several women poured out of their buildings to gather around and bargain. It was noisy, everyone talking at once.

On a few occasions throughout my travels, I would see this kind of truck in various neighborhoods away from village centers with the loudspeaker going. Once I saw a woman leaning out her third-floor window, waving. The produce seller stopped. She lowered a basket on a thin white rope. He read her note on a scrap of paper and put in the requested goods. She pulled it up and then, a moment later, down came the basket with the money inside. This is a regular ritual in southern Italian and Sicilian villages: daily delivery of fresh, local provisions. Sometimes a driver is selling bread made just that morning; sometimes it's a small refrigerated truck with a butcher driver who cuts meat to order in front of the buyer's house.

All this passes by on Via Libertà between seven thirty and eight o'clock. Eventually, the bar across the street opened. I got my morning coffee and *cornetto,* and when I came out the men were beginning to cluster, as usual, around the front of the church. Lucio was in his regular spot, rhythmically tapping his cane against the side of the metal bench. We waved, and I continued on to the *pensione* to pick up my car for the nearly two-hour drive to Alimena. I doubted I could solve the mystery of Maria Messina's birthplace there, but the day was clear and warming up to a respectable temperature for a late Sicilian spring, and the drive through the wide-open countryside promised to be leisurely and relaxing.

The drive to the southwest—first along provincial road SP176 then along SS120 and finally onto SS290—was, as expected, through wonderful hills and fields, all turning a deep green that was flecked with the occasional white patches of sheep. Alimena suddenly sprang out of this greenness, a cluster of small houses with the usual churches here and there dominating the skyline. Sicily is full of villages like this: seemingly isolated and almost hidden in the tucks of hills. When a traveler gets off the autostrada and, armed with a good map, takes these small provincial and state roads, there is no telling what they will find. Many times I have stumbled into a really small place with only a few streets lined with medieval structures and sat down to a remarkable meal in a tiny trattoria with perhaps three tables. Alimena was like that.

I drove into the town square and parked in a spot fronted by a sign I didn't understand. As I got out of the car, a man, walking stiffly and using a cane, and dressed in a dark jacket and wearing a Sicilian cap, came toward me, waving his free arm to get my attention. It was a parking spot reserved for someone important was all I could discern from what he said. Move the car over one stall, he said, gesturing to the one next to where I was parked. There were no painted lines indicating there was a stall there. No problem, the man said with a smile. I moved the car; he watched approvingly, nodding his head as I emerged. I thanked him for his good advice. No police, no ticket, he said. We shook hands. He moved across the street and into Bar Da Pino, looking back once and offering a final wave.

Usually, the first place I head is a bar, to order an espresso and perhaps get some information. Alimena is one of the smaller ones I visited, barely more than two thousand souls. This time I decided first to walk up Via Roma, temporarily turned into a pedestrian street to make room for an outdoor market.

There were stalls where folks were selling everything from fruit and vegetables to shirts and socks. The stalls were in the street, in front of the usual small stores: a tobacco shop, a dress shop, a small bar or two. It was lively. It seemed that every one of the two thousand Alamenesi was walking along this patch of pavement.

I liked the feel of the place and walked to the end of the market at a major cross street. I bought a gelato; the pistachio was superb. Everyone seemed to know each other. This was a day for the locals to meet, greet, and stock up on supplies. People noticed me, the stranger, the foreigner, but, as it had been with the elderly man at the parking spot, it was smiles and nods all around.

I walked over to another street and there stood the Mother Church, dedicated to Santa Maria Maddalena. It had broad steps and a long open space all the way down to a street at the bottom, Via Calascibetta. I sat on the steps for a bit, leaning back and enjoying the morning while listening to the sounds coming from a block away of the market along Via Roma. Then, the sound of tinkling bells aroused me. I sat up, and along Via Calascibetta came a flock of sheep, perhaps twenty or thirty. A lone man with a tall, straight staff was driving them through the heart of the village, from a field on one side to a field on the other. I was so engrossed in the scene unfolding in front of me, I forgot about my camera. A missed shot. The flock wheeled around a corner and disappeared, the tinkling bells growing faint.

It was time to ask someone—anyone—about Maria Messina. I returned to Bar Da Pino, ordered the obligatory espresso, and carried it outside to a table shaded by an umbrella. It was getting hot; the umbrella was essential. Soon, the man who had served me came out to clean off the tables. I got his attention and asked if he knew anything about the writer Maria Messina. He shrugged his shoulders. No. He then looked across the small triangular square and saw two men. *"Un momento."* He called them over, pointed to me, and went back to clearing the tables.

I told them who I was. One young man spoke excellent English. They were village employees. Giacomo Ippolita said he was the assessor and director of the environment. With him was Francesco Federico, who he said was the vice mayor. I asked them if they knew anything about my writer. They both said no. Feeling defeated, I asked them to recommend a restaurant. "Follow us," Giacomo said. Then, before we left the bar, he was on his cell phone.

"I called Mari Albanese, a friend who is a writer. She said she knows about Maria Messina," he said. He was almost as excited as I was. "She will call you in an hour." We went to the restaurant. I devoured a plate full of spaghetti *con asparagi e carciofi,* asparagus and artichokes, a local specialty. Wonderful.

Giacomo told me his mother, also a friend of Mari's, knew

English very well, he said, because she lives in Chicago some of the year and in Alimena the rest of the time. He asked if I was on Facebook. He whipped out his phone, and within a few seconds we were "friends." We exchanged phone numbers and addresses. My two companions left. I returned to Bar Da Pino to wait for Mari Albanese's call. A few moments later, the phone chattered. Mari spoke no English. Language confusion led to her saying *aspettate* (you wait). She hung up. I called Giacomo to ask if he could help; his mother, the lady from Chicago, answered. "Don't worry," said Lillina Messineo. "Mari just called me. We will both meet you in thirty minutes." Whew. Once again, I had wandered into a place unknown and unknowing. I asked questions and someone knew something or someone, and wonderful things were happening.

Lillina and Mari arrived. Mari, a professor of philosophy, taught in Palermo, a quick ninety-minute drive along the autostrada. In Alimena, she served as a village counselor. I found out she had written a major paper on Maria Messina that, unfortunately for me, was in Italian and well beyond my translation skills. She gave me a copy for the day, she said with a smile, when I became fluent.

She told me, through Lillina, that Messina's father was born in Alimena. As for his daughter, "We think she was born here but we are not sure." I suggested that someone in the village administration should research property records to determine where the father's family house was located. Also, I added, perhaps church records could be found in some archive that would give details on the birth as well as the christening.

I was surprised that this kind of work had not been done. Maria's biographic notices in various publications were not much more than a few paragraphs. Mari agreed. "It may be possible." If the village were to do this, I said, that would be a way to make it more desirable for tourists to come. Even if she really had been born in Palermo, she might have spent time here during vacations in her father's family house. There could be a plaque on the home, perhaps a small one-room museum with copies of her books and memorabilia of the time.

Some time after my visit, I talked with Elise Magistro, a professor in Italian at Scripps College in Claremont, California. Elise is the translator of that collection of Messina short stories that brought the village of Mistretta to life for me. She had spent several years translating and studying what little is known about Maria's life. The professor, who also has visited Alimena and made a brief, fruitless search for records, made it clear that nothing is known about where Maria lived between her birth and moving to Mistretta when she was sixteen. The assumption must be made that she was born in Palermo where her father was a teacher and later, when he was promoted to a school inspector, the family moved to Mistretta.

A house with a plaque that clings to the possibility that Maria spent even a short amount of time in Alimena would be enough to draw a few tourists, provided the father's family home was found. I thought about my visit a few years earlier to the preserved home of the Sardinian writer Grazia Deledda, the only Italian woman to win, in 1926, the Nobel Prize for Literature. Her house, in Nuoro, Sardinia, was simply restored, and the small museum inside did Deledda great honor.

Mari and I agreed that Maria Messina needed to be discovered by new generations of readers, no matter whether she ever lived in tiny Alimena. Our too-brief meeting drew to a close. Mari handed me a copy of her thesis. Then, she paused, thinking. "Can you come back soon?" she asked. "I want you to hear some wonderful music that is unique to this village." Eager to learn new things about Sicilian culture in these remote villages, I am not one to say no to such an offer. She set a date and time for a few weeks later. We left it at that and parted, best of friends after only thirty minutes of conversation.

I took one more walk up Via Roma, now deserted in the growing afternoon heat. With the sidewalk merchants gone, the street was open to one-way traffic, but there was hardly any to contend with. Near the top, at the point where earlier I had turned to go to the Mother Church, the usual collection of retirees was clustered around a few tables at an outside bar. A card game was under way, but its players were unusually quiet as they calmly slapped down their cards, one by one. I had a final espresso and walked back to my car. As the older gentlemen promised when he helped me move it, there was no ticket. The drive back to Mistretta was as calm and leisurely as it had been earlier in the day, and the countryside, like always that time of year, was just as beautiful.

A few weeks later, I returned for that promised private concert, where I would hear for the first time a group of men, *i lamentatori,* sing. Mari was away on business, but a colleague met me at Bar Da Pino and led the way to a large church, the Convento, set back on the shallow slope of a hill overlooking the village. The church was plain, essentially unadorned except for two niches on each side of the entrance, and the large front doors of well-weathered wood were bereft of any paint or varnish. The stones making up the façade were rough and chipped, and clumps of grasses and weeds grew out of cracks in the vertical walls and in the stone steps up to those ancient front doors.

A few dozen feet away from the front stood a Christus, a large statue of Christ. Instead of his hands being held out away from his side, palms outward in a welcoming gesture, as they are in traditional statues of that genre, this one's arms were held in front, shoulders high and palms outward, almost in a gesture of "Stay away." That meaning is not likely, however; I sensed it was a representation of Christ showing the nail marks on his palms, an act by Jesus making a dramatic statement: He is risen.

The eighteenth-century church, with the full name of Chiesa dell'ex Convento di Santa Maria di Gesù, was built in the 1730s. It had been shuttered for the past ten years for a reason I never understood. Perhaps, like many churches in Sicily, it was closed because of damage from earthquakes. The good news: In late 2017, the region of Sicily announced it was providing 225,000 euros for its restoration. Perhaps on my next visit I will be able to see the interior.

A smaller building, attached to the church's left side, was once a convent. Its front doors, in much better shape, were wide open, and a couple of men were waiting inside. My guide introduced them to me and then took her leave, saying she had an appointment. I was on my own language-wise, but not too concerned. One of the men showed me around the large, open, ground-floor room with decorations hanging here and there showing symbols of their confraternity, or church-service organization, Ecce Homo (Behold the Man).

Photographs pinned to the wall showed the members in white robes, with red fabric covering their shoulders and tied in the front. They wore white scarves around their heads, wrapped around their necks, allowing the fabric to flow down their backs. Two men in front held long, unlighted tapers. Another photo showed the men with small boys, their sons, dressed in miniature costumes like those of their fathers: the next generation.

These gentlemen I was meeting were a subset of that larger group, specialists in singing lamentations, particularly during Easter processions, in this tiny community. More men arrived, including a teenage son. No one was in costume, of course; they were simply wearing work clothes. Many were farmers who came in from their fields, at Mari Albanese's request, to show me a small piece of their culture. We shook hands all around. They formed a semicircle and, at an unspoken signal, began. The singing, a guttural brand of throat singing, beautifully rich in harmony, from high tones—the highest provided by the teenager—through tenor and baritone. The sound reverberated against the stone walls and off the high ceiling of this former convent. The only word I can think of to describe it is "stunning." This went on for several minutes.

They finished one lament and began another. The power of those seven or eight voices was overwhelming. It was like the time I was in a tiny club in a neighborhood of New Orleans where a brass band held forth, nonstop, for nearly an hour. The sound captured me, surrounded me. I couldn't have turned and left even if I had wanted to. In this small, one-room convent, their voices held me tight. I stood, looking from man to man as each one dominated then gave way to another.

They presented me with perhaps thirty minutes of this magnificent singing of music each knew by heart. The songs are *lamentanze* (laments); the men are called *lamentatori* (lamenters). This kind of music is found elsewhere in Sicily, and often there are festivals featuring it, such as one Alimena hosted in the summer of 2015—*il Festival delle eredità immateriali* (the Festival of Intangible Heritage)—where lamenters from throughout the island gathered. In a report about that festival, Mari Albanese spoke warmly about this "treasure," and praised the presence of many young people who are embracing the tradition.

I expressed my gratitude. Some shook hands, a few others embraced me, doing what Sicilian men do, with a light kiss on each cheek. The last one, locking the convent doors and offering a wave, drove away. I sat on those steps, wondering what was inside that locked-up church.

Nello Turco, my host in Mistretta, offered, one bright morning that promised a hot late-spring day, to drive me to the cemetery on the the village edge. There, he wanted to show me the grave site of Maria Messina. I had been surprised she was there; the last I knew, she had died in Pistoia, in northern Tuscany, on January 19, 1944. She had lived in Mistretta only from 1903 to 1909, leaving at age twenty-two to go with her family to the Italian mainland, where her father had been transferred to another village. As far as I knew, she had never returned during her lifetime.

First, though, Nello said he had a surprise. We drove down Via Libertà and stopped in front of a small, street-level office. Inside waiting was Nino Testagrossa, an official with the Mistretta Cultural Association. With him was Maria Alfieri. She introduced herself, speaking excellent English, and said she would act as interpreter for my conversation with Nino about Maria Messina.

Within thirty minutes, I discovered why and how Maria's remains ended up in Mistretta. It seems the cultural association decided they did not belong in Pistoia, where she had died of multiple sclerosis. Apparently her widowed mother, Gaetana Traina, had been with her there, her last stop in a series of Italian towns—Arezzo and Florence among them—seeking a cure to the disease that made it impossible for her to write. Gaetana died on December 20, 1932, eleven years before her daughter. Through the help of Mistretta native Giorgio Giorgetti, who was in Pistoia, the cultural association was able to arrange the transfer of Maria's and her mother's remains to Mistretta in 2009.

According to Elise Magistro, who talked to me long after my trip and who spends part of every year in Mistretta, the people there were overwhelmed at the prospect of having their village be the famed author's final resting place—in the Sicily she loved and the place that formed and shaped many of her stories and novels. She focused on the subservient role of women, of both high and low birth, in the culture of this island during the late nineteenth and early twentieth centuries.

Nino Testagrossa, another key figure in that transfer, said it was one of his proudest moments. He said the association now chooses to honor an Italian woman writer annually—a writer who describes how women live in Italy and how women's roles have changed over the last century. Maria Messina was the first to be honored.

Nello took me to the cemetery. It had been awhile since he had been there, so we wandered a bit looking for Maria's tomb. It was a rough-and-tumble place. Some graves were well maintained; others look like they haven't been touched in decades. "Families leave, and the descendants are far, far away, and there is no one to maintain their ancestors' resting places," Nello told me. Of course that is true everywhere, not just in Sicily.

Nello suddenly stopped, thought a moment, then pointed up-hill to a long bank of small boxes. "There," he said. We walked up, looked at the names along the row, and there it was. MARIA MESSINA/*SCRITTRICE* (writer) and the dates. On the line below: GAETANA TRAINA/*MADRE DELLA SCRITTRICE* and her dates. Mother and daughter together. Ironically, right next to their spot was another box front with the name Giorgio Giorgetti, showing he had died at age seventy-three in 2013. *"Molto appropriato"* (very appropriate), this closeness of resting places, I said to Nello.

I knew that just before Maria died, she was moved from her Pistoia apartment because of heavy Allied bombing during the height of World War II's Italian campaign. Bombs fell in October 1943 and again on January 3, 1944. Her apartment was destroyed, and along with it all her correspondence, manuscripts, and photographs—everything. She had been moved to a house in a safer area and, unable to care for herself or write a word, she died sixteen days later. Her writing career had lasted twenty years with a prolific output of dozens of stories and a handful of novels. Only two, a novel and a collection of stories, have been translated into English, one in 1989, the other in 2007.

Elise Magistro, during a discussion a year after my time in Mistretta, laughed as she told me that as a graduate student seeking a subject for her dissertation, she wanted to write about an Italian female writer. Her committee members scoffed and said the only one worthy was the Sardinian writer Grazia Deledda. So that is what she settled on. Over the years, she came across the writings of Maria Messina, thanks to Leonardo Sciascia, who rediscovered her in 1981, thirty-seven years after her death, and urged publishers to reissue her works, ending her fifty years of literary obscurity. She had fallen out of favor with publishers in the 1930s as they grew weary of the negative, sad realities of the *verismo* movement. Truth is sometimes painful.

I asked Elise what it was that she thought Sciascia saw in Maria's work. After all, like many Italian men and in the tradition of Verga and Capuana, who—until Maria came along—paid little attention to women writers of their time, Sciascia also was not known for his appreciation of many women writers.

"Sciascia was passionate about anyone or anything, any art, any music, that was Sicilian. He saw an authentic voice in Messina." Elise told me. Sciascia then, like Verga, was open-minded enough that when a wondrous work hit his eye, he was willing not to judge the gender but to embrace the art.

So how did Maria develop as a writer during a time when women of the bourgeoisie wore long black dresses bound tight at the throat and could not leave the house without a father, uncle, or brother accompanying them? Or, during a period of mourning for a dead family member, women were confined to the home for six months, drapes drawn, no light allowed to enter. A woman whose husband died wore black until the end of her days, and it was unheard of for her ever to marry again. If a daughter did not marry, she would spend her spinsterhood in her father's house, never leaving the family home to be on her own. There was no place to go, no job available so she could support herself.

It was a time when girls did not go to school. Any education took place in the home, but only if a father or mother offered to teach. We know that Maria's mother taught her when she was very young, and her brother, who went to school, shared his lessons with her. But she was mostly self-taught. She was reared speaking only Sicilian, and she taught herself Italian, a separate language. That she could write such powerful stories in that language while in her early twenties and virtually unschooled, is remarkable. Verga was, in the modern vernacular, "blown away" by the strength in her writing. He knew her story. Some of the letters she wrote to her mentor described what her childhood was like.

From writings of her niece, Annie Messina, we know that Maria's home life was unbearable. Her father and mother were unhappy in the marriage; her father stayed away as much as he could. The family, like nearly all families of the time, depended entirely on the father's income. Then, compounding this rough upbringing, he died shortly after they left Sicily for the mainland. Mother and daughter managed to survive, with the help of Maria's brother, but he, too, was often gone, working in the Middle East. As Maria's health began to deteriorate, in the late 1920s, the pair moved frequently, in search of a cure. Annie Messina reports that they spent time in Naples, which was a good time for them, but the debilitating sclerosis worsened, hence the moves to places like Arezzo and Florence, and finally, at rope's end, Pistoia.

Elise Magistro describes what happened when Maria burst forth as a writer in the tradition of *verismo* championed by Verga and Capuana this way:

The male writers of *verismo*: Verga, De Roberto, Capuana—a trio not particularly friendly to female writers—in their works you see females defined in a certain way, either saints or as fallen women. Messina comes in and redefines this; she is more valid. She is observing her own society and the women around her. This new writer is very authentic, because unlike Verga who ran to [Sicilian folklorists to get] his material about the lower classes, she is actually observing what she is writing. Verga would never have interacted with people lower than him. Hers is a more authentic voice.

So what did Messina learn from Verga? "She admired Verga's ability [while writing in formal Italian] to make his prose sound like Sicilian in syntax, using certain diction, and Messina is very good at that—note the ellipses for silences," Elise said.

She emphasized that Maria was an observer. She watched everything: the lower-class people, the peasants, how they interacted, how they spoke to one another. She knew the seasons and what was harvested when, and she could relate that to the reality of the people. She observed the middle class and how the women were kept in their houses, able only to sit on a terrace hanging over a dark lane where sunlight often could not reach, and knit. And she observed the people of the upper classes, many of whom had lost their family fortunes and who lived in great houses but had to put on a show so others would not know their economic reality.

Elise said Maria saw it all and wrote prolifically during those long days in the family house. She never married, never had children, and never left her mother's side. Shortly following our conversation, I received this note from the professor:

In spite of seemingly insurmountable physical, social, and psychological challenges, she produced a body of work that was extraordinary for a woman of her background and times. Her short stories weave the varied threads of a complex and painful Sicilian reality into a rich tapestry of Sicilian life at the beginning of the twentieth century. Anyone wishing to discover Sicily, to understand Sicily as it once was, needs look no further than the works of Maria Messina.

I understood her statement perfectly. For years, I have advised friends and readers that in order to truly understand Sicilians and their mind-sets, they should read *The Leopard* by Giuseppe di Lampedusa and watch Visconti's faithful film of that book. I would add Verga's *I Malavoglia*—the English translation is *The House by the Medlar Tree*—and to see Visconti's film version, *La terra trema*. Camilleri's Detective Montalbano novels give a huge insight into modern Sicilian culture. Now, I must add to that list the available works of Maria Messina for all the reasons enumerated by Elise Magistro.

ELEVEN

Riesi, and Racalmuto's Serrone

Cu' nesci 'rrinesci: Who ventures forth succeeds.

—Sicilian proverb

Rosy Trovato's message urging me to visit her Sicilian town could not be ignored. We had become acquainted through mutual Sicilian friends, and she had followed my work on another book about Sicily. But we had never met face-to-face. Without her appeal, I would have bypassed Riesi, located in the south-central part of the island, between inland Caltanissetta and coastal Licata. With a listed population of around eleven thousand, it was larger than the small villages to which I typically gravitated. In a series of messages, however, she convinced me to drop by for a few days. The visit turned out to be well worth the time.

Riesi is a hardscrabble town surrounded by land that once was a center for sulfur mining—an industry that, for three centuries or longer, trashed the hills throughout the area and demeaned its workers and their families. Sicily in the 1800s produced 75 percent of the world's sulfur supply. Production finally shut down in the early 1980s. Those hills are in full recovery, turning green and productive every spring, and that once burned-over land now shows off almond groves and wheat fields.

The people, toughened for generations, survived despite the debilitating effects of sulfur mining, despite warring World War II armies during brutal fighting in and around the town, and despite a postwar economic crisis that forced hundreds, if not a few thousand, to emigrate to larger cities on the Italian mainland and elsewhere in Western Europe and Scandinavia.

It would take a few days to learn about the people of this town: what kind of tough, hard-nosed stock they came from, their independent approach to Catholicism, and their rough times with a deeply entrenched Mafia. I gathered all this through a long afternoon conversation, with Rosy Trovato interpreting, with a priest who is also a historian.

Before that conversation would take place, however, I wanted to get acquainted with this little corner of town I was a guest in for four days. It was a cursory glance, much like speeding down a highway and seeing something interesting alongside the road as you zoom by, but you don't stop and go back to better absorb the view. Four days isn't enough time anywhere, but even the briefest time can leave impressions that are unforgettable. That's what happened to me in Riesi: indelible impressions.

Once ensconced in Palace B and B Veneziano on Via Principe Umberto, after spending an hour or so locating a parking spot in the height of a post-*riposo* afternoon traffic, I wandered. This part of Riesi was fairly level, no hills to struggle up in the hot Sicilian sun. The buildings, a mixture of postwar and medieval, were dark-stoned versus the mellow golden hues in many hilltop villages across the island and the mainland. Here, they were like the darker buildings of Palermo as opposed to the warmer stones of Catania.

Heading out of the hotel and up Via Pasqualino for one short block, a large, pleasant piazza opened up on my left, Piazza Garibaldi. The obligatory church stood tall across the way. Along the other side of the square were a restaurant and several *circoli,* or private gathering places, for the pensioners of various professions. There was the storefront with the usual array of card tables and chairs for the *lega pensionati,* or metalworker retirees. Next to it was the Circolo Artigiani, where various craftsmen gathered. And next to that was one that, it seemed, was for everyone else: Circolo Pensionati di Riesi. There were a few more such clubs located around the square; it seemed Riesi had an abundance of older citizens. This fit with what I had learned a few days later: Young people, when through with their secondary education, typically leave in great numbers for elsewhere in Italy or in the West. In fact, just months after my visit, Rosy Trovato and her husband left for Boston, Massachusetts, with their two teenage daughters. Their number in the visa lottery turned up, and they are now making a new life in the New World.

I walked across the square toward a gelato shop on the far edge. Three elderly men standing in the center of this vast open space, heads close together and talking with great animation, saw me. As if on a silent signal, they turned and walked toward me, intercepting me in midstride. With friendly greetings, they asked me where I was from and what I did for a living. I told them I, too, was a *pensionato,* a retired newspaper journalist. They wondered why I, as someone with no ancestral ties to Riesi, would want to come to their town. I said a friend had invited me, and that I was enjoying myself.

One man took me by the arm, and the three walked me to

their *circolo*. We sat down outdoors at a well-worn wooden table
that appeared to be from another century. One man disappeared,
just to return a few moments later with four *espressi* in small plastic cups with lids. We tossed the contents down in one gulp, the
way espresso is supposed to be consumed. They asked more
questions; I answered as best I could. I once again learned about
the kind of hospitality that is rare in my country. Whenever I
visited that square over the next three days, those men were
there. They would shout a greeting.

Rosy had someone she wanted me to meet. One afternoon we
drove out into the countryside to a large house with a gate across
the driveway and a wall shielding the home from the road. Greeting us was Padre Pino Giuliana, seventy-nine years old at the
time of our visit. We entered a large book-lined living room filled
with comfortable furniture. Padre Pino is a historian, someone
who knows everything important about Riesi and the culture of
its people. After formalities, we settled in for a couple of hours
of discussion: the padre speaking Italian only, Rosy interpreting,
and me asking a question or two as best I could at my language
level.

There was a time in Sicily and on the Italian peninsula,
particularly in the south, when millions died because of mosquito-
borne malaria. Padre Pino said that, because of this killing
disease, much of Sicily's interior was virtually abandoned for
centuries, during the time when the Sicilian Muslims ruled (they
were then replaced by the Normans). "There were almost no
roads and no bridges over the streams that flowed through here

in those times," he said. It was called *reis,* a word at the time that meant "abandoned land."

In the 1600s, it began to change. Spanish rulers, always eager to find ways to raise cash, started selling to nobles the rights, or licenses, to vast stretches of land where they would establish populations. A Spanish don, Pedro Altariza, got the license for the area around Riesi.

It started small, of course. There were one hundred inhabitants in 1647, twenty-five thousand in 1948 just as the major postwar diaspora began, and just twelve thousand in 2016, a number that continues to decline. Riesi today has enough buildings, empty and still standing, to house a population three times that large. Housing, by European and U.S. standards, is a bargain at a few hundred to a few thousand euro in these villages. What is *molto caro,* or most dear, is the cost of restoration.

"When people emigrated, they believed in their hearts that they would come back with a lot of money, that their children, having grown up somewhere else, would prefer to come back and live here," said the padre. "Then they made money in America and bought a house and their kids learned English and made American friends. They didn't come back. A few might return to visit, but the next generation saw no future here. So the houses that had been in the family for generations are now empty"—a modern-day *"reis,"* or abandonment.

In those early centuries, Padre Pino said, there was no middle class, just affluent land owning families at the top and farmers or sulfur workers at the bottom. This peasant class could not own land until the 1950s. In more prosperous areas of Sicily and Italy, the farmer made money from his crops that he could then spend for goods and services. In the area around Riesi, people were paid in grain, a product that did not lose value even in the worst of times.

From my studies and writings about Sicily, I knew about the sulfur industry. Sicilian authors such as Luigi Pirandello, whose father owned sulfur mines around Agrigento in the deep south, and Leonard Sciascia, who grew up in Racalmuto, some thirty miles to the west of Riesi, wrote about the impact the industry had on the land and the people.

The heat inside the mines often drove the workers to work in the nude, hammering large chunks of sulfur out of walls, creating pillars they hoped would keep the ceilings from caving in on them. The greatest tragedy was that, well into the early twentieth century, boys as young as ten worked alongside these men, sometimes with aprons draped over their bare shoulders to protect their unclothed bodies from those large chunks they carried out to the surface. There is a wonderfully executed statue on the edge of the town of a young, nearly naked boy with a large chunk of sulfur on his shoulders. It is part of a larger monument honoring those miners. Racalmuto has a *circolo* for these retired miners, their numbers rapidly dwindling year after year. It has pictures of these naked workers down deep in the mines, working sunrise to sunset, sleeping in the mines on carved-out platforms, Monday through Saturday.

Padre Pino nodded when I told him what I knew about that brutal work. "There was a certain amount of pride," said the priest, who is old enough to have known many of these men, these elderly and physically stooped-over survivors. "They were proud they could do such difficult, dangerous work every day. Many survived, despite being the lowest class."

Padre Pino closed our discussion, waxing poetic about the uncertainty of Riesi's future. He believes the future is in archaeology—not the digging up of stuff, but "digging" to find the original value in the culture. "This is why older traditions are important; we have to keep them alive, not only for ourselves who stayed but for those who left and return occasionally with their families to share them with us: Easter and its processions and the festival of Mary of the Chains in September." In my experience, in places like Riesi and Racalmuto and Mistretta, where religious processions and festivals are local and not necessarily designed to draw tourists, their real meaning is never lost but constantly renewed, from generation to generation.

Some time after my Riesi visit, I felt the need to go to Racalmuto, a village I have returned to many times over the years. It was there I met a couple of the retired sulfur and salt miners who had worked on the outskirts in now-closed mines. I had met the daughter of writer Leonardo Sciascia, her son, and husband for an afternoon at the Sciascia family home in the *contrada* of Noce outside of the village. It was always pleasant to go to my favorite restaurant and be remembered, visit after visit, or to have the woman behind the bar at the head of the village's main street look up as I pushed my way in through the hanging beads of her doorway and exclaim with a smile, "Oh, you have returned!" And I would once again greet my friends, Giuseppe Andini and Paola

Prandi, owners of Racalmuto's B and B Tra i Frutti (Among the Fruit). During this trip, they knew me so well that they let me stay, as their only customer, in my usual room in the large main house when both were away on a long trip.

Before he and Paola left, however, Giuseppe took me to meet a friend of his. The visit was a surprise. Over the years, while driving to and from the village center and the B and B just a few miles away, I had passed a tiny church at the top of a hill. A sign along the road said the area was the *contrada* of Serrone. That small stone church had always captured my attention. It obviously wasn't a regular church for the residents since it was always closed and no sign indicated any hours of worship. I figured that this tiny church and its history would remain a mystery.

I mentioned it to Giuseppe. He nodded, saying he knew what I was referring to. Then, one afternoon, he offered to take me there. The surprise was that his friend, Alberto Alessi, owned it with his family and had agreed to show it to me. Next to the church was a large solid gate. It swung open, ever so slowly, and we drove up a hard-dirt path toward a large, three-story *palazzetto* almost completely surrounded by olive trees. This home and olive grove were tucked away into a cleft on a hillside and almost unnoticeable from the road that I had driven a few hundred times.

Alberto was waiting for us. Fifty when we met, he is slender with thin facial features and dark, slightly gray hair. He worked for many years as an environmental engineer specializing in water treatment. Eleven years before our meeting, he left his profession and decided to use his family estate to grow olives.

Alberto waved for us to follow, and we entered this remarkable centuries-old home, modernized but not overly modern in the interior. It can best be described as "tasteful." It was a comfortable mix of the past and present. This family obviously cherished its heritage. As we visited, he explained, with Giuseppe helping out with interpreting, that the name for the *contrada*, Serrone, comes from the Spanish word *"cerro,"* which means hill. When the Spanish ruled Sicily, they gave that name to this area, and it stuck over the centuries, eventually being transposed into Italian.

His ancestor was Salvatore Sferrazza, who, in the late 1800s, bought the land, house, and church that had been there since 1641. Now Alberto and his family are fourth-generation owners. Interestingly for me, Salvatore's grandmother was the sister of the great-grandfather of Leonardo Sciascia. The connections I've discovered with this great Sicilian author (1921–1989) continue to grow. My closest friend at home in Utah, the historian Leonard Chiarelli, is a distant cousin of the writer who still corresponds regularly with Sciascia's daughter Laura. I have spent time with each of Sciascia's daughters and his grandson. And now I have met another of Sciascia's distant relations. It is certainly a small island in the sense of relationships.

I got a brief history lesson during this visit. Alberto's great-grandfather Salvatore had no sons but four daughters. Three did not marry. The one who did married Alberto's grandfather Alessi. Salvatore, in the mid- to late 1800s, was a high official at the Vatican in Rome, where he served as first counselor to four popes. The title is long and impressive: *cameriere segreto di cappa e spade,* or roughly, secretary of hood and sword.

As a side note, Salvatore traveled extensively for the popes to such places as Turkey, Greece, and the Middle East, but the cost of those trips was borne by Salvatore, not the papacy. The original size, in 1641, of this Racalmuto estate was nearly five hundred acres. Today it stands at nearly thirteen acres, plus the house. Salvatore had to sell much of the land to pay for his journeys on behalf of the Holy Fathers.

That little church, not in great shape after nearly three hundred years of life, was rebuilt in 1896. Additional wings had been added onto each side of the original house; one was added when the church was rebuilt near the turn of the twentieth century. Alberto gave a quick tour, detailing his plans for future renovations.

We went outside, into the midst of the olive grove. Sitting on this hill, near that saddle in the mountain that the Spanish called *"cerro,"* is a paradise of trees, some one thousand that are beautifully pruned and maintained. A few trees, Alberto said, were centuries old—I saw them with the gnarly trunks and twisted limbs that I love about olive trees—but most are only twenty years old and have hundreds of years of life ahead of them. Originally, the land was covered with an almond grove and vineyards for grapes. Alberto made the decision to grow only olives—and the oil they produce must be organic, he said.

The ground around the trees is covered with lush, green undergrowth of fava bean plants. "When do you harvest the beans?" I asked. Alberto laughed. "Never," he said. "We plow the plants and the beans back into the soil. That is the fertilizer. No chemicals. It is purely a biological approach." The plowing, which takes place in April, reduces the threat of wildfire. I once stayed at a small *pensione* in Sardinia that was built in the middle of an olive grove dating back almost five hundred years. The owner's biggest worry was the wild grasses that grew among the trees turning brown and fire sparking from a tossed cigarette. These grasses had to be cut down to the dirt every year before the heat of summer.

Alberto's olive trees were not irrigated. "The rule is, no watering. Only the rainfall," Alberto said. To irrigate would produce more olives at harvesttime, but the oil, he said, would be lower quality.

He still has a few acres where he can plant more trees once the rocks and boulders are removed. Plus, he hopes to recruit other olive growers in the Racalmuto area to his organic approach. That would mean organizing a cooperative to grow, harvest, and press the fruit.

"The elevation here is five hundred meters (1,640 feet) above sea level. Olives grow best at 350 to 700 meters (1,148–2,296 feet) above the sea," he explained. Production in this relatively small area and the demand that olives be grown organically and without chemicals means production would be limited.

Now it was time to see what had long eluded me: the inside of that tiny church. We walked along the pathway from the house to the gate. Alberto pressed a remote control button and the gate swung open. The late 1800s rebuilding was a good one. It was not crumbling a bit; the gray stones were solid.

Alberto said the church is used for family weddings, and once a year he and his wife host a party where all Racalmultese can come for food and to see the open church. No one is excluded. I thought that would be a great time to be here.

The interior, as expected, was tastefully furnished. The pews were original, and the only pictures on the wall represented the

Stations of the Cross. The altar area was backlit with a gentle blue light. On the wall behind the altar was a painting of the Madonna with child, its origins unknown. The altar itself was simple, unadorned. In a small room behind the altar area stood a confessional, likely dating back a few centuries. We went up a slender stairway to the floor above that back room. The view out of the window was impressive: a sea of olive trees, young and just beginning, at twenty years old, to produce a full crop. I had seen, while back at the house, a stack of perhaps twenty boxes containing bottles of the previous fall's pressings. They were going to be shipped, Alberto said, to a distributor on the East Coast of the United States. "Where will they end up?" I asked, hoping to know where I could find a bottle or two for my own use. "I don't know," he shrugged. "It is up to the distributor."

TWELVE

On Tourism's Cusp

What contempt the people who think up souvenirs have for other people.

—Diane Johnson

IT QUICKLY became apparent, during my first hour in Sambuca di Sicilia—a village of some six thousand along the southwest edge of the province of Agrigento—that it was more attuned to tourism than most of the villages I had been visiting. Large tourist buses, like clockwork and just a few minutes apart, arrived one after the other as I sat, midway up the main street, nursing my first double espresso of the day. I had been spared such a sight during all my weeks on the island, but here the large crowds of tourists, speaking French, German, and Spanish, climbed off those buses and slowly made their way uphill toward the top of the village and its beautifully restored Arab Quarter. Tour guides holding the traditional umbrellas high above their heads led each group.

I later learned that this dramatic influx of tourist crowds was likely drawn here because, just a few weeks before my 2016 arrival, Sambuca di Sicilia had won the honor as Italy's Borgo dei Borghi, or Village of Villages, awarded by one of the national television channels, Rai Tre. This means it is considered, subjectively of course and for at least a year, the most beautiful of Italy's thousands of villages.

Charming and friendly it certainly is. I had no idea that it had won such an honor before I visited; that knowledge came a few days later. Frankly, I doubt if knowing a place had won such an honor would induce me to visit. I discovered, also later, that Gangi, a village I hadn't stopped at, had won the honor in 2015. Even much later I discovered that the very first village I spent time in, Castiglione di Sicilia, was Sicily's entry in the 2017 competition. Alas, Castiglione did not win the Italy-wide online vote. It placed fifth. The honor went to Venzone, a village of barely two thousand people in the northeast Italian province of Udine, within the Friuli-Venezia Giulia region, deep in the mountains above the head of the Adriatic Sea.

This sudden arrival of mass tourism, beyond catching me by surprise, caused quite a stir in Sambuca di Sicilia on that May 1 Sunday morning of my first day there. The street had been quiet, almost empty, when I parked along Corso Umberto I next to a municipal garden known as Villa Comunale and walked up a few dozen feet to a bar. As I sat there, enjoying the day's growing warmth despite occasional scatterings of rain, a flurry of activity began to build: doors on storefronts were opened to the sunshine, an employee at a small museum across the Corso set out one of those sandwich-style signs announcing its newest exhibit, and a local police car slid into a parking spot, disgorging five officers, who immediately started to pull wooden barriers out from the street's sides, closing the roadway to traffic. Then, they milled around the upper edge of Villa Comunale, where a snack truck had just parked and was open for business.

This was all happening when the first tour bus arrived, then the second, and then the third, perhaps five minutes apart. Within an hour, the tourists had wandered up the street and back again, hundreds of them, all the way to the Arab Quarter on the town's northeast summit and to Terrazzo Belvedere, which overlooked the valley below and its long sections of vineyards. Some ducked into shops along the way. A couple came into the bar and ordered drinks, quaffing them quickly before heading down toward the buses at the end of the Corso. The hour over, the tourists were gone.

Minutes later, the only activity along the street was the shop owners locking their doors and the lady folding up the sandwich-style sign, hauling it inside, and then locking her door. In a flash, these entrepreneurs were all gone, and the street—it was a Sunday morning, after all—was abandoned. Just my bar was open. I could almost visualize dried-up tumbleweeds, like we have in western U.S. deserts, blowing down the wide deserted boulevard.

I had not yet shown up at the *pensione* where I would stay for the next five days, but I had a name and phone number. I called Vito Savelli to ask directions. He spoke no English and immediately handed the phone over to his brother-in-law, Romeo Danielis, a vacationing economics professor at the University of Trieste in northeastern Italy. The route was a bit complicated, so they agreed to meet me near the outskirts of town at a roundabout I remembered passing en route to the village's historic center. Within minutes, the pair was there, leading me up a small, local street, then through a postwar housing complex and up a country road well into the hills high above Sambuca di Sicilia.

We stopped at a gated driveway, and Vito pointed to my

parking spot. He and Romeo grabbed my luggage, hauled it into a large country house, up some stairs, and into my room, which had a view of the swimming pool, still not ready for warm weather, and the Belice River Valley far below, full of vineyards and olive groves. The village was off to the east, stunningly spread across the top of a plateau much lower than this country house. It was a perfect setting. I had a desk that afforded me the view while I worked, access to the internet, a comfortable bed, and a good-sized shower. Nothing more was needed.

Vito handed me a key but said it was for the gate if I returned late at night when it was closed. A key for the house? "You don't need it," he said in Italian. "It is always open. Someone is always here." I met his wife, Elisabetta Giacone, and Romeo's wife, Patrizia Giacone. They asked me what my plans were for dinner. I said I would return to the village. Could they recommend a restaurant that serves local specialties? Nonsense, Elisabetta said. "You will eat with us." That was not part of the reservation, but it wasn't important to them. I became their houseguest for five days and had several meals with the two couples and sometimes a few of their friends, both for breakfast and dinner. Vito and Elisabetta, I suspect, were taking advantage of Romeo's facility with English and knew we could have evenings filled with good conversation. We did. It was an engaging, conversation-filled stay, one of many during my three-month trip.

The rain kicked up again. I made quick visits, in between rain showers, to the village to wander about or wait out the cloudbursts while sitting on a stone bench under an awning and enjoying a short Tuscan cigar. I was especially interested in the Arab Quarter, which has been restored to perfection. It dates back to the late A.D. 820s when the Muslims began to take the island away from the Byzantines. There is a record in the archives in Palermo that shows the town was registered as "Lasabuca." But at some point it became Sambuca. Until 1928, was called Sambuca Zabut. Either way, the second half of the name reflects its Arab origins. Mussolini, as he did with villages all over Italy, wanted all names to be Italian; Sambuca di Sicilia is the result here. In fact, the dictator took it a step further and demanded that the names of Italians must be Italian. I personally know one elderly man from Tuscany who was named "Walter" at birth; his family, in the time of Mussolini, had to rename him Qualtiero, the Italian equivalent. Meanwhile, the origin of the name "Sambuca" is shrouded in myth: Is it named for the elderberry plant that is the basis for the liquor? Is it named for the Greek stringed musical instrument? Or does it come from an Arabic name, as suggested by Sicilian writer Leonardo Sciascia, who said it derives from *al-Sabuqah,* for "remote place"?

Despite the rain, a couple of restaurants and the two bars I visited in the part of the village along Corso Umberto I had outdoor seating under well-placed large umbrellas. I frequented a ceramic shop that had examples of the magnificent plates and bowls created in one of Sicily's ceramic capitals, Caltagirone.

One bar, where I became a "regular" and thereby was warmly welcomed every time I came in, proudly displayed a pastry creation for which the village is famous: *la minna di Virgine,* created in the early eighteenth century by the Sambucese nun Sister Virginia Menna. In Italian, it can be called *il seno di Virgine* (both expressions referring to the "breast of the Virgin"). It is cream filled and, obviously, shaped like a female breast. On top is a layer of *crema di zucchero* (sugar) flecked with bits of dark chocolate. The story goes that the nun, influenced by hills scattered around the valley overseen by the village, created the pastry in honor of the marriage of a local marchese.

Some in Sambuca believe the word *"minna"* is a play on the nun's last name, Menna. But it is a word that also describes a traditional pastry from Catania, *la minna di Sant'Aita*. It is part of the February feast of Saint Agatha, Catania's patron saint. Months after my visit to Sambuca, my Sicilian American friend Allison Scola set me straight, pointing out that both pastries are not the same, in appearance or in origin. I learned that the Cantanesi pastry, appropriately, represents Saint Agatha's breasts, while the Sambuca version represents hills. The ones in Catania appear in the same shape as Sambuca's, but they are covered on the exterior by a white or pink icing with a red cherry on top. Usually two are presented together on a plate since some paintings and other representations of the saint show her holding a plate with two.

The saint's story does not speak well of the Roman overseers of Sicily. Agatha, the daughter of a wealthy family in Catania, reportedly rebuffed a Roman prefect's advances. He then condemned her to a brothel because of her unfailing Christian faith. Ultimately, in A.D. 251, she was tortured and her breasts were cut off. At one point, and despite the intervention of Saint Peter, who healed her wounds, she later was rolled over hot coals and was to be burned at the stake. But a timely earthquake stopped that spectacle. Despite these miracles, Agatha died a few days later.

I had only one *minna di Virgine* during my time in Sambuca.

And I've never been in Catania during Saint Agatha's festival. But I enjoyed the storytelling barman who sold Sambuca's version to me with my espresso, and his delight in telling me about its origins inspired by the shape of the surrounding hills. Over the days as I wandered through the village, I saw that every bar and every restaurant proudly displayed the pastry, made fresh early every morning but Sunday. Maybe the one I had was a day old.

For at least two consecutive days out of the five I spent in Sambuca di Sicilia, the rain toyed with me, refusing to stop entirely and always threatening to build up to a new attack. It was delightful during the night, offering a soothing sound through the open screened window next to my bed. But, occasionally during the day, the rain would slow down, allowing me to take a quick walk around Vito and Elisabetta's grounds. They had a huge garden that the four family members were in the process of planting, setting long rows of tomato and bean plants.

The grounds also had massive foliage that thrived in this southern Mediterranean climate and various trees bearing fruit, as well as a two-hundred-year-old pine tree with a massive branch that hung over the tiled roof of the house, like the sword hanging over the head of Damocles. If it were my house, that massive branch, several feet thick, would make me nervous, but there is no way I would remove it. Vito and Elisabetta certainly were not worried about it. The tree was healthy and stunningly beautiful in its advanced age; I suspect it still had a few hundred years to go.

Near the edge of their pool stood a large tree with heavy fruit covered by a warty yellow skin. At first I thought they were overgrown lemons that should have been picked weeks ago, but Romeo set me straight. It was a *cedro* tree, a citrus fruit similar to a lemon but decidedly different in taste. We have the Greeks and Romans to thank for introducing these citrus varieties to the island, but it was the Muslims who planted the trees on a large scale.

The fruit inside was a bit bitter, Romeo said, but what people used was the thick wall of white pith that surrounded the pale yellow fruity interior. That pith, three or four times wider than the slight band around the fruit of the lemon, can be sliced up and eaten, perhaps with a dash of salt and a drizzle of olive oil.

As he talked about how Sicilian cooks use it, I could see how an individual *cedro* could be used in a risotto dish, utilizing the entire fruit. The zest would be trimmed off in slices and finely chopped, the pith cut into slivers a few inches long, and the juice squeezed. It all would be set aside and saved to add to the risotto, along with finely diced fennel and celery stalks. A few leaves of sage would be added at the end. One recipe I saw while searching the internet in my room during a particularly heavy rainstorm called for a bit of vermouth to offset the mild bitterness of the zest. It was something I would have to try one day, provided I could get a *cedro*. I am still looking for one.

The effect of the near-constant rain in the view out of my window was pleasant and helped pass the time as I sat at the desk trying to work. Often, it poured down, hitting the light beige tiles surrounding the pool in great splotches and bouncing back up knee-high. Across the valley, to the east, a dark, rumbling cloud hung over the village, which I could tell was being bombarded with great sheets of water. Then, quite suddenly, the rain died away. Shafts of sunlight hit those pool tiles and, within minutes, a gentle steam started to rise as they warmed up. It was midspring in the heart of the Mediterranean, after all, and the temperatures were warm and climbing.

I took advantage of this break and headed outside and through the open iron gate and started walking along a country road surrounded by trees and, beyond, wet fields of green. A short distance away, I noticed fences, haphazard and leaning this way and that, surrounding an abandoned farm, much like the one that had intrigued me weeks earlier outside of Palazzolo Acreide. The patch of land around the crumbling buildings was fallow and full of weeds and wildflowers. The buildings were nearly squashed flat into the earth, looking like a remnant from the war. The structures were beyond rehabilitation. It was impossible to determine their age, or the age of that rusted, blasted-apart fence. Fifty years? Five hundred years? Perhaps the descendants of the early owners were somewhere in America with no idea what their family once owned or even still owned.

I walked back to the house, left my muddy shoes at the door, and was heading upstairs when Elisabetta invited me to lunch. It was a tubular pasta that I hadn't seen before. The chunky sauce was full of small black olives with the seeds still inside, chopped cherry tomatoes, and nuggets of well-cooked eggplant. It was a stunning dish, in looks and in taste. Surrounded by good friends and wonderful conversation, I quickly devoured it and the small Sicilian cookies set out for dessert with espresso.

The large window in this comfortable living and dining space showed dark clouds once again forming on the horizon. It started to rain, the sound of drops slamming into the roof tiles, grabbing our attention. Their gardening would have to wait. I headed upstairs and got in an hour's worth of work before the sun once again broke free. The sky turned blue, and I decided I would drive down from Vito and Elisabetta's hilltop home and more thoroughly visit the town. There were things I needed to see, and I wanted to say hello to the folks at the bar.

There was a parking spot in front of that establishment. I went in, ordered my coffee and a regular non-*minna* pastry, sat outside, and enjoyed the afternoon. Patches of gray clouds skittered across fleeting glimpses of blue sky; I worried that rain would erupt at any moment, but it seemed to be holding off. The Arab Quarter was a few hundred yards up Corso Umberto I. It made for a sturdy walk up that hill, which topped out well beyond the quarter's entrance. The belvedere was a few dozen feet beyond with its wonderful view of the Belice River Valley's compact vineyards.

One enters the Arab Quarter through Piazza Navarro. The piazza, I discovered while reading a historical marker, was named for a prominent physician and writer, Vincenzo Navarro (1800–1867), who led a campaign to get farmers in a valley near his birthplace of Ribera, known as Valle di Verdura, to abandon growing rice—a crop the Arabs had introduced in Sicily a thousand years earlier. With all that rice, the Arabs created, among other wonders, a dish that is still popular all over Italy and, most particularly, Sicily: *arancini,* or lightly battered rice balls holding cheese and various combinations of vegetables. But those ancient paddies and the vast amount of water they required drew the mosquitoes responsible for countless deaths over the centuries from malaria.

Despite his efforts, the disease continued to be a problem well into the twentieth century. Mussolini had it nearly eradicated throughout Italy in the 1930s. One of his methods was to import, from Australia, thousands of eucalyptus trees whose roots can absorb lots of water, thereby helping to drain the soil in the marshes around Rome. This success caused them to be planted elsewhere in Italy, including Sicily, where today they dominate some low-lying areas. Ribera is just about an hour's drive on today's roads from Sambuca. Navarro ended up getting married in this village and living out his life here.

The good doctor's square was small and attractive. It was placed in front of a well-wrought stone arch that serves as a dividing line between medieval and Saracen. The streets and pathways quickly shrink down into a twisting mixture of beautiful stones, tying together rows of ancient houses built on Muslim foundations. The nearby Terrazzo Belvedere is now a wide-open, attractive space that likely was where the Arabs built the castle. Nothing on the surface remains of what was probably a large stone structure with an imposing view of the valley below.

The pathways in the quarter are hardly big enough for three or even two people to walk abreast. They are not called *via* for street, but rather *vicolo* for alley or lane, and there is only a slight change in their names: Vicolo Saraceni I, Vicolo Saraceni II, Vicolo Saraceni III, and so on. The buildings, mostly just two stories tall, are beautifully restored. Their façades are either well-finished natural stone, or are covered with fresh paint ranging from white to light Mediterranean yellows and blues.

There are smaller arches tying together one building to another, spanning the walkways, sometimes in balanced juxtaposition to each other. Numerous small, wonderfully paved courtyards spread out in front of each section of houses, and the three steps up into each home are faced with marble set on rough-stone blocks. Potted plants in large wooden planters and well-shaped wooden benches are plentiful, adding to the visual appeal of this place.

This part of the village seems to be the most recently restored, perhaps as an attractive chip in Sambuca's quest to win the Borgo dei Borghi competition in 2016. Other sections are medieval in look and well cared for, but not with the intimate feel of this quarter first established by the island's Arab conquerors in the late ninth century A.D.

I was walking downhill when the rain, in a fury, started up again. Lining the Corso were a couple of tiny shops for craftsmen. I glanced into one where an older man sat repairing shoes. The shop was cold and had poor lighting, which made it stand out in contrast to the finer shops farther down the street that sold ceramics, tourist souvenirs, and clothing. This elderly man, concentrating on his work, didn't look up as I glanced inside. He was repairing a shoe, sitting at an old sewing machine next to a table piled high with a clutter of leather material. The scene reminded me of my visit weeks earlier in Vizzini with shoe repairman Francesco Giallo. Their craft is obviously not a major moneymaking profession.

The sky, once so blue, suddenly darkened and the drops poured down in a repeat of the heaviness I had earlier witnessed at the house. I jumped to the side of the Corso and found refuge under a scaffold covering the wall of a building in the midst of restoration. There were three open doors in this long façade;

inside men were plastering walls, the smell of the white mud pleasant as I glanced into the doorways. At one, a worker was standing, leaning against the jamb, smoking a cigarette. He saw me in my drenched condition, clutching my camera and notebook beneath my jacket.

"*Entra. Entra,*" he said, motioning with his hand. I stepped into the small room, water dropping off me and onto the dusty marble floor. He finished his cigarette; I offered him a short Tuscanello cigar. He smiled broadly and took it gratefully. We both stood there, watching the rain roar down the steep Corso in a small river, and made conversation. I learned that I was standing in a sixteenth- or seventeenth-century building that would become offices of some sort. He remembered as a small child when it was last restored and now, he laughs, he is grown up and doing the work.

The three men working on inside walls, plasterers' hawks in one hand heaped with mounds of wet plaster, were using rough trowels to slap the mud onto the surface, followed by another worker who smoothed out and blended in the mixture. I figured that the man in the doorway must be the crew *capo*, or boss, since he could stand there for fifteen minutes without working while we smoked the short cigars.

I thanked him for the brief respite and trudged down the street in what had devolved into a light rain. My exploring was done for the day. By then it was late afternoon and, despite it being the end of *riposo*, no one was about. The shops were open, but no customers. I expected business would pick up early in the evening, particularly if the rain stopped. Businesses close late in Sicily, and restaurants usually don't open until nine o'clock. The farther south one travels in the Mediterranean world, the later people seem to eat. Restaurants can be bustling well after midnight. If I didn't eat at the house, I'd come back for a full meal in the village. My hosts had been so generous that I had yet to do that.

On my last full day in Sambuca the sun was out with no rain expected. I decided to take a thirty-minute, twelve-mile morning drive to a small village that boasts as its favorite son a famous Sicilian American. It is Bisacquino, birthplace of the American film director Frank Capra (1897–1991).

Like Sambuca, Arabs established Bisacquino in the mid-ninth century, building up a small village around a farmhouse they named Busackuin. I am told that name means "rich in waters." Surrounded by fine-looking fields full of a variety of crops, fruit orchards, and vineyards, it sits along the flank of a domelike hill. I must admit that I was drawn there simply because I knew it had been Capra's birthplace. It was well worth the visit, but again, the frustration of heavy traffic in a small, compact village was a distraction. After a lot of back-and-forth driving, I found a temporary, fifteen-minute spot along Via Roma, in the heart of the beautifully paved main square, Piazza Triona.

I expected to see a statue of the famed America director, but there wasn't one—just the Mother Church of San Giovanni Battista and a handful of small shops, including a pastry shop. I didn't want to get too far away from my car because of the time limit, but after a circuit of the square I spotted a parking policewoman with the ubiquitous ticket book in her hands. Remembering my positive experience of talking to a parking cop in

Calascibetta, I walked up, introduced myself, and pointed to my car. I told her I was only here for a few hours and would it be possible to leave the car there because all the other long-term spots were taken. She smiled and said something to the effect of: "OK, but only for two hours. Then I will go to lunch and someone new will replace me and they might not be so nice." Delightful. I wandered around this village of five thousand people without the car's plight hanging over me.

I had done my basic Capra research. I had no idea whether his family home had been identified with a marker, but I suspected it was in the countryside outside of the village's historic center. Capra's father had been a fruit grower, and the family likely was not well-off. Capra, who had been born Francesco Rosario Capra and was called by the traditional nickname Ceccio, left for America at age five with his family. They traveled in the ship's below-deck steerage, the cheapest ticket available. His biographer quotes Capra describing the smelly, crowded conditions in steerage, calling the thirteen-day journey one of his worst experiences ever.

The family landed in New York Harbor and eventually made their way to Los Angeles, where his father was a fruit picker and Ceccio sold newspapers. After high school, his father wanted Capra to work with him, but he opted for college, and the rest is film history.

I do not know how many people emigrated from this village to America and what the population was before the great diaspora of the late nineteenth and early twentieth century, but in my wanderings I could see that Bisacquino also had abandoned buildings just begging for someone to take them over and renovate.

I made it back to Piazza Triona and saw a lot of late-morning

activity. There were peddlers' carts full of toys, candy, and a variety
of nuts. One fellow was making fresh nut bars on a hot plate fu-
eled by a propane burner. I bought a small piece with the nuts held
together by a concoction of peanut butter and honey. Delicious. I
also purchased a jar of local Sicilian honey that I would wrap
carefully and ship home with other souvenirs and documents.

I relaxed on a bench near the edge of the Mother Church and
watched the frenetic activity all around me. Eventually, a pastry
shop on the piazza's edge caught my eye. This little café sold
everything a person would need for a quick meal: *caffè*, of course,
beer, pastries, *spremuta* (fresh-squeezed orange juice), and panini
(sandwiches put into a heated press and served warm).

The café had three smiling, very busy workers who knew
nearly everyone who came in over the hour I spent there. And
they knew what each one would order, handing them a beer or
a pastry with an espresso. I was studying the contents of the pastry case, and one of them, a lovely young woman with long black
hair and wonderfully dark eyes, came over and happily told me
the name of everything and how it was all made in the shop. I
decided on two things: an *arancino* filled with cheese and chunks
of ham, and a small pastry with pistachio cream inside and speck-
les of chopped nuts on top.

A few years ago, in Palermo and in the café where Lampedusa
sat in the late 1950s writing *The Leopard*, I had an *arancino* with
cheese and small squares of ham, and it was one of the most wonderful things I had ever eaten. In the years after, I always searched
for an equal to that experience and usually was disappointed.
But here, in Bisacquino, birthplace of one of America's greatest
film directors, I found it.

THIRTEEN

Sicily Meets Its Last Conqueror

We set to anchoring behind several large volcanic pillars just a stone's-throw away from where the Tyrrhenian Sea kissed the east of the island. A handful of wishes scattered the skies as we approached the shores of Aci Trezza.

—RJ Arkhipov

T HINGS WERE winding down. Only four villages remained: Calatafimi-Segesta in the island's southwest; a revisit to one of my favorite east-coast villages, Aci Trezza; Agira, the birthplace of the Greek Sicilian writer Diodorus Siculus, who lived during the Roman period; and Castel di Tusa, on the northwest Tyrrhenian coast, where the journey would end. I wanted three more months to see even more new places and make more friends, but only a few weeks were left. According to Italian law, I can only stay up to three months at a time on a tourist visa.

Some visits during this trip were just the right length; others were not long enough. I had wanted to spend more days in Mistretta just sitting in the sun and talking to the *pensionati* about their work and lives. Ah, and what about Calascibetta at the island's center, sitting on a plateau with the much higher town of Enna hanging over it? Of course, there was Sambuca di Sicilia, where I must return when rain does not interfere. And some day

trips to places that sincerely grabbed my imagination, and where
I did not spend the night, should have been expanded. One in particular was Mezzojuso, where, if I had only known, I could have
easily have split my Easter Week time with nearby Piana degli
Albanesi. I learned that I preferred the two towns' noncommer-
cial approach to Good Friday processions where there were few
tourists, if any, among the locals.

Except for a few nights in Palermo at the beginning and end,
I would only revisit two places, both favorites, where I had spent
considerable time in the past. I could never say no to Aci Trezza,
a still-functioning fishing village a few minutes north of Catania
that has lost none of its charm and where the warmth of its people
has never cooled. And, of course, Racalmuto, where, despite perhaps a half-dozen visits over the years, I always see and learn
about something new, like the organic olive grove hidden behind
that little stone church. But now, with the frustrating end in
sight, I still had places to go and friends to make.

One of those friends was Gianluca Giangrasso, a thirty-
something I met during my time in Calatafimi-Segesta. My
host, Salvatore Cudia, suggested that Gianluca could show me
around. This part of Sicily was as far west as I traveled during this
long, fruitful trip. Nearby, as reflected in the town's modern
name, is the ruin of the ancient Greek city of Segesta with its
lone, unfinished temple and rough theater hewn out of a large,
sloping hillside. It was a site I had visited at least three times over
the years and didn't need to see again. So Gianluca made up for it
in his proposed itinerary with a stop at the memorial marking
the battlefield where Giuseppe Garibaldi and his Expedition of
the Thousand, on May 15, 1860, had their first battle and their

first victory over the Bourbons. It was a struggle that led to Sicily eventually being united with Italy.

The memorial sat atop a hill, Pianto Romano, and looked across the battlefield, now a broad slope of tall grasses billowing in the breeze. This was also a burial site for the fallen during the struggle that took place just four days after Garibaldi and his northern Italian volunteers landed at Marsala. And just the day before, in the tiny village of Salemi, Garibaldi declared himself dictator over Sicily in the name of King Vittorio Emanuele II of Sardinia.

The battle was inconclusive; each side saw close to the same number of dead and wounded, but the Naples-based Bourbons had fielded three thousand combatants compared to Garibaldi's twelve hundred Redshirts. Despite it not being a clear victory for Garibaldi's forces, it was demoralizing for the Neapolitans, who had been attempting to hold on to the control of the island. By the end of May, Garibaldi defeated them in the battle of Palermo, ending warfare on the island and shifting the theater to southern Italy and Naples.

Gianluca then led me to Salemi, eleven miles south. This village began in days shrouded in the haze of time and likely was built by Greeks, who called it Alicia, over the top of an earlier indigenous settlement. Salemi was close to and allied with the mixture of Greeks and indigenous people at Segesta. Alicia/Salemi was the scene of many battles between Segesta and the southwest Sicily Greek town of Selinus, now called Selinunte, which boasts of being Europe's largest archaeological site. Greek cities were independent of one another and, at least for a few early generations, were closely allied with the city-states in Greece from which they migrated. National unity was rare; city-states often fought with one another, leading to battles between far-off colonies in Magna Graecia, as southern Italy and Sicily was later called by the Romans.

Salemi today still shows significant damage from a 1968 earthquake that devastated much of southwestern and central Sicily. In fact, several years ago, a mayor proposed selling many of the damaged, uninhabitable buildings to outsiders for one euro each, as long as they promised to restore their purchases within two years. There were few takers at the time, although, as we have seen in Castiglione di Sicilia, Gallodoro, and several other villages with abandoned, crumbling structures, there is a new movement in that direction.

After a stop for coffee and conversation, we pressed on to Gibellina Vecchia (Old), also known as Gibellina Antica (Ancient), a ruined town just seventeen miles to the east that has been turned into a massive art project. The original Gibellina was destroyed in that monstrous 1968 earthquake. Survivors among its four thousand residents were relocated about twelve miles to the west, where the modern town, now called Nuova Gibellina, was built. In the 1980s, something remarkable happened at the ancient site: The Italian painter and sculptor Alberto Burri (1915–1995) covered over the rubble of the ruined village with chest-high cement, keeping intact the streets, alleyways, and footpaths between the blocks. I first saw it in 2009 from a hillside a few miles away. This sea of cement, gleaming under the hot July sun, glides up the slope of the hill.

When Gianluca and I visited it in 2016, the cement work had been expanded at the bottom, finally encompassing the entire vil-

lage. We drove down to it and walked along some of those ancient streets and pathways, some marked with signs showing their
original names. I could imagine how nostalgic that could make
former residents, now quite elderly, or their descendants, who,
knowing the street names where they or their grandparents once
lived, could visit, within a few feet, where those houses once
stood. Visiting Gibellina Antica, in its uniqueness as a major ar-
tistic undertaking, is a somber, quiet experience. Gianluca and I
spoke in hushed voices during our brief time there, often walking along the pathways in silence. We had the place to ourselves
with only the breeze-carried sound of birds to keep us company.

Gianluca is a wise young man, a deep thinker who knows his
island's culture well. As we visited the various sites over a four-
hour tour, he spoke at length and profoundly about Sicily. He
quickly figured out that while I enjoyed seeing "places" and understanding history, I wanted to dig a bit deeper into the Sicilian
soul. He didn't disappoint.

"When the scirocco is blowing, people become grumpy, short-
tempered," he said. "When it is too cold, people do not want to
work. Also when it is too hot." This he said with a chuckle. "Of
course, they do work, but *riposo pomeridiano* is very important."

This was his understanding of the culture of his people who
are Mediterranean islanders and who do not consider themselves
Italian in the familiar sense. The scirocco, a hot, dust-laden wind
from the Libyan deserts that blows across Sicily, Malta, and Italy,
has worked over the centuries to silently shape the mind-set of
these islanders. I once wrote about what the writer Leonardo

Sciascia described as "the scirocco room" that can be found in many Sicilian houses. Other than a narrow door, the room had no openings to the outside. Here, a family "would take refuge against the wind." Sciascia adds this melancholy note: "The scirocco, too, is a dimension of Sicily."

I can picture family members huddling together in these quiet, windowless places waiting for this dry, hot wind to subside. It pulls them together, strengthens their trust of and loyalty to one another. In Sicily, families come first, then the village, then the province, and then the region of the island itself. They almost never feel loyalty to the state based in Rome, which almost always, in Sicilians' view, does nothing for them. Now, in some respects, the European Union does more for them than Rome—but not always.

Gianluca continued with his cultural lesson. "The identity of each town is tied to the town's patrons." As an example, he said, "The dates of the [religious] festivals are the same, but how each town honors them is unique to that place." And, he added, dialects of the Sicilian language also tie people together. "We talk the same dialect in our small area: Calatafimi, Vita, Salemi, Alcamo. This, too, ties us together."

There was a time, I suspect, when someone from a village deep in the interior would venture to a village or a town perhaps a few dozen miles away and feel as if they were in a foreign place. When Italy was unified in 1870, Tuscan Italian, the official language of the new nation, heavily influenced what was spoken on the island. And Mussolini, in the early twentieth century, mandated that teaching and speaking Italian was obligatory for all schools. Despite these century-old pressures, village dialects remain.

I have a Sicily-born friend who told me that when he went to his ancestral village in the early 1960s, people from one side of that place spoke a dialect different from that of people from the other side. This, today, is gone. But dialectic phrases, mingled with formal Italian words, still exist, sort of a "proto-Sicilian," meaning the language is evolving. An Italian speaker from the north of Italy can easily communicate with people in the far south in this modern age of universal education, but if those folks shift into their local dialect, that visitor would be lost.

For his part, Gianluca was pleased when I told him what my friend George had told me in Caccamo about how Sicilians, once closed to outsiders, are beginning to open up. This was something I had seen happen most dramatically from my first visit in 1986 to now.

"They are opening to foreigners," Gianluca confirmed. "And it is not only to encourage tourism. They understand their culture is not just Mafia. Tourists can change characteristics of our [once-closed] culture. If one hundred people a day come to see our landscapes that we have always taken for granted, this will slowly begin to change us by opening us up. A worker on the land can only see the economic side of that landscape; a tourist can see the beauty, and this changes us. Tourism is our future."

Shaking loose from the Mafia stereotype has been difficult for these islanders, who know it is still there, under the surface. And they know who its members are. The elderly men sitting on benches in countless villages in the sunshine can pick them out as they walk across the town square. Only once did someone point out a Mafia *capo* to me. He had been sitting across from me in a tiny barbershop in a rough-and-tumble Palermo neighborhood—a portly middle-aged man with a week's stubble, wearing a tight-fitting, stained polo shirt, looking nothing like anyone in *The Godfather*. Everyone who entered the shop greeted him with kisses on both lightly whiskered cheeks. He paid no attention to me, a stranger who was simply waiting his turn for a haircut.

I told Gianluca this story and he told me the Greek myth of the Medusa as a way to characterize how good can transform into evil and back to good again. "From the blood of Medusa is born Pegasus, the winged horse," he began. "From something so horrible can be born something beautiful." Medusa was once beautiful, but vain, and because of a personal slight, Athena turned her into horrible creature with hair of writhing snakes, and if someone looked at her they would turn into stone. One version of the myth says that when Perseus beheaded her, the blood from her severed neck created the beautiful Pegasus.

Gianluca told me these things while we sat at an outside table at Salvatore Cudia's house far out in the countryside in the *contrada* Barchetta, perhaps five miles from Calatafimi-Segesta's historical center. Salvatore, who served us wonderful espresso, calls his place Casale Cudia. It sits on a hillside with a wonderful view far out into the interior showing wide-open agricultural land and few houses.

We had finished our tour by driving around that village center and now my guide and new friend described how the village of more than six thousand Calatafimese is actually arrayed over three hills: Monte Tre Croci, or Mountain of Three Crosses;

Monte del Castello, where the partially restored castle sits and its slopes make up the historical center; and Monte San Vito. The Saracens first settled on the hill, calling the village Qal 'at Fimī, meaning Eufemio's Fort. There are thirty churches in this small village, including one—the Sanctuary of Santissima Maria of Giubino—that sits on the top of Monte Tre Croci. Priests hold services there only from June to September, when parishioners shift from a church in the village center to this country church about three miles away. When they make the shift, they walk the three miles in a procession carrying their beloved saint, a co-patron of the town. In September, they walk back, holding their saint high on men's shoulders.

On my final day in the idyllic countryside surrounding Salvatore's home, I drove into the village. I needed a tie to wear for a meeting in Palermo with a member of parliament to discuss her work to help establish *albergi diffusi* in villages with abandoned structures. My Castiglione di Sicilia friend Nunzio Valentino had advised me that a tie would be appropriate. I parked in a spot with a fifteen-minute limit and set the paper time clock on the dashboard. I looked around, and just a few feet away, standing in the doorway of a men's clothing store was a well-dressed elderly gentleman who watched me closely.

I approached. He smiled and warned me that the traffic wardens patrol this street several times a day. "Do not overstay your fifteen minutes." I thanked him for the advice and asked if he had ties. Of course, he said. He pulled down a large box from a top shelf, opened it, and showed an array of nice silk ties. I liked one of them. "Fifteen euros," he said. I had a twenty-euro bill. He reached into his pocket. He had only a ten. He gave it to me, making my purchase only ten euro. He shrugged, wrapped the tie in brown paper, and handed it to me.

I wanted to explore a bit. And perhaps I could get some change to pay him the five euro I still owed. He suggested I leave my car key with him so he could adjust the time on the paper clock on my dashboard if he saw the parking policeman coming. Why not? I would be back in an hour, I said, handing him the key fob. I walked around a bit, exploring a part of the village I hadn't seen with Gianluca and discovered a tobacco shop. I took out my ten-euro bill, bought a small box of Tuscan cigars, got a five-euro note as change, and returned to the haberdasher still standing in the doorway, my key in his hand, and my car still safe. I took the key and handed him the five. He smiled and tucked it into a well-worn leather pouch. We were now whole. I often think about that honest white-haired gentleman standing in the doorway, watching people go by as the afternoon slowly dissolved into the lilac of early evening.

I needed to drive to Catania for a brief stop, en route to Aci Trezza, to witness a puppet show. I was on my way to spend a few days in that hardscrabble fishing village on Sicily's Ionian coast just a few miles north of Catania. But some friends of a friend told me that a puppet performance was scheduled for a shopping galleria in the heart of Catania; I had seen only one such show before, in Siracusa, and had been bowled over by the cleverness of the puppet masters: how the crusader swordsmen could engage in a one-on-one duel with foes, dancing back and forth with swords banging and then, suddenly, a quick swipe and the dreaded enemy's head would fly off. I had no idea what the narrator was saying as he told the story, but the theatrics were amazing, and the puppeteer's skills were remarkable.

Now, in Catania, I would have a chance to see another show and perhaps talk with puppeteers about their art. So I timed my nearly four-hour drive from Calatafimi, taking the southern route through Sciacca and Agrigento, then north to Caltanissetta, and on to Catania via the dreaded autostrada.

One of my acquaintances gave me an address. I promptly programmed it into the rental car's navigator as I approached Catania's outskirts. I was apprehensive about this part of the drive; I felt comfortable driving in Palermo but, frankly, Catania's traffic scared me. A few decades earlier when I had rented a car for a long weekend and asked a colleague at the navy base, where I spent two weeks, about driving in Sicily, he had told me, "Catanesi drivers do not observe stop signs or traffic lights, and the traffic is very heavy. Just remember this: Never make eye contact with another driver. If you do, you have given up the right of way."

Over the years and throughout many trips to the island I had followed that advice religiously, and it works well. I would zip through intersections knowing another driver wanted to be in the space I was heading for and barged on without a look in their direction. I always won. Neither scrapes nor near misses. When I forgot and happened to glance at the other driver, I would lose. Invariably. But it is nerve-racking in a crowded, convoluted city like Catania with its few wide boulevards and ancient, narrow streets that probably were first laid out by the Greeks and then tossed about by earthquakes, covered over by lava flows from nearby Etna, and then rebuilt for medieval carts.

So I dropped off the autostrada and into the bowels of the city, following the beautiful, lissome voice of the navigator with her reassuring English accent. She took me along wide, traffic-choked boulevards, turning this way and that. I easily passed through crowded intersections, never giving other drivers even the brief- est of glances. I flew right along; at this rate, I would arrive at the puppet show thirty minutes early.

Then, Miss Directions had me turn off a main, four-lane street onto a small one-way side street. Hmm, I thought. This doesn't look right. I kept moving. She had me turn left at an even smaller street that had cars parked along the right-side edge, cutting the road down even more. I pushed buttons and pulled in my side-view mirrors. The street came to a small T intersection. She wanted me to turn right, saying my destination was just ahead. This couldn't be correct. This was a rough neighborhood, not anywhere near a shopping galleria.

I pulled forward and realized I did not have enough clearance with my moderately sized French car to make the turn. I backed up a bit but came terribly close to the building on my right, threat- ening my car's paint job. I pulled forward a bit and it finally dawned on me that I was stuck. I sat there for a moment thinking the silly thought that the only way out was to call for a helicop- ter to drop a line down and pull my car out. Despite my predica- ment, I chuckled at the fantasy.

A much smaller car approached on that tiny street to the right wanting to drive through the top of the T that I was blocking.

He stopped, looking at me with a quizzical expression. I looked back and, in very Sicilian style, I shrugged my shoulders. At that moment, a miracle happened, and it didn't involve the arrival of a helicopter.

To my left, two young men, jammed together on a tiny scooter, arrived. The driver stopped, looked at me, and motioned for me to back up so he could move around the front of the car. I shook my head and pointed to the wall behind me, just a couple of inches from my rear bumper. He looked where I was pointing and did his version of the shoulder shrug. I rolled down my window and said the only thing I could think of: *"Aiutami, per favore."* (Help me, please.) This young fellow, perhaps eighteen years old, wearing a black T-shirt with the name of some rock band on the front, his hair cut short to the scalp on the sides and long on top, complete with faded blue jeans with the knees stylishly ripped out, parked his scooter out of the way. He walked over and started giving me hand directions so I could back up. It was impossible. My shirt was soaked with perspiration; my nerves were shot. All I could do was curse that lovely-sounding, mysterious English lady trapped in my navigator.

I stopped. Opened the door, climbed out, and motioned for the young man to get in. He smiled, tilted his head in a "why not?" position, got in, shut the door, turned in the driver's seat, looking to the rear and started inching: backward, forward, backward again, forward again. It took him perhaps a minute. He had the car free and had turned it left toward the main boulevard with plenty of room to spare.

He stepped out of the car with a smile and started toward his scooter where his friend was waiting. I intercepted him, embraced him, and kissed him, as Sicilian men do, on both cheeks. He kissed back. I handed him a twenty-euro bill. He glanced down at it in his hand, shook his head, pressed it back into my hand, and said, simply, *"Buona fortuna."* (Good luck to you.)

I called the fellow who had given me the address and told him what had happened and how I was going to have to miss the puppet show, which likely was almost over by this time. I told him the address he gave me. Oh, he said, I misspoke. He had transposed a word or two. No wonder the navigator lady took me to the wrong place. When I told him where I was, he said something like, "Wow. That is a rough part of town. You are lucky." "Please," I said, "there was nothing but good people where I was. I was in a place where the people and in particular a teenager with a wonderful soul restored my faith in humanity." I never saw a puppet show on that trip. What I experienced in that tough Catania neighborhood was much better.

Santo Valastiro and I have been friends for several years now. We met when I went to Aci Trezza to work on my first book about Sicily. I stayed in his newly opened B and B, Epos, just a few dozen feet from the center of this tiny village of fishermen. I have stayed with him many times since. This time, I wanted to take a short break and unwind a bit in Aci Trezza after nearly three months of nonstop travel before I headed up to the north coast to Castel di Tusa, ending my time in Sicily. I have written a lot about Aci Trezza and its relationship to the Cyclopean Greek myth of Odysseus as well as the village's role in Giovanni Verga's masterwork, *I Malavoglia,* and the 1947 Visconti film made from it, *La terra trema.*

Santo greeted me and got great enjoyment out of my tale about being stuck on that tiny street in Catania. I asked him about Salvatore Vicari, the retired fisherman who, as a boy of ten, played the part of Alfio the Boatboy in Visconti's film. Unfortunately, Santo said, he had passed away since my last visit. Santo had introduced a friend and me to him one evening in the small square in front of the Mother Church of San Giovanni Battista. He was then an exuberant man, well into his eighties, an illiterate fisherman and member of a dying breed of men who, from childhood, went out to sea in small boats, sometimes for days at a time, rowing against the wind and enduring storms. Sometimes, as in *I Malavoglia,* some didn't return.

Salvatore loved the fact that people, because of his tiny role of playing the small brother of the main character who fought against the middlemen who got rich off the fishermen, wanted to meet him. My friend took the photograph of him that appears in my first Sicily book.

Now, just a couple of villagers who appeared in that film were still alive, Santo said. One, Agnese Giammona, is the wife of a restaurant owner. She played the significant role of the male protagonist's younger sister (the character Lucia). In an iconic black-and-white image, she is standing near to her real-life older sister, Nelluccia Giammona (the character Mara), at the front of a handful of black-robed women looking out to sea from a windswept point of land waiting for their loved ones to return—a well-remembered subject of posters. Agnese and her sister were ill, Santo told me. Agnese's apartment was just across an alleyway overlooking her husband's restaurant. A few months after my last visit, Santo sent the sad news: The sister, Nelluccia, eighty-six, passed away in August 2017.

I walked down to the square where I had often over the years sat on steel benches among the village's *pensionati*. Ironically, these benches faced away from the sea and the harbor with its tall, jagged boulders of ancient lava rock that the blinded Cyclops Polyphemus, in his rage, had flung at Odysseus's escaping boat. Instead, they faced the church. Perhaps in designing this square, the villagers who had enough of the sea and its perils during the day wanted it behind them and the church in front as they sat and conversed with friends and neighbors during their evening walk-abouts. The benches were full, except for one occupied by two elderly men. I approached and asked if I could sit there. No, they said. They were saving the seat for a friend. Unlike the men on the benches, I stood with my back to the church and looked out across the Ionian Sea that was beginning its evening dance of shifting colors as the sun dropped behind Etna, which stood high, smoldering, above the village. I glanced over toward the men waiting for their friend and saw him slowly, painfully, pushing his walker roughly across the paving stones. His friends jumped up and helped him into his reserved seat. Perhaps fifteen minutes later, my eyes still out toward the darkening sea, I heard the shout, *"Signore, signore!"* One of the two men on that bench pointed to the empty seat beside them. Their friend had gone. I sat down and thanked them.

Soon I was alone and still did not want to leave that little square, which over the years has become almost as familiar to me as my living room at home.

I reflected on what being alone while traveling means to me. It is best, and most efficient, to travel alone when I am working on a project. I do not get distracted and am free to quickly move about, changing plans or directions at the spur of the moment, all without having to explain or compromise. It also means money saved, since B and Bs and hotels here tend to charge per individual. Such savings can mean an extended budget and a longer journey. It's a selfish pursuit, I know.

Early on, such solitude gave me a sense of freedom. Now, sitting alone on this bench in Aci Trezza and, despite feeling comfortable here, this aloneness begins to weigh on me. Perhaps it is a function of growing older.

I would eat much later; the restaurants were beginning to shake off the inactivity of winter and stay open until midnight. My favorite, Ristorante Lachea, would open around eight or nine o'clock. I had plenty of time. I looked across the main street toward the restaurant owned by the husband of the woman who, as a child, was in Visconti's film. To the right, and on the first floor above the street, sitting behind the glass of French doors that opened onto a small balcony, Signora Agnese Giammona sat, looking out at the people below and, perhaps, out to sea. I was in Aci Trezza for a few days, and I saw her there at that window for most of each day and early evening, occasionally reaching to open a glass door to let out her two tiny dogs or to coax them inside. I wished I could speak with her about Visconti and her experiences in that magnificent film made in the black-and-white harshness of Verga's *verismo* literary style in hard-to-watch realism of the life and time of Sicilian fishermen and their families. It could never be. Months later, I learned that she was quite ill and often was no longer seen through her window. I keep hoping to find her there during each visit.

One morning after breakfast, Santo and I settled down for a conversation about Aci Trezza, where he grew up and now lives from spring to fall during the tourist season to run his family B and B. The rest of the year he is in Rome. We had never talked like this before, but now Santo knew me and knew of my love for this place and its people. So he shared some insight over espresso and *cornetti*.

"Fifteen years ago," he began, "there were many fishermen from Aci Trezza. Now there are just a few boats. There is one that is larger that goes off for several weeks at a time to, say, the waters off Greece to go after big fish. There are some small ones, with perhaps two on board, that go out late at night with nets to get the smaller fish remaining in the Ionian Sea—anchovies that go for a few euros a bag."

The morning before, I had stood on the raised steps of a building next to the port and watched a fisherman below surrounded by a pressing crowd of locals and a few restaurant owners vying for those bags of anchovies. "Yes," Santo said, his mother often goes there to buy the tiny fish. "Today she tells me we have enough for lunch, so we don't need to go down and get any."

He said the frustration for any individual fisherman nowadays and what keeps younger people from going to sea are the controls imposed on them by the Italian government, which is under pressure from the European Union. "The EU has arrangements with Japanese fishermen who work from large modern boats that ply the Mediterranean at will.

"I have seen, in Tokyo fish markets, large red tuna that sell for perhaps ten thousand euro each." EU pressure keeps locals from engaging in this kind of fishing. Santo's words, tinged with a bit of bitterness, made me think of how I had once felt when I learned, a few years earlier, how Rome and the EU enter deals with a country like Morocco to sell Italian cars there. In exchange, Morocco sells fruit and produce to Italy and Sicily, bypassing Sicilian growers. I remembered the sadness a local resident of Venice shared with me about how the Belgium-based EU was clamping down on tiny fresh-pasta shops on that island, making them either purchase expensive modern equipment or shut down. And close they did. It is not always Italy driving these kinds of changes. It is the EU.

Through all this depressing talk, Santo managed a smile. "When Italian fishermen come upon a Japanese vessel, they would sometimes cut their nets. But, now, not so much." Even the fishermen on the smallest boats owned by families that have fished for generations must pay for expensive licenses, and so fewer and fewer do that. "A large commercial boat's owners can sell their licenses to someone else from a place far away for forty thousand euro, so they do and leave fishing."

Now I hear the same refrain about the future for this village and others in Sicily: The future is tourism. This makes me think of the grizzled retired fisherman I met several years ago who, for twenty euro, rowed his small boat with two of us as passengers around the boulders tossed into the sea by the Cyclops, mingling

with other boats with scuba divers and people heading for pic-
nics among those rocks. He didn't fish anymore. He just showed
up at the docks every day and waited for a tourist to approach,
like my friend and I did. A few years later, with a couple of other
friends, we walked down to the pier and there he was, waiting.

The morning of my last day in Aci Trezza found me, as usual,
in the small square. The elderly were there in their usual spots,
along with a handful of tourists. This time, a large crowd filled
the road and the steps of the church. A hearse stood at the curb;
flowers lined the steps. Within a few minutes, the great doors
swung open and a priest and acolytes came out, followed by a
gray casket carried by men in dark suits. The bells, the same ones
that sounded so forlorn when they chimed in Visconti's *La
terra trema,* started their long, diligent clanging. I looked around.
The elderly were lined up along the front edge of the square; the
benches were empty. The casket was placed onto the hearse's rollers and pushed inside. The door closed. The priest and his reti-
nue of white-smocked young men and boys led the way, then the
hearse, then the crowd of perhaps a couple hundred mourners
falling in close behind. The elderly men, who likely had just lost
one of their own, joined the procession.

Within moments, the square was empty, traffic was normal
along the street, and the bells of San Giovanni Battista were silent.

I was in a hurry to get to Castel di Tusa for my final three days
before going to Palermo for one night so I could meet some
friends before heading home. I drove out of Aci Trezza toward
Catania on the coastal highway, then turned west toward the

autostrada and a two-hour drive to Castel di Tusa, where I wanted to catch a religious procession of the Madonna with child. I wasn't sure of the occasion, but I had heard about the procession while exploring the interior a few weeks earlier. I figured it would be a nice capstone to this Sicilian odyssey.

A sign along the highway caught my eye: the exit to Agira would be just ahead. I had taken that exit a few years earlier when I realized halfway to the village that if I continued, I would arrive late for my B and B reservation. I drove there anyway, but moved quickly through the village, stopping only a few moments to admire the view, and then headed back down to resume the long drive to the west coast, near Trapani.

It was a quick glimpse, but intriguing, and my bigger interest was to see the village where the Greek-Sicilian historian Diodorus Siculus (90–30 B.C.), whose twelve-volume Loeb Classical Library set of books sat atop my bookshelf, was born when Rome controlled the island. Now, with more time to spare, I figured I could spend a few hours there and still easily make my way to Castel di Tusa long before evening. I also remembered that from the road that curved its way up the mountaintop where the village sat high and mighty there was a spectacular view of Mount Etna. I wanted to see it and its snow-covered western slope one last time before heading home.

The town is one of the largest that I had visited on this trip, with fewer than nine thousand Agirini. I was attracted to it because it is deep in the folds of the once sulfur-rich Erean Mountains in the island's center, and the late-spring drive promised to be a beautiful one. It would be my last foray through the island's interior with its gloriously colored grain fields, now mostly golden-yellow with bits of green still left to show that spring hadn't quite departed. In other fields sat large round bales of hay; already in early May there had been a first cutting. As one who grew up working on Idaho farms full of wheat, hay, and cornfields, I always found it emotional to drive through hills such as this. The sight of a light breeze blowing uphill, kissing the tops of maturing wheat and making the illusion of endless waves rolling across a sea, touches me to the core. A confessor once told me, "You are a man of the soil." I suspect that is one of the reasons Sicily touches me so.

Agira completely covers a high mountaintop like a knit fisherman's cap or the bowl over one's head to guide scissors for a haircut. It is northeast of Enna, just nine twisting miles from the autostrada. It appears in the distance just a mile or two away from the exit. The drive was slow, which allowed me to soak in the beauty around me. A large truck and trailer was lumbering ahead, rattling mightily every time it hit a series of potholes. It was loaded with several olive trees, each with roots held together by thick wooden slats. They were young trees, perhaps only twenty or thirty years old, and could have been nursery grown or simply dug up to make way for construction somewhere far away and hauled for replanting in one of the olive groves at the base of Agira's mountain.

The town sits on top of the ancient Greek village that in turn was built atop a Sicel village the Greeks called Agyrion. This name comes from the name of the Greek tyrant Agyris, who ruled central Italy in the fourth century B.C. The Romans, when they arrived a few centuries later, Latinized the name to Agirium. Agira also is a relatively new name in the span of Sicilian history.

The village, since medieval times at least, had been known as San Filippo d'Argiriò. This name, in turn, came from a translation of what the Arabs named it when they arrived in the ninth century A.D.: Shanta Fīlibb, which refers to San Filippo of Agira. Confusing runs of names, changed over and over through the millennia to reflect whomever happened to be conquering the island at the moment, can be found throughout Sicily. It has been Agira as recently as 1861. Why was it changed once again? It's a mystery.

The town's view of Etna is profound. I could sit for hours—if I had that kind of time—on a rampart looking at that vast slope, still white from snow near its top, and its smoking craters. I stopped and did just that, but only for the time it took to enjoy my short Tuscan cigar. It was a Sunday, and traffic, as expected in a town this size, was heavy. Open parking spaces were few. I drove around for a half hour, searching slowly and making my way through crowds of people, either coming from or going to church or shopping in stores that, surprising to me, were open on that day of rest.

Just ahead, only a block or so from the town square, a spot opened up. It did not have a sign with a specific time limit. I parked and walked up the slight incline. At the top I saw sidewalk tables arrayed outside of a couple of bars and restaurants. People were having their morning espresso or sitting down to heaping plates of steaming pasta or fillets of fish. I ordered a double espresso, sat in the only empty chair I could see, and watched the life of this small town unfold around me.

There was the ubiquitous traffic warden, a middle-aged woman with stern features, prowling the area, warning drivers not to linger along this stretch of street. Drivers would stop and implore her to let them double-park for *solo un minuto,* just a minute. She was firm, unlike the more gentle wardens I had found elsewhere, like that woman in her well-pressed blue uniform keeping an eye on my car in Calascibetta, just a few dozen miles to the southwest, and allowing me to stay for hours in a fifteen-minute zone. But here, this warden had a whistle and used it every few seconds, sounding like a tweeting bird. I grant her this: In the hour I observed her darting and tweeting, I never saw her write a ticket.

I ordered lunch: pasta *pomodoro* with fresh, crisp asparagus on the side and a lovely apple torte for dessert. I finished with another espresso, and headed for my car. There were two others double-parked behind me, their drivers nowhere to be seen. I couldn't move. Typical. I leaned against the hood, lit another short Tuscan, and waited. One man came out right away, nodded at me, and smiled. I smiled back. The second driver appeared fifteen minutes later. He saw me, shrugged, climbed in his car, and waved. Very civilized, I thought, remembering the advice of my friend in Mineo: *"Tranquillo,* John, *tranquillo."*

Afterword

A traveller I am, and a navigator, and every day I discover a new region within my soul.

—Kahlil Gibran

I AWOKE on my first morning in Castel di Tusa, and when I went downstairs in my B and B—my last in this journey and with the wonderful name "Camelot"—and stepped outside and looked over the wide Tyrrhenian Sea with the sun, low in the east and casting a glister of bouncing light across the dark blue water. I inhaled deeply and breathed in the sweet air of Sicily. I could almost taste lemons in that breath, a scent imbued with the spread of wildflowers still going strong on this north-facing slope looking over the vast sea beyond. On one side of the beautifully designed square—we would call it a "patio" back home—outside Camelot's front door was an outdoor kitchen, three-sided with a long open front and sloping roof. Agatha Cangialosi was busy there making coffee. On the other side, next to the main structure, was a table, placed in shade I was grateful for in the growing heat of a Sicilian morning in mid-May. Sitting and polishing off his first coffee of the day was Agatha's husband, Giuseppe Lo Piccolo. His sister-in-law, Agatha's sister and owner of the

Camelot, Annamaria Cangialosi arrived with a welcoming smile.
Eventually, we four sat, savoring our *espressi,* and made conversation: convivial with brief explanations about our lives. This trio
of new Sicilian friends gave me room to flail at their beautiful language. We got along fine and understood each other perfectly.

I relate my time in Castel di Tusa not so much to describe another village. After all, it is a tiny beach community with homes
for summer residents, a few small apartment structures, one
really nice bar with a great selection of pastries, a hotel just off
the stony beach, and a small warren of homes on the other side
of the main Messina-Palermo rail line. It is fairly nondescript. But
the people aren't. I was here to witness a procession beginning
in front of the village's main church, Santuario Maria Santissima
della Catena, or as it properly translates into English, the Sanctuary of the Lady of the Chain.

I tell this story here because what happened during this visit
reaffirms my faith in people, something that is not hard to do in
Sicily, as I never came across anyone who was not warm toward
a stranger. But it was particularly poignant.

I asked Annamaria where I could purchase shoelaces. "Not
here," she said. "There is no store. You will have to go to Santo
Stefano di Camastra. It is just nine kilometers [5.5 miles] to the
north." I groaned. I simply wanted to hang out on benches along
the sea and unwind a bit before beginning the long process of
heading home in three days. But my shoelace had snapped, so off
to Santo Stefano I went.

It was a quick drive and a beautiful one along that Tyrrhenian
coastline with patches of Sicilian pines whipped into all kinds of
shapes by decades of sea winds. Santo Stefano is larger, with about

five thousand residents. Its main street is lined with shop after shop displaying ceramics. In fact, the sign at the town's entrance proclaims it as the CITTÀ DELLE CERAMICHE. I did not know this, that Santo Stefano has a ceramics tradition like Caltagirone in Sicily's center or Sciacca along the southern coast near Agrigento.

I eventually found a lone parking spot and went into a couple of shops to see where I could find shoelaces. After three or four tries, someone directed me to a children's clothing store just across the street and next to an appealing-looking bar where I might find my second espresso of the day. I went, entering the shop with a tinkling bell over the door. A man came out from the back room. He reached under the counter and pulled out a box with a jumble of shoelaces. One was the right color and looked long enough. Success. I would fix my shoe problem and head back to Castel di Tusa for a day looking out to sea and visualizing the centuries' worth of seafaring traffic that had sailed past here.

I would have a lot to dream about. It was along this coast that the Norman king Roger II was riding in a storm-tossed ship that was forced to land on the beach at Cefalù, just along the coast a few miles west of Castel di Tusa. In his prayers, the legend goes, he promised that if he survived this storm at sea he would build a cathedral at the spot where he found refuge. Thus, Cefalù has one of Sicily's most glorious cathedrals, with stunning mosaics that are on par with the Cathedral at Monreale, which interestingly enough was built at the behest of Roger II's grandson, King William II (William the Good).

But I digress. I took the shoelaces next door to the bar, ordered my coffee, and sat at a tiny table perched along a sidewalk. There was a happy, laughing group of folks a few feet away taking their morning break. I unlaced my shoe and, bent over, started threading the new lace when, suddenly, I noticed blood dripping onto my shoe and the sidewalk. I grabbed my nose and realized I was in the middle of a major nosebleed. I've rarely had them and they are usually quite small. This one wasn't. All I had was a slim napkin, which I pressed against the offending nostril, but it was quickly saturated.

A couple of women from the other table noticed. They jumped up and, with napkins in their hands, gathered around me, pressing the paper against my nose. One ran inside to get ice, a man commanded me to hold my head down. Another said I should sit upright and tilt my head back. I fumbled with more napkins someone kept pressing into my hand, but the blood kept flowing. My shirt and pants were turning scarlet. Then, into my view, arrived an older woman who, I found out later, was just passing by. She took charge. She had me tilt my head back and pressed a new supply of napkins hard against the nostril.

She ordered a young woman to run across the street to the *farmacia* to get a *"tampone."* I heard "tampon" and figured, what the heck, one of those should do the trick. It seemed like just a few seconds and the young woman was back with a box of small squares of gauze that I found out later were designed to *"stop hémo."* And they were called *tampone* and were different from what I had first imagined. This wonderful woman who took charge was pulling on a latex glove—where she got it, I don't know—and then she tightly rolled that cotton swab. The next thing I knew she was jamming it, hard, into my right nostril.

That did it. The flow was halted. Meanwhile, someone else was pressing pieces of ice wrapped in a bar towel against my nose.

I noticed that two of the women from the next table stood on either side of me, their comforting arms around my shoulders. Another young woman had wet napkins and was wiping blood from my mustache and beard. The crowd around me started to break up. The folks from the next table went back to it. I looked around; the woman who had taken charge was gone. She had swooped in, rescued me, and, with her job done, disappeared. I got up and walked over to the other table. I thanked them profusely.

One woman said, *"Signore, questa è la Sicilia. Aiutiamo. Dite alla gente che la Sicilia non è la mafia."* (Sir, this is Sicily. We help. Tell people that Sicily is not the Mafia.) I told them that I knew this, and that tourists who stereotype the island with misguided fascination about the Mafia bother me. Why the Mafia came up, I have no idea, but these were people who obviously were sensitive about an outsider's view of their island. I offered to buy them all *espressi*. Politely, they declined. Their break was over; work beckoned.

I sat at my table to finish installing the shoelace. The barman came out, smiled, and shook his head at the sight of the *tampone* sticking out of my nose. He gathered up all the bloody napkins, hauled them inside, and returned with a gelato cone. "On the house," he said in English. I walked over to the *farmacia* and asked the pharmacist for a box of *tampone*. I now carry one of them in my wallet and the box is stashed in the cupboard—just in case.

The next morning, I was sitting at an outside table at the pastry shop in Castel di Tusa. I looked up. A woman was striding toward me. It was the angel who had saved me the day before. "How are you doing? How is your nose?" "It is fine," I said. No more problems. I reached into my shirt pocket and pulled out a paper-wrapped *tampone*. "It is my new friend, *nuovo amico*," I said, pointing to it. She laughed. I thanked her, and then she turned and started to walk away.

"Wait," I said, doing my best with my limited Italian. "What is your name?" She didn't stop or look back. "Rita," she shouted as she opened the door to her car. "Like Rita Hayworth." And, once again, she was gone.

ACKNOWLEDGMENTS

It would be impossible to enumerate and thank all the many friends who, with the courtesy and patience that never desert a Sicilian, have given me information, explanation and assistance.

—Henry Festing Jones

The words of Henry Festing Jones ring as true for me as it does for my friend, Karen La Rosa, an organizer of small tours of Sicily, from whom I "borrowed" the quote. She was a major, indispensable help for this book. She suggested places to visit and gave me long lists of people she knows in Sicily who could enlighten me in my explorations. There are other "indispensables," folks who dove headfirst into the waters of my journey and plied me with villages to visit and whose language skills, matched against my basic Italian, saved me more than once. I'm thinking of Professor Santi Buscemi, who urged me to go to Mineo and learn about its native son, the nineteenth-century author Luigi Capuana.

Most important, Santi gave me the name of Ninni Maglione, who provided lodging and guided me around his beloved village. He, in turn, introduced me to Salvo Andrea Leggio, a twentysomething master pastry chef who showed me the countryside around Mineo, introduced me to his large family, fed me wood-oven pizza made for a dinner at the family home, and responded brilliantly to my many questions via email after I returned home. Plus, Ninni took me to the village *biblioteca* and introduced me to Maria Giovanna Cafiso, who shared the richness of ancient and modern books.

When my journey began in Castiglione di Sicilia, I had no idea how important Nunzio Valentino, owner of the *albergo diffuso* Borgo Santa Caterina, where I lived for eleven days, would be. His suggestions about places to visit paid off handsomely. He knew people in every village on my initial list, and he called and arranged for them to spend time with me. My gratitude toward Nunzio—who would greet me on the phone or at the *albergo* with, "Hey, Mr. John!" I would shout back, "Valentino!"—is immense. He got me off on the right foot with my three-month journey and led me to stories I could never have gotten on my own. He arranged a meeting in Motta Camastra with Venera De Luca, a most able guide who has a special sense of place in her delightful village. When he suggested that I go to Gallodoro, I met Antonella Siligato, my guide and interpreter. His lifelong friend the mayor, Alfio Filippo Currenti, opened more than one door for me in that delightful tiny village high in the hills with its magnificent view of the Ionian Sea.

George Giannone needs special mention here. I met him, quite by accident, when I arrived in Caccamo for a several-day visit. He became a dear friend who taught me the history of his beloved village, shared meals, and showed me, from his immense collection, photographs of church interiors and other places around Caccamo. We stayed in touch. About one year from the day we first met, I saw a social media post that he had died. I had been looking forward to the day I could return and hand him a copy of this book so he could see the impact he had on my storytelling. Rest easy, George.

In Vizzini, I met Alfredo Giarrusso, a pharmacist who was my host in the house I stayed in for several days. He introduced me to people who told me their family histories, and he shared the history of his own family and the house he was restoring that had been in their care for generations.

I must mention Giuseppe Andini, whom I have known for several years. On this trip he arranged for me to meet the man whose family owns a small, private church in the outskirts of Racalmuto. A delightful day.

Many others helped to various degrees. This is where I worry that I will forget someone, but I must start with Nello Turco of Mistretta, who helped gather a lot of local information about the early-twentieth-century writer Maria Messina. Nello and his wife, Enza Constantino, were my hosts; and they went beyond their duties as *pensione* owners and prepared one of the finest Sicilian meals I have ever eaten. During a conversation with a cultural official in Mistretta, Maria Alfieri served as a most able interpreter. In Riesi, Rosy Trovato, in addition to doing a powerful sales job to get me there, arranged interviews and shared history of this once sulfur-rich area.

Others who helped were small-tour operator Allison Scola,

Michela Musolino, Rochelle Del Borrello, Mari Albanese, Giacomo Ippolita, Lillina Messineo, Louis Mendola, Jacqueline Alio, and Elise Magistro.

I close with the names of three very important people in my life, the people in my dedication: Sicilian-Americans Leonard Chiarelli and Alex Caldiero; and my wife, lovely, patient Connie-Lou Disney. Leonard, an authority in the history of Muslim Sicily and head of the Middle East Library in the Marriott Library of the University of Utah, has done significant research for me over the years, responding to my excessive emails quickly and with good humor, and he helped me during our many discussions while we sat on my front porch smoking cigars. Sicily-born Alex, a poet and artist in residence in humanities at Utah Valley University, whose knowledge of the Sicilian language is total, has long supported my efforts with translations and has offered his insights into Sicilian culture. I have known these gentlemen for many years; they are among my closest of friends. Connie-Lou, a brilliant book designer, helps me stay centered while urging me on and protecting my time at the computer, keeping me safe from interlopers.

—John Keahey
January 2018

SELECTED READING

Abulafia, David, ed. *The Mediterranean in History*. Los Angeles: Getty Publications, 2003.

Attlee, Helena. *The Land Where Lemons Grow: The Story of Italy and Its Citrus Fruit*. Woodstock, VT: Countryman Press, 2014.

Braudel, Fernand. *The Mediterranean in the Ancient World*. Translated by Siân Reynolds. London, UK: Penguin, 2001.

Capuana, Luigi. *The Marquis of Roccaverdina*. Translated by Santi V. Buscemi. Boston: Dante University Press, 2013.

Chiarelli, Leonard C. *A History of Muslim Sicily*. Second Revised Edition. Sta Venera, Malta: Midsea Books, 2018.

De Angelis, Franco. *Archaic and Classical Greek Sicily: A Social and Economic History*. New York: Oxford University Press, 2016.

De Roberto, Federico. *The Viceroys*. Translated by Archibald Colquhoun. London, UK: Verso, 2016.

Goethe, Johann Wolfgang von. *Italian Journey*. Translated by W. H. Auden and Elizabeth Mayer. New York: Penguin, 1992.

Grady, Ellen. *Blue Guide Sicily*. Ninth Edition. Taunton, Somerset, UK: Blue Guides Limited, 2017.

Lampedusa, Giuseppe di. *The Leopard*. Translated by Archibald Colquhoun. New York: New York: Pantheon, 1960.

Lewis, Norman. *In Sicily*. New York: St. Martin's Press, 2000.

Maraini, Dacia. *The Silent Dutchess*. Translated by Dick Kitto and Elspeth Spottiswood. New York: Feminist Press, 1998.

Mazzucchelli, Chiara. *The Heart and the Island: A Critical Study of Sicilian American Literature*. Albany: State University of New York Press, 2015.

Mendola, Louis and Jacqueline Alio. *The Peoples of Sicily: A Multicultural Legacy*. New York: Trinacria Editions, 2013.

Messina, Maria. *Behind Closed Doors: Her Father's House and Other Stories of Sicily*. Translated by Elise Magistro. New York: Feminist Press, 2007.

———. *A House in the Shadows*. Translated by John Shepley. Marlboro, VT: Marlboro Press, 1989.

Nicklies, Charles E. "The Church of the Cuba Near Castiglione di Sicilia and Its Cultural Context." *Muqarnas: An Annual on Islamic Art and Architecture*, XI, 1994.

Norwich, John Julius. *Sicily: An Island at the Crossroads of History*. New York: Random House, 2015.

Ridley, Jasper. *Garibaldi*. New York: Viking Press, 1974.

Seume, Johann Gottfried. *A Stroll to Syracuse*. Translated by Alexander and Elizabeth Henderson. London, UK: Oswald Wolff, 1964.

Siculus, Diodorus. Translated by C. H. Oldfather. Vols. I–XII. *The Library of History*. Cambridge, MA: Loeb Classical Library, Harvard University Press, 1939.

Swick, Thomas. *The Joys of Travel and Stories That Illuminate Them*. New York: Skyhorse Publishing, 2016.

Verga, Giovanni. *Cavalleria Rusticana and Other Stories*. Translated by G. H. McWilliam. New York: Penguin, 1999.

———. *I Malavoglia: The House by the Medlar Tree*. Translated by Judith Landry. Sawtry, UK: Dedalus, 2008.

———. *Mastro Don Gesualdo*. Translated by D. H. Lawrence. London, UK: Dedalus, 1984.

INDEX